THE CLARINET

Excellence and Artistry

ROSARIO MAZZEO

Copyright © 1981 by Alfred Publishing Co. Inc.
Printed in the United States of America
        Alfred Publishing Co., Inc.
        15335 Morrison Street
        Sherman Oaks, California 91403

Current printing last digit: 10 9 8 7 6 5 4 3 2 1

Library of Congress Cataloging in Publication Data

Mazzeo, Rosario, 1911–
   The Clarinet.

   Bibliography: p.
   Includes index.
   1. Clarinet—Methods.   I. Title
MT382.M347   788′.62′071   80-27569

ISBN 0-88284-133-5

TO
MY TEACHERS,
FOUR WONDERFUL GENTLEMEN

JACK C. LYNCH, who in the very earliest years of my music-making headed me towards the correct compass direction. GASTON HAMELIN, GUSTAVE LANGENUS and FERNAND GILLET, each gave me of their best, carrying me further along in my career, and setting standards which I have all my life tried to reach.

TO

HARRY RANDALL, Editor of THE SELMER BANDWAGON, whose idea, and whose invitation it was, which caused me to launch the writing of THE CLARINET MASTER CLASS articles. Over the years the response has been such as to make their appearance in book form seem almost pre-ordained, thus placing him almost in an "I told you so" position. For greater unit cohesion here they have been almost entirely re-written.

AND TO

KATIE CLARE, my ever-patient and inspiring wife, who so many times has come forth with exactly the needed scholarly information, just when it was needed, and whose charming drawings carry their accompanying messages to full clarity.

CONTENTS

PART VI — REFERENCE MATERIALS

PART VII — ACOUSTICS

PART VIII — SONGS MY MOTHER TAUGHT ME

PART IX — PERIPHERAL VIEWS

APPENDIX 1

APPENDIX 2

BIBLIOGRAPHY

ACKNOWLEDGMENTS

INDEX

FOREWORD

A most heart-warming part of my life has been the continual stream of letters received in warm response to THE CLAR-INET MASTER CLASS series in the Selmer BANDWAGON. Over the years these have run literally into the thousands, and have made me realize how earnest and devoted to the study of the clarinet were these widespread players and teachers. The publication of the articles spanned more than a decade, the subject order was random, and it was chosen to some extent in response to the letters and requests. Therefore more attention was given in some directions than others, and no attempt was made to cover all aspects of clarinet playing. I had especial pleasure in learning how many non-clarinettist teachers found the material helpful in their teaching.

When considering the sequence for this volume I felt that a more coherent subject order was indicated, and have so proceeded in this new setting. Occasionally the same subject material will be found in more than one chapter. I have allowed this to stand, since the statements in their original context were necessary to re-enforce, or complete, the immediately surrounding text.

Now, no attempt is being made to expand this into a more complete statement, or full-scale method. My more than half-century involvement with the clarinet has allowed my attention to focus particularly on areas which were of greater interest to me. And it is to these that I now address myself. Emphasis is mostly towards basic concepts for each of the controls necessary in successful playing. These are the foundation stones. Since the subjects included here are of a rather diverse nature, but all needing attention at every level of playing, I hope that they will be read by players of every category, and by woodwind teachers with pupils at any stage.

THE CLARINET MASTER CLASS number 11, which reported a meeting of the International Clarinet Society,* has been omitted. However, I urge every serious clarinettist to become a member and thus to be acquainted with their publication *The Clarinet*. In a few short years it has become a very important reference source.

The articles concerning reeds, ligatures and literature have been wholly re-written. The discussion of reeds has been extended to cover the subject in general, rather than confined to an isolated type. The proliferation of ligatures in this past decade or two clearly indicated the need for an up-dated statement. Much is happening, and more should happen with the development of reeds and ligatures. As to literature, the many new conveniences and efficiencies of the publishing field have made available an absolutely incredible array of material. Whereas in my

* Publisher, James Schoepflin, Department of Music, Washington State University, Pullman, Washington 99164.

youth one could hope to collect (with reasonable expectation) *everything* of one type (e.g., concert pieces for clarinet alone) it is now manifestly impossible. No one can have that many tentacles extended for information. Catalogues show an infinite exhibit of instrumental groupings. Chamber music is found with all manner of tonal coloring. Gone are the restraints of writing only for conventional groups, such as string quartets or woodwind quintets. You will understand the problems of cataloguers when you have to cope with groups of which one member is listed as "silence," another with "dog" (real!), yet another with a tuning fork (played by the clarinettist, if you please), or with such esoterics as the early Joseph Beer's *Quintet* for clarinet, horn, and three viole-d'amour (a lush combination!), or the recent William Hibbard's *Bass Trombone, Bass Clarinet, and Harp* for—(you guessed it) bass trombone, bass clarinet, and harp. More power to the composers. No one's muse should have to hedge.

My own credo for teaching is a simple one. If you cannot explain in words understandable to your listener *exactly* what is to be done, the chances are that you do not really know *exactly* how to make him bring it about. True, your pupil's musical instinct, and possibly very apt motor controls, may allow a certain degree of imitation, but he could do it even better if he clearly understood each and every aspect of the controls. And for

the pupil who has not this "natural" grasp the explanation and illustration are more than ever necessary.

And this brings me to another general credo—less is best. You cannot set more than one brick at a time into your wall-building. Every bit of study should offer a path to some one fundamental *attainable* benefit. Constant repetition, unless properly focused, can allow the continuation of some faults which may be part of your involuntary contribution. Each repetition of such fault serves only to build-in that particular fault. Obviously, playing from one end of an etude to the other is meaningless unless you have *continual* focus. But this focus need not be the same each time you play! True, each etude probably has one general main purpose. However that does not stop you from studying it from any number of viewpoints, each contributing towards full mastery.

Increasingly the professional music world is being peopled by members of both sexes, therefore in order to avoid the constant repetition of "ladies and gentlemen" I will use the generic term to include both.

Because the illustrations and examples involve only the soprano member of the family I have used the octave identification most in use by clarinet players.

PART I
CONCEPTS

Chapter 1:
STUDYING-PRACTICING

Early in 1925 (quite a few years ago), I began to play the clarinet, and as a result have thought about it each day ever since. Some days more than others. Some days almost exclusively—and some rare vacation days almost (but not quite!) not at all. I remember the initial impression when a clarinet was first in my hands. The dark, mysterious wood; the fascinating key forms, irregular in shape and action—all manner of mystery seemed wrapped up in it. I loved it. I still love it, only now far more than ever. It seemed as though I could never solve some of its mysteries. But I am still trying. The instrument has brought me into contact with a fascinating array of personalities—some completely dedicated, perceptive and sensitive, others bordering on the odious.

Teaching has been one aspect of my clarinet life which I have enjoyed enormously. It has been a passion with me, and my pupils (most of them!) have added greatly to my pleasure in music, and more than that—my perception of its problems. My life has had many dimensions, many not directly connected with the clarinet. It has been extremely interesting to compare the approach to learning of the die-hard clarinet players with that of people in other professions. My general impression after all these years is that we are a pretty narcissistic lot. There is a great need to share some of the solutions, and even the giver will be the better for it.

Therefore in commencing this book I am going to try to avoid the personal advice, unless it is also rooted in substantial observations of others. How one person does something is not necessarily the way the very next person should do it. We have different mental capacities, different degrees of curiosity, of perseverance, different jaw formations, oral cavities, motor controls, and above all different musical inheritance. Therefore my approach will be to explore solutions based on a wide avenue of experience with many personalities.

My beginning will concern itself with two aspects of clarinet playing: one philosophical, and the other physical. First, the philosophical.

STUDYING–PRACTICING. Most players don't stop to evaluate the difference between these two words—and it *is* significant! How often I have seen a player try something over, not be able to play it, and yet continue to play it many, many times, repeating what he couldn't do well (and therefore making more of a habit of his failure) as well as what he could do. I recall one instance backstage at the concert of a very famous orchestra. The 1st clarinettist was practicing what was indeed a very tricky short passage. He played it once, correctly—second time, correctly—third time, missed—fourth, correctly—fifth, missed—sixth, correctly—and so on for about ten times. Then he walked immediately onstage to perform. What must have been his state of mind? Was the eleventh try (onstage) to be a missed one—or correct? It was pure chance—and he happened to miss. How much better if he had taken the passage apart at some earlier time, and studied the actual problem. 'Studying' is more concerned with *examination* of a problem, and 'practicing' more with the *repetition* of certain motions or actions, to make them a habit. These are fundamental definitions, which remain despite modifications of them. Therefore one's first thought (when faced with a passage not mastered) should be *not* to practice it. If you do you will only practice (make a habit of) the errors as assiduously as you do the parts which you *can* play, and which can really be improved by repetition.

In studying, make liberal use of a mirror, and a metronome, and a teacher, or colleague. Take the problem apart, analyze each element separately—posture, finger motions, embouchure, breathing, and blowing (yes, they are to be treated as two entirely separate conscious actions). Analyze the sound, compare it with known examples which you admire, don't merely try 'blindly' to make it better—think *how* and *what* you should specifically do to make it better. Remember that you do not play the clarinet with only your lips, or teeth, or fingers, or breath, or jaw, or diaphragm—you also play it with your mind and ears. The largest part of teaching the clarinet is 'subtractive,' that is, calling attention to and removing those involuntary actions which are gratuitously added while trying to do what is asked.

Most of the 'additive' advice can be written (note Keith Stein's superb book *The Art of Clarinet Playing*); it is the 'subtractive' part which necessitates direct observation. How many talented players, and quite proficient too, suffer some handicap merely because someone, blinded by the good qualities, allowed the talent to develop with the accompaniment of the deficiencies. For example: there is a demonstrably scientific way in which the fingers can be moved so that the lines of force are followed, thus making for the greatest efficiency—subject, of course, to minor adaptations because of pecularities of individual hands. Yet I have seen quite good players who didn't even begin to realize their full potentials because of truly faulty hand positions. Some teacher, somewhere, because the player was better than the surrounding pupils, allowed him to go on and build-in the fault, or deficiency, by years of practice with it. Think how much better a player there would have been if some pruning had been done in his early study days.

Another example is rhythm. How many times a youngster has learned to play a passage merely mimicking, by virtue of such musical talent as he possesses, and yet being unable to fully decipher the solfeggio aspects! My general feeling has been that if you cannot explain the process in words, you probably do not have really clear thoughts about it. You are trusting only your instincts, and these may let you down when you face the same problem in a different context while playing. Spell it out for yourself. If you do not have really clear thoughts, you cannot give clear directions to your motor controls. This may seem elementary, but it is the elementary aspects of your controls which are the foundation of your technique. When you are satisfied that each element is being thoughtfully controlled and efficiently performed, and your mind and ear are satisfied with the result—*then* you have something!

In the matter of motor controls, I have noticed that everywhere in the world clarinettists (and for that matter, woodwind players generally) play with more accuracy and cleanliness when playing passages with down-moving fingers. There is an easy explanation for this, and it lies in the fingering charts in all methods. The fingering for a note is given as that which is used to sound the note. Thus, for

example, the fingering for  is given as

This is true *only* when you are playing this note without connection with other notes. Consider now that you are playing this G in a legato after F

What is involved here, by way of action, has nothing to do with the book fingering for G. All that is needed is a clean up-motion of the first finger right hand. Yet invariably, and because the book image is so strong, you will notice an involuntary movement downward of the three fingers of the left hand. This can only remove attention from the needed motion of the first finger right hand. Cleaner action can be attained by thinking of fingering as being attention *only* to those fingers, or finger, which needs to be moved. Think also that *up* should equal *down* in preciseness. Your fingers should move in either direction with equal energy. Recall the matching down-motions of a pianist's fingers; they are easiest to visualize. You may even do what I have done with some pupils—attach a lyre at the top of the upper joint and another at the bottom of the lower. Join these with a long ruler at an appropriate height and have the pupil move his fingers down to the wood of the clarinet, and up to strike the ruler—in each case with equal impact. The impact itself, and the height of the motions, will vary depending upon your tastes and opinions. All you are trying to do is to make the pupil aware of the needed same-ness of the up or down strokes. Watch a very good player in such a passage as this, from the "Unfinished Symphony" of Schubert.

Ex. 1

Notice how much more cleanly and smoothly the down-motions are made. Even the tuning of the notes produced by down-moving fingers will seem more certain because of the more definite motions. There is no reason why the up-motions shouldn't be the same. In my life I have found the greatest master of this control to be Fernand Gillet, for many years the distinguished first oboist of the Boston Symphony. His was the most immaculate fingering, and I'm sure it contributed a great deal to his beautiful and extraordinarily consistent playing.

Chapter 2:
THINKING WILL MAKE IT SO

The other day I was sitting on my mountain-side watching the sunrise on the Pacific Ocean and thinking about thinking. Before I get to writing about thinking I had better explain this business about sunrises in the West.

We live 500 feet above the sea on the west side of a mountain which rises steeply to a little over 1700 feet. Our beautiful sunrise colors the ocean to our west because the sun shines over the mountain, right above our house, and directly on to the ocean, which then reflects the light back to us. About an hour later we get direct sunlight. Our sunsets (also in the west!), which are fabulous, we get directly without benefit of an intermediary. Now about thinking.

Music is an art in time. Thus, it is never still. And *there* is the beginning of a technical problem from which many players suffer. Their minds are implanted with the idea that music is a matter of motion. How a beginner's eyes open wide when he hears really rapid passages being played on the instrument on which he can move only slowly! How much emphasis is placed on rapid fingering, general agility and quick maneuverability!

I have written about moving fingers more quickly—but *not* sooner. Quicker and sooner have entirely different meanings as you will realize when you reflect. The point I want to make is that of *living* a tone, no matter how short its duration. By so doing, you will not only improve its quality, but also you will find (because of greater tonal consistency and security) that you can manipulate between tones much more quickly. After all you are dealing with a 'something' (tone) which when thus

played is more solid, therefore more easily and securely dealt with. Your passage work will be infinitely more clean and sure. Let me explain.

Many players are so taken with the need for motion that they think only in terms of continual motion, with the exception of obviously long tones. Try playing a simple scale, perhaps one quarter tone value per second.

Ex. 1 ♩ = 60

Each tone sounds a quarter of a second (minus travel time between tones)—certainly not much time for thinking. In fact the finger movement usually takes so much attention that the tones themselves get very little concentration. Now play the same scale at MM40.

Ex. 2 ♩ = 40

Breathe where necessary

Focus *all* your attention on tone quality, tuning, solidity of sound and absolute stability (no wavering). Only at the very last milisecond give yourself the absolute minimum of time to move your finger(s) to the next position, and when you do so, have them already poised so that you move with the greatest quickness and adroitness. Except for this absolutely necessary minimal time for motion, get your mind to consider that *most of the time you are not in motion, the tone is being sustained.* Picture tone as a horizontal something, a steady, unchanging quality of sound going forward in time, but appearing to be timeless by its unchanging quality.

Then the scale will assume a different feeling in your mind and playing. It will be a series of 'somethings'—tones of a completely controlled quality. There will be a more sustained and settled feeling about your playing, your tone will sound larger, fuller and richer. This is the valuable result of *not* considering the thoughts for finger motion as being more important than those for sustaining sounds. It is of the utmost importance that the player gets this concept clearly in his mind, and in the feeling of his fingers.

The sounds will be both more definite and easier of mobility. For example, consider how difficult it is to play a complex moving passage with a mushy reed. The tones blur together, fingers seem to trip over each other, etc.—and all because you do not have a sufficient definiteness of sound. Take a firmer reed, for a moment put aside its other playing characteristics, and consider only how much more easily the same passage can be played (note: you are playing at a comfortable *mezzo forte* so as not to introduce problems of nuance control). What I am saying is that with a concept of a tone as a 'something' living in time, which you may want to *exchange* frequently for another 'something' living in time (thus a rapid succession of tones), you will have a wholly different feeling about your playing, especially passage work. It will all be more poised, far more clear, and more maneuverable.

The problem is in not sufficiently recognizing the difference between 'moving in quick succession' as opposed to just 'moving quickly.' A scale is nothing else

than a series of *held* tones (horizontal sounds, if you will) moving either in slow, or quick succession. The tones must be held out as full values, whatever the speed of succession. A quick scale is nothing more than a succession of tones (call them 'short' long tones!), each of which is your whole universe during the moments you are playing it. Then the tone will be really sufficiently wind-nourished and stalwart, enough to withstand the inevitable buffeting it gets when the fingers move from one tone to another. Try this next scale in exactly the same manner as examples #1 and #2 and see if you can play it as cleanly.

Ex. 3

Coloring is a subtlety which is not the concern of this moment. First we want health and substance in a tone. Only afterwards should we concern ourselves with variations in quality and color. If you will permit me a visual example: a person of no particular training who leaps across a brook alights on the other side with arms extended for balance, occupied in teetering into a solid and settled position. A superbly trained ballet dancer making the same leap lands with apparently effortless and settled poise. No teetering. That's the way you should arrive on each tone. Pause in your motion, live out the tone, enjoy it. At the appropriate time move on abruptly to the next one. Think a little Zen during each tone!

Which reminds me of another problem of thinking—or not thinking. I often see or hear about players who are trying desperately to achieve some general goal; but who merely get more and more bogged down in specific passage repetitions which may or may not slowly improve. It is so much quicker if you isolate. When something is not satisfactory, try to focus on only one aspect of your playing. Think about that single aspect. Think about it a lot. Do not think about anything else. Play with that single thought in mind. Invariably *that something* upon which you are really concentrating will improve sooner. Then go ahead and concentrate on another aspect, etc. Only after you are satisfied with *each* should you proceed playing with more than one thought at a time.

For instance, if you play the very first measure of the Brahms Sonata in E♭, Opus 120 #2, and find it not quite to your liking (or maybe anyone else's), try it again, first attempting to see if you can make the notes with equal resonance and aliveness. Not so easy because of the variety of tonal response! Then recognize that you are trying to make equality with:

Ex. 4

1. movement (F to E) by lowering one finger on a ring—no mechanism moving.
2. movement (E to G) by raising two fingers—right hand rings move.
3. movement (G to F) by lowering one finger—right hand ring moves.
4. movement (F to A) by raising four fingers, thumb, register key, and tilting to press the throat A key— various mechanisms move.
5. movement (A to D) by tilting away from the A key, lowering six fingers

and thumb, pressing register key— various mechanisms moving.
6. movement (D to B♭) by raising six fingers, thumb, releasing register key, tilting to the A throat key and pressing right hand B♭ lever. Of course I am not considering for the moment the addition of the left second and third fingers to add resonance to the regular B♭ played with the thumb—various mechanisms moving.
7. movement (B♭ to E) by tilting away from A throat key, releasing the B♭ key and pressing the thumb and first left ring. On the Boehm-Mazzeo model— tilt away from the A key, raise right hand first, second and third fingers, press thumb and first finger left hand ring—various mechanisms moving.

How different from a pianist who makes each of these notes with single fingers! Can you make all these movements equal to each other in tone-level and clarity?

When you can play these notes with equal resonance and aliveness, fingering them so that the finger motions sound exactly alike, *then* you are ready to give them the musical emphasis, shading, etc., which your artistic nature wishes to achieve. You are no longer the victim of involuntary differences of sonority, finger attack, etc. You are not the victim of the clarinet—its sounds are truly made and regulated by your thoughts. You are now in command . . . and all it takes is thinking: isolating each problem until mastery of each, and only *then* blending them to make your desired performance. Nothing is left to chance.

The most important thing about thinking is think-time. It is so important when attempting to improve a passage that you take time *immediately* after a transition, to think, to evaluate your success (or lack of it) in making that particular transition.

After a studied movement, pause on the next tone, forget rhythmic context for the moment, and give yourself time to evaluate what you just did—in the very instant after you did it. Consider what specifically you are going to change (improve), and focus upon it. When you do play it again and it does not improve, do not repeat it again without some new thinking. Some little element of control must have been missing, otherwise you would have improved the passage. This think-time must be used *before* you cloud your thought process and memory with the next several motions. It is more important to have one full minute of thoughtful editorial scrutiny to five seconds of playing than the reverse. If you do immediately proceed to the next motions, they will blend into each other and you will recall no more than a general impression—not the fine examination which concentration on a particular movement allows. It does little good to waltz your way through a difficult passage, scale, or whatever—and then try to evaluate the whole. Your memory will work best with *immediate* re-capture, *immediately* after the experience. All of the above is merely to say that since playing the clarinet successfully is not all *that* natural to most of us we must ponder continually the specific mastery of controls, physical and aesthetic.

Which brings me to another point in my present emphasis on thinking—articulation. It is sad to meet the player who, because of his innate musicality and talents, has learned to play well, yet when faced with original problems is not able to solve them. And why? Merely because he learned to play principally by rote, by talent alone. Heaven knows that there is never really enough talent, but consider my oft-repeated statement—that you will be your 'most' teacher. It is you who will be with yourself all through life, you whom must solve all the problems of playing which come your way. Your formal teachers will long ago have separated from you. Therefore, if you are not able to articulate each problem clearly, and then join the solutions into a coherent and successful whole, you cannot really be a successful teacher (however popular!) of yourself or others. Instead of just 'trying it again' (a form of gambling) try instead to see what is needed for each element of the passage. Isolate and state each problem. Success will come far sooner, and be more stable.

Chapter 3:
THE DEVELOPMENT OF
TONAL CONCEPT

Pupils with whom I am working for the first time are often confounded when I point to their instrument and say "What is it?" Almost invariably they first identify it by brand name. Then, noting that I am not satisfied, they say, "Why it is a clarinet." I say, "No, I mean *basically*." "Oh, I know—it is a reed instrument." When I am still not satisfied, there is a long pause (during which they are re-evaluating their decision to study with me). When no answer is forthcoming I ask, "Would you consider saying that you are playing a wind instrument?"

Why such persistent questioning? Because sounds take place in time—a continuum, and in the absence of a perpetual-blowing apparatus, the player must supply a constant force, continually replenished. A shortage at any time results in embarrassment. The raw material of tone is air, supported and projected outward by various muscles surrounding our supply of it. The mouth is but a passageway, and to some extent a control. Consider, if you will, the tone as a solid substance which you intend to modulate, divide, raise, lower, and otherwise variously treat. All of these treatments are 'controls'—it is the *wind* which is the basic source of tone. Therefore (and now the reason for my apparently naive questions) whenever

you have any problem with sound, even certain fingering problems, *first* suspect blowing. More often than you may believe, some deficiency in blowing is the basic cause.

Since 'technique' means *all* controls—spiritual, philosophical, and physical—your first step should be a few reflective moments for analyzing the problem; otherwise you may apply a wrong solution, or at least an inadequate one. This is a good time to stress again the importance of cassette or open-reel tape recorders for study purposes. Your hearing is better if you are not encumbered with the effort and mechanics of making the sound. You are able to sit back and make a more reflective, and comparative, judgment. I urge all to make use of as good a tape recorder as possible for serious practice (or teaching) sessions. You will be pleased beyond words to notice the difference it makes in your editorial judgment.

Whatever the error or shortcoming, I find that attention to the wind source and control is at least a partial initial correction, if not the whole. Even a wrong note often occurs because of wind exhaustion, with its consequent effect on your brain signals to your fingers. Except for such contests as 'eating the most doughnuts,' 'holding your breath under water,' etc., I do not find any virtue in breathing only when you *have* to. By that time it is too late. Breathing (in music) is no more than punctuation, and unless you are reciting Gertrude Stein, you probably speak with a sense of punctuation. Therefore it is important that you breathe to accommodate the rising and falling inflections of your phrasing. It will make your phrasing more natural, certainly more eloquent, and physically no burden. It is amazing how many places in a phrase will accommodate breathing (punctuation)—and how much they depend on the quality of the immediately preceding tones. It is not difficult to play your last tone (or tones) with an 'on going' quality which clearly indicates those notes immediately following the breath. Most players suffer from what I call a pre-breathing diminuendo—if not in quality, at least in resonance. This makes each breath a stopping point rather than a transitional inflection. Consider the subtle differences of your spacing when you read aloud. Note the differences between commas, semi-colons, colons, periods, and even paragraphs. Music breathing should reflect this same kind of inflection.

TONAL CONCEPTS

Forty or fifty years ago we were able to hear fewer of our best players. They were not as ambulatory, nor were they broadcast, nor recorded, as are today's. At that time it was relatively easy to identify a player almost at once as a pupil of this or that teacher. This was both a virtue and a drawback. A virtue in that a player had seriously pursued a course of work toward a known objective. A drawback, perhaps, in that it may have inhibited the player's natural instincts in producing his own individual tone quality.

Here we come to a philosophical question: Is a player more free after obeying a strict discipline, and only then taking off on his own? Or is he freer in never having undertaken a strict objective discipline? I incline to the former, and for these reasons: In adopting a method of performance, nothing is 'frozen;' there is almost no habit which cannot be rechanneled when the player is sufficiently mature to make a competent judgment, and he has the control which comes from developing

within a known discipline. In fifty-five years of teaching the clarinet, I can readily say that the pupils in the second category have the greatest trouble in identifying problems, and in exercising control. There are some who by virtue of native talent are fine players—but with certain 'dead-end' attitudes and controls. Therefore the very act of seeking to emulate an admired sound, done objectively, can itself make you freer to follow your own later bent.

Almost always the second group is tempted to adopt the same instrument, same mouthpiece, same reed as the player they choose to follow—but alas, they may not be the same type of player. Certainly some of these physical changes are warranted but if you make careful comparisons between two fine artists, you will find that greatness (or sameness) is in the players' native qualities, rather than in their outfits.

It is certain that one of the most important aspects of music-making is the production of beautiful sound—not just beautiful sound, but a completely controlled tonal palette; for this century's new music demonstrates that great music is always expressive, but not always conventionally 'beautiful.' Many of us get side-tracked by the various techniques of sound production and so lose track of the final and fundamental purpose of music—which is to evoke in a listener a feeling identical, or at least akin, to that experienced by the composer. That feeling need not be concerned with 'beauty;' it must only be genuine, even if it concerns ugliness or some other generally non-admired characteristic. Instruments are but tools to build the kind of tone (and therefore music) which we imagine. They are extensions of ourselves.

We are currently experiencing a major thrust towards expansion of our music vocabulary. Notice that I say 'music' rather than 'musical.' Somehow 'musical' has been so often coupled with 'beautiful' that many people believe non-beautiful sounds are 'not music.' Even today's dictionaries define noise as being a number of 'discordant' vibrations, yet we are all old hands at accepting discords as part of completely effective music. Those of you who agree with my definition of music will understand the need for *full* tonal control, as it makes any controlled 'noise' a means of 'music' making, a way of evoking an emotional response. Do not confuse the final goal (music) with its secondary aspects, such as techniques of any kind.

Before getting down to the matter of tonal control let me remind you that, while I am dealing specifically with the clarinet, many of my remarks will be equally applicable to any instruments, especially winds. It may be interesting to begin by analyzing the full cycle of tonal concept, even the naive beginning stages. I want to examine every stage, and if my sequence does not agree with yours I hope that at least my general logic will be obvious.

Given a sound, and coping with a clear realization of it, we may find our first conscious thoughts are of its pitch (high or low), duration (long or short), and volume (loud or soft). Unless there is an extreme we do not bother even to identify it, beyond recognizing its existence. This is the birth of our tonal consciousness, not as listeners, but as music-makers—of whom I expect an aggressively analytical thoughtfulness. Possibly our very first conscious effort will find us identifying pitch differences. We continue to make our first tones, possibly aspiring to put them into a recognizable sequence, perhaps even a melody. Such matters as beauty

of tone, dynamic controls, etc., are not immediately present, but we do get a clear idea of the verticality of pitch relationship, even though our tones may be played in sequence (horizontally). There is a certain satisfaction about achieving any definite sound, whether or not it is the intended one! Now you are launched.

The next two items will vary in order according to the individual's priorities, but usually the time factor is noticed first. How long should a tone be held? Notice that I say 'tone.' A 'note' is a symbol which the player transforms into a 'tone.' Awareness of chronological sequence is easily noted by everyone, and we start talking of 'beats' or pulses, perhaps at one-second intervals. This is an easy concept, making it no problem to move further towards the next awareness—volume. At first the only concern has been loudness or softness, later becoming a graded series. It is generally better at this stage to have the player aware of terraced levels only. Now we have pitch, time, and volume working for us.

It is the moment to move on to the inauguration of a tone, its release, touch, or attack. It is a pity that last word is commonly used, since it generally adversely affects the start of notes played in certain moods. 'Release' is much more accurate. 'Attack' generally indicates violence, a forward thrust, etc., and in common use denotes a posture of offense. True, the wind does go forward, but it is usually the tongue going *backwards* which most definitely initiates the sound.

The manner in which a tone begins, and even how it ends, influences the total timbre formation. It becomes obvious that the tongue affects the characteristic overtone formation. True, though the initial 'touch' sound disappears almost at once, there is a difference in a sound without the 'touch' effect. This is one of the reasons an artist produces a more beautiful tone than a beginner. Since the *visualization* of the touch of a string player or pianist is somehow more real than dealing with an out-of-sight tongue, and perhaps for other reasons, the word 'touch' seems to work best. Anyhow with the control of time and volume of tones properly started we have made a significant move towards expressiveness.

A next easy step is to identify time variance, acceleration, and deceleration. Acceleration seems to be built into many people, and deceleration usually seems to be attached to 'beats' only, and not the total contents of that beat. An example is a *ritardando* in quarter note time in which there is a succession of four sixteenth *notes.* These look alike, but should be played as four sixteenth *tones* of increasing lengths, a bit of accuracy often overlooked.

Fig. 1

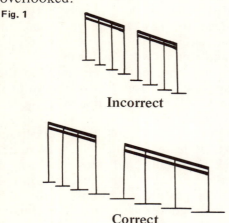

Incorrect

Correct

Somewhere in here comes tuning, since the player has by now probably moved to a fairly stable control of tone production. His hearing will not only distinguish one pitch from another, but will begin to distinguish the flatness or sharpness (flatness usually first) of an individual tone in a series. Since pre-hearing is an absolute requisite in the production of fully controlled tones, this discrimination is crucial in aiming for a 'center' to each tone, which in addition to being in pitch has the greatest resonance and the best potential for full control as detailed later in this text. There must be a mental image. Everything heretofore has been very basic; now we can proceed to a more involved expertise.

First are contrasting levels of volume within an entire section or period, not of individually selected tones: a number of loud tones followed by some softer ones. Then we have levels of 'touch:' note beginnings with differing degrees of abruptness, achieved by variances in the finger (and sometimes breath) action.

The next easily understood refinement is that of *graduated* changes in touch, volume, etc. This takes us beyond the previous rather block-like approach, which had the great virtue of making possible the clean identification and separation of each control factor. Keep in mind that I am still speaking of a very elementary level of performance.

Now we move on to that frequently misused word *staccato*. The word itself means 'to separate' or 'to detach.' The separator is the space, the time interval between the tones. The remaining sound lengths (separatees?) are determined by musical taste in following the composer's directions, or if playing with a conductor one conforms to the conductor's idea of the composer's wishes. Merely identifying a tone as staccato is too general in the early stages of music-making. True, fine professional artists can use the word singly, but only because their rapport is such that each will understand it in the context of the style of that moment in their music-making. The very act of producing a *'staccato'* tone on a clarinet has an influence on the 'touch' effect, a control which should be dealt with separately. I find it most effective, especially in the earlier stages of learning, to qualify the word with an adjective—long, short, shorter, etc., and leaving the stylistic remarks like crisp, light, vigorous, etc., as separate requests. This produces far more clean-cut controls, not overlapping ones. There must be a full range of tone lengths as well as a full range of 'touch' (tonguing) controls. Furthermore, not all such tones should be played with a 'horizontal' volume level. Often, and most sensitively, such tones are each played with a decay of volume and resonance, making a very voice-like effect. This removes the stiff, military-like effects so easily possible with wind instruments.

So far I have been discussing physical controls, though without reference to the details of their achievement, and not really addressing myself to the matter of esthetics. Do you remember your very first effort in imitation of a fine player when, without clearly identifying which controls were involved, you tried to match his mood? Perhaps you tried to play a lullaby with the feeling of a lullaby, instead of just its pitched tones, or a march with a real martial spirit, or a waltz with a real swing to it. That was a great time, and it was probably followed by your noting, or being told, which of your controls needed more attention to produce the desired result. The artist in you was beginning to emerge. You had moved from a secondary aspect of music (controls) to its principal one (projection of feeling, mood, emotion, etc.). In my teaching I have found this to be the most fertile moment. The player really becomes effectively discerning in his search within his own controls to bring about the desired result. Now there is a newly awakened sense of texture, variety of tone quality,

and their full fusion with all previously known controls. Since we can modify the interactions of our reed, air supply, and vibrating air column, we are on the threshold of eventurally unlimited controls.

Tone is a personal concept. It exists within us. There are two general approaches to the subject of control of tonal characteristics. One is a direct imitation, leaving the burden of responsibility to the pupil. The other is verbalization in the presence of imitation. I do not believe in the former, so will discuss only the latter.

The pupil hears the teacher and tries to imitate him, with more or less success. There is the danger that the pupil may have a certain imitative talent and will produce something like the teacher's sound. Invariably he will not know how he did it. While it is imperative that he have examples of the best, a pupil is, after all, his own best teacher—at least he is going to be his own pupil longest. Therefore it is absolutely necessary that he understand what he is aiming for, and what controls are necessary—else when he is away from the immediate example he will flounder. What I am really harking back upon is to recognize *which* controls do *what,* and how and when to use them. You must be able to operate each separately or in conjunction with others.

A first step is for the teacher, in the presence of the given example, to describe it in words. That is the start of building a vocabulary common to the teacher *and* pupil, so that in giving future advice the teacher knows they are discussing a shared experience or example. Analogy is a fine method to deal with various aspects of the tone being described. Almost everyone can be induced to draw from his own stored impressions of sounds he has heard and these can be the basis for making comparative judgments. *The ever-developing concept of good tone is not an immediate transfer of knowledge or example, but a constant nudging in the desired direction.*

I often speak of instrumental teaching being a partially 'subtractive' process. The additive part is easy—each fact, each step must be broached at the appropriate time so that a solid structure of learning is built. The subtractive part is the constant 'pruning' a teacher *must* do to remove the involuntary actions of the pupil which hurt (or destroy) fine playing. The pupil invariably does not see nor hear these until told. I am referring to involuntary physical movements, or music judgments made while pre-occupied with trying to apply a requested control. Editing comments are a must at such moments, to encourage the development of the characteristic tone the pupil could or should try to achieve, given his unique combination of vocal cavity, jaw formation, tooth structure, mouthpiece, reed, instrument, and embouchure—to say nothing of his esthetic objectivity. Therefore the teacher must have the tools (words) constantly to nudge the performer toward ever better controls over a fully malleable tone, with unlimited possibilities for variety of the individual harmonics. The make-up of this multitude is influenced by the player and instrument, and can be minutely described.

We have come finally to what I really am talking about, a concept of tone in all of its ramifications.

First I will set forth my definition of mastery of the clarinet. "You have only to be able to play every note* over the entire register of the instrument, in every nuance, at any speed, with any articulation, with every kind of start and close, and with all changing gradations. Add to this whatever musical talent you have, and mix thoroughly."

* Remember, when you play a note it becomes a tone.

Projection requires producing a healthy tone. This must include the overtones which add richness, fullness and individuality. Initially when we were told to 'blow' into the clarinet we reverted to our past experience such as blowing out a candle. What was sufficient for such purposes is utterly inadequate for producing a healthy tone on the clarinet, which must be supported continually by the whole force of air within the lungs. I liken this support to the squeezing air out of a football by an unremitting pressure on the side *opposite* the opening in the bladder. Translated to the clarinet, and without getting into the complete physiological process of pressing air into the clarinet, this means exerting pressure from the bottom of the lungs so that the wind being ejected is fully backed and under constant pressure from the player. There must be no moments of wind starvation to depress or interrupt tonal continuity. I work on the simple premise that you must have more material available than you mean to use, so you can apportion it at will. A cabinet-maker must have more wood than is actually required for the finished product, else he cannot possibly cut, plane, and sandpaper to size.

The sound must have, both for you and the listener, an apparent roundness throughout its life. This is especially true of the initial moments of the tone. Unless there is a special circumstance, the first moments of life of the sound must be full and resonant. Imagine the wind ejected being a solid column of air in the shape and proportion of a truncated cone of substantial diameter (A), accurately cut at right angles to its axis and moving forward small end first. When viewed head-on the truncated cone would look like a disc as opposed to, let us say, an ice-cream cone (B) approaching point first. I find it helpful to imagine this truncated cone packed with tiny straws, each breathing life forward to make the tone thoroughly nourished.

Fig. 2

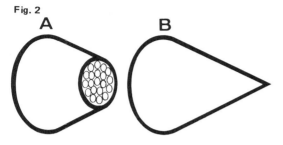

You can further benefit your concept of sound if you will reflect that the clarinet sounds best when played near the peak of its pitch, while other woodwinds are played nearer their centers of pitch and can thus be manipulated towards either flatness or sharpness. Recognition of this distinction can only help you to produce a more efficient and richer tone.

If the tongue can act with sufficient expertise, you set the reed in motion by a succinct and deft *rearward* stroke. Voila! a tone which sounds full at the first instant of its life. It is critical that wind delivery be truly immediate—in fact it is good practice at first to 'pre-blow' before and while setting the reed in motion, to assure true fullness and aliveness at the very start. My point is that only by being able to successfully *inaugurate* a tone with maximum aliveness and intensity can you proceed to the infinite variations required by sophisticated music-making. You must feel that you are producing the tone from the center outwards. You must be focussed on the very core of the sound. Otherwise you will find yourself with a tone which is superficially smooth, but hollow, lacking in intensity and resonance qualities, and leaving little possibility of good projection.

Putting aside all questions of mechanical aids such as oscilloscopes, the now ubiqui-

tous fine quality tape recorders are an almost ideal method of examining your tone. It is best to hear your tone exteriorly and simultaneously search your memory for sensations of control felt when you produced it. Hearing your tone at the actual moment you produced it is not sufficient for complete judgment, because there are influences of various external and internal factors, such as bone conduction (especially true for those who play with teeth directly applied to the mouthpiece). Another example is your own speaking or singing voice. When you first heard it on a recording it seemed unfamiliar. While listening to taped clarinet sounds, recall your precise feelings as to control when you were producing the tones; in other words juxtapose the two experiences. Now you have a more accurate relationship of cause (controls) and effect (the resulting tone).

It is a truism that if you do not have a clear mental concept in which you can identify all the qualitative factors of the sound, and apply to these the specific controls, *each* necessary to produce its contribution to the overall quality, you will not successfully pre-hear your tone. Notice how many players are surprised (and probably annoyed) at moments in their tone production, as though the production itself were an accident, or dependent on external factors. It probably was. They had not identified properly the specific controls necessary to achieve their objectives. They had not accurately pre-heard it.

At this point please notice that I have concerned myself mostly with basic tone only, not with its infinite variations of timbre, resonance, the effects of 'touch,' tuning, vibrato, volume, etc. These aspects should not be considered until you have achieved a healthy, honest, forthright delivery of tone at a substantial level of volume, sufficient so that you know the tone is not being starved. At that time you have enough wood to commence building your cabinet!

Now you can proceed to those limitless subtleties of each control: timbre, which may be adjusted to make for better blending with certain instruments (example— different for playing with a flute than with an oboe); tuning, which in its finest form is never static, though giving an always satisfying esthetic sense of rightness; resonance of individual tones, each of which may vary within itself to suit a particular circumstance; 'touch,' which can have such a decided effect on one's sense of tone quality; and vibrato, which when used should have an infinite variety (within its limits) of pitch, intensity and speed. If you have control sufficient to make all of these effective on command, you will have made it possible to build yourself a tonal image which can directly relate to the musical style, such as Mozart in contrast to Debussy. You will have succeeded in truly 'tailoring' your tone, with individually identifiable controls, and from a known 'recipe.'

Chapter 4:
DIVIDE AND CONQUER

A. WHEN?

In addressing ourselves to the subject of general improvement in playing an instrument, the last thing we should allow ourselves is to be general. The basis of good tone production is efficiency *at each step,* and the elimination of waste motion or air in *each detail.*

The body and mind are inefficient during the early stages of playing because both tend to respond together and instinctively to an unfamiliar challenge. An instinctive response tends to involve all, or at least many, parts of the body working in sympathy with each other. For example, we recoil not just by shrinking away, but also by throwing up our hands or closing our eyes, moving away, or any number of other movements. Most are thoughtless, the result of a lifetime of experience.

In the case of the clarinet (and the clarinet *is* a challenge) we face a whole new series of physical actions and mental activities—many of them unfamiliar, and none of them having been combined before in these particular ways. These must be isolated or combined in various unnatural degrees. Certainly a good deal of attention has been paid to developing each of these many requirements, and also their use together, but not enough attention has been given to the *means* of isolating them for efficient study. It is the means I want to discuss here, as they enable us to work for specific single objectives—always a better policy than to study and practice for general improvement. It goes without saying (*almost* without saying!) that one can improve somewhat by striving for general improvement. But then it is much easier, in the early stages, for bad habits to creep in. These are increasingly difficult to remove as time goes on and they become embedded. The teaching techniques I will describe enable us to edit faults before they become habits.

First let us tackle the question of when to play. We normally read music in association with the production of our first tones. But I strongly believe that we should commence producing tones in association with written notes only when we can pulse the music properly, and have a good concept of the pitch relationships—that is to *solfège* it. Otherwise the concentration needed for planning *when* to play *what* tone, will seriously detract from the attention available for the physical control of the instrument. You must be free to concentrate solely on the clarinet at this early stage. This separation of the clarinettist from the clarinet is the first of the many separations I propose.

There are many excellent works which one can use as texts in this connection, but for me the best is *Rhythmic Training* by Robert Starer. Ideally it would be best if one could study all the material in the entire book before tackling the clarinet, but that would not be in the order of most people's enthusiasms. However I would consider it mandatory that at the very outset of playing an instrument a substantial amount of work with this book should already have been done. Because the visual, tactile (relating to motor controls), and audible mean so much among our senses I think that the solid development of their coordination is absolutely mandatory during any solfeggio study.

My method of working with the Starer book is simple and graphic. Because the visual and the audible mean so much to our senses, I think both are absolutely essential to the solfège study which precedes the study of an instrument. The equipment needed—a pencil, surfaces for producing three different sounds when tapped upon (perhaps a hard-bound book, a paperback, and a pamphlet), the Starer book and a music stand. Notice that at this time we are concerned with rhythmic training only. The pupil should be unencumbered by a clarinet or by any pitch relationships, except for the differentiation between the three sounds. I ask that they tap out the indicated rhythms of the lower notes using the hardback for the prime pulse, the paperback for the secondary pulse, and the pamphlet for the weakest beats—meanwhile singing a 'tu' syllable in a monotone for the values indicated by the upper notes. For example the taps in a 5/4 measure would be thus:

Ex. 1

H=Hardback

S=Softback (paperback)

P=Pamphlet

Once the initial pulsation is grasped you have a firm basis for proceeding to subdivisions such as:

Ex. 2. Visual, aural and physical coordination must be fully mastered.

Then progression extends to such complicated patterns as:

Ex. 3

A metronome is imperative at the outset, and until the pupil has developed the ability to maintain an even beat series, without speeding or slowing, in a reasonable tempo, such as ♩ = MM72. As soon as the first half-dozen or so pages have been mastered, begin work with pitch relationships, using any of the well-known solfège study books—each teacher usually has a favorite. The rhythmic demands should encompass no more than has been mastered in the Starer studies. After a couple of weeks of this, one can safely start with the clarinet.

There is such a multiplicity of clarinet methods that I hardly need to suggest material for beginning. For my own teaching I use the *Méthode* by Eugene Gay (see Chapter 17 for a description). The rhythmic problems there have been already met in the Starer book.

B. HOW?

Pay considerable attention to the choice of the first sounds, in whatever method you use. They must be sounds which the student can sing accurately, set in rhythmic patterns he can beat. At this stage tones which are going to be played are readily within the range of any voice. It is vitally important that the habit of 'pre-hearing' becomes solidly entrenched. The player must be able to hear the pitch in his imagination—before he plays it on the clarinet. Alas, many players await (with wonderment and curiosity) the sounds the clarinet will produce, rather than have a clean-cut concept in advance. This habit is critical not only to tuning but also to good sound production, rhythm, and of course later, phrasing, etc. If they cannot give proper evidence of performing by singing and tapping, they should not play the tones on the clarinet! Thus you see our first absolute requirement is that we 'separate out' the subjects of rhythm and pitch before proceeding with the mysteries of the clarinet itself.

When a novice is poised in that moment before making initial sounds, trying to focus attention on ever-too-many unfamiliar and unnatural actions, the single most important thing for him to bear in mind is the idea that the clarinet is a *wind* instrument. As described in chapter 3, it must be blown with very solid backing, utterly unlike blowing out a candle or match. These latter actions probably represent the player's blowing experience to that moment. They are, of course, only 'mouth' blowing, while the air blown into a clarinet has to be fully supported by the whole reservoir of air in the lungs, and by the strength of the lung walls and diaphragm. For me the easiest method of presenting this idea has been to ask the pupil to imagine a football, with the nozzle uppermost. The project is to get the air out of the football with an absolutely steady pressure, with the greatest possible wind speed. It is easy for a pupil to understand that this is done by maintaining a consistent, unyielding pressure from the walls opposite the nozzle, and of a strength to maintain an unrelenting stream of air. He should imagine his wind production as a long solid cylinder.

The suggestion of density is, at this point, of utmost importance—the idea of wind continuity, speed and density being critical. This is not the time to worry about any other aspects of playing, since there will not have been time yet to develop any continuing bad habits with other controls. I find it useful to have a pupil hold his hand up about six inches from his mouth and eject a *blast* of air from his lungs, so he can feel the intensity, meanwhile being acutely aware that the source is not his mouth, but the constricting lung walls. The mouth serves only as a passage, and by use of the throat and lips, a focuser. Here another useful trick is to have the pupil stand in a draughtless room and hold a piece of typewriting paper (the lightest possible) about ten inches in front of his mouth. By carefully focussing and fully backing his blown breath he should be able to make the paper stand still at any chosen angle (see illustration Chapter 14). The evidence is so graphic that this is a good exercise to take home for study and experimentation the first week of playing.

We have separated out a clearly identifiable objective, and in the matter of making a sound we have put the first thing first. In general my method of teaching is to emphasize only one or two ideas at each meeting, which should serve as basis for the greatest attention during a week of study and practice. Obviously the aim is to do less *better,* not to disperse efforts over *more*. Refinements in blowing I will deal with further along, but meanwhile let us proceed to the concept of embouchure.

Everyone has heard of 'look ma, no-hands' bicycling,—'no-pressure' playing of various instruments,—'relaxed' this, and 'relaxed' that type of playing. Not for a moment do I want to overlook the value of relaxation, either as a direct technique in performance, or as a constructive time away from the effort of playing. But this is the point where the pupil must be made to realize that muscles not commonly used are going to have to come into play. The embouchure formation requires tensing of certain neck and face muscles. While it is obvious that this is not the time to get into the refinements of this positioning, it is the time to establish the idea that this subject is a must. No playing should be done without considering all aspects of this mouthpiece, reed, and clarinet positioning. 'Re-building' the embouchure of a player who has had several years of playing with an incorrect, inefficient positioning is very hard on the teacher, and even harder on the pupil. Make continual use of a mirror. Few people are sufficiently aware of the isolation of the particular muscles involved; consequently they must see on themselves the positioning which the teacher is trying to establish.

No two embouchures are alike, since jaw shape, condition of teeth, shape of normal 'bite', etc. all play a part. Only a capable teacher can, by observation, be a proper judge of this positioning for the individual. It is difficult to make a pupil understand that 'tensing' does not mean 'biting.' By carefully adopting the advice of the teacher, producing sounds while viewing himself in the mirror, and noting his embouchure position when the teacher indicates correctness, the pupil can set the first solid stages of embouchure develop-

ment. Obviously refinement will continue until he is a well-developed player.

It is imperative to see that the embouchure position is *fully formed* before the onset of each sound, and it must remain in position until after the sound has ceased. Otherwise there will be a pitch and tone quality change at each end of the tone involved. I go to the extent of insisting on a real moment of reflective editorial silence *after* the embouchure is formed and *before* the tone is produced,— and a similar silence *after* the tone has ceased and *before* the muscles are relaxed. It is a very easy habit to acquire at this stage, and the resulting purity of pitch and tone quality throughout the life of the tone are a sufficient reward for the effort. You will find that it is not very difficult to create an awareness of the individuality of effort of the blowing apparatus, and the muscles involved in embouchure formation. It clearly separates out the embouchure identification in the player's mind and feelings.

Because of differing physical equipment—teeth, jaws, general physique, etc.— it is almost mandatory that each player have a 'tailor-made' modus operandi. With today's excellent tape recorders (particularly the almost ubiquitous small cassette recorders) and by the use of a mirror for embouchure and throat analysis, it is possible for a player to hear himself exteriorly, without the confusion added when the mouthpiece is being played, with the resulting felt vibration. Thus he can relate what he hears from the recording to what he saw and felt when he played. We are in the process of witnessing a break-through in the form of photographs taken interiorly with the wonderful new cameras, adapted from those being used for surgical purposes. They will help us rid ourselves of many misconceptions, irregularities, and vague generalities of throat, tongue, lip (and tongue) use with which we have had to live. I have read some of the findings of the talented and alert university-based wind teachers who, together with some sympathetic scientists, are hard at work in this area.

Now comes the problem of the correct use of the tongue. Since birth we all have been accustomed to use the tongue and mouth muscles in conjunction with one another. There are practically no normal human actions where one uses one without the other. Consequently requiring each to move alone takes, at first, an abnormal effort, and few people fully succeed at this stage. A few moments of having the pupil move the tongue freely, using small strokes against the back of his teeth, at his command, all the while keeping the mouth closed, and the face muscles immobile, followed by doing the same thing with the lips parted (but not moving one iota) generally succeed in having him understand and *feel* the individuality and potential independence of the tongue motion. This then is the ideal time to have him sustain a long, held tone, meanwhile just touching the reed lightly at spaced intervals, using some rhythmic pattern to accustom the tongue to independent command—and all the while watching the mirror to see that there is absolutely no sympathetic mouth or jaw motion. Do this until there is really *no* sympathetic motion. The idea which I try to impart is that the jaw and mouth positions *must*, before, at the onset, at the close, and *after* the end of the tone, be in the same position as they are in the middle of a well-played tone. The use of the tongue must in *no* way disturb this. It is merely a valve acting independently. True enough, there are circumstances later in one's career when one may wish to 'bend' a tone, or otherwise control the embouchure—but not at this moment.

Each teacher will have his own way of proceeding with the development of the tongue use, to make staccato sounds, etc. I have dealt with this subject in chapters 12 through 15, but I do want to touch on one important point here. In a succession of articulated (tongued) sounds where some are staccato and some are joined, it is important that the student realize that the tongue action for *starting* each of these tones is exactly the same. It is only *after* the tone has begun to sound that the question of legato or staccato ending becomes pertinent as far as tongue action is concerned. This approach will result in a far more agile staccato, and will give more tonal coherence to the overall passage. Somehow many players tend to use a softer tongue action on the first of the group of slurred tones, resulting in lack of clarity, agility, and consistency.

Ex. 4

The matter of fingers and general posture must be dealt with early in a career. Keep in mind that because no one of us was built to play a clarinet, it behooves us to adopt a bodily posture which is as natural as possible. Any eccentricity can only breed problems. The breathing must be in no way inhibited, and the arm and finger positioning must be not strained. The actual manner of manipulating the fingers will vary from person to person.

Most people probably assume that since they use their fingers for any number of other purposes they can use the same familiar motions in playing the clarinet. Not quite; actually one or two simple thoughts ought to be entertained.

The first is to use the fingers in as simple and efficient a manner as possible.

Many teachers allow their pupils to use what I call the 'unwinding' method. A finger is brought to the instrument with each joint contributing a little to the overall motion. The result is very imprecise control of timing, and an inefficiency in closing the required hole.

My observations lead me clearly to the conclusion that those players with normal sized hands are most successful when the fingers are slightly arched so that the individual whorls of the fingers come into full and instant—and silent—contact with the *entire* ring or hole. Your finger is only going to the wood, not through it! Pay attention to the whorls' contact with the far side of the rings or holes—that is the side opposite the hand involved.

I find it meaningful, as a regular exercise, to study and practice the raising and lowering of the individual fingers on a surface—even your knee will do—being very conscious that *all* movement is at the base of the finger. This joint acts as a fulcrum or axle. There must be no sympathetic movement from any other joints or fingers, and each finger must act as an individual, as though sprung to either close or open instantly. The time spent in movement must be as close to zero as possible, and the springing (agility, deftness) must be as developed on the up-motion as on the down (most players have better control with the downward motion). Remember that the fingering for a given tone is that which involves the fingers needed to be moved to reach the new tone from the last one, *not* the fingering of the fingering charts (unless it is a tone after a silence). One hundred percent of your attention must be directed to the specific finger(s) to be moved. Movements between tones will be cleaner, thus, among other things, making it easier to play tones in quick succession.

Needless to say, this action should be repeated with each finger of each hand. At first practice only on the ringless holes, since it is then easiest to judge the effect of your finger action. When you move on to the keys, you must be sure to recognize that it is not the instant when your finger touches the key which matters, but only the instant when the pad touches, or leaves, the wood. Remember when 'practicing' that you do not just want to 'improve' (everything). If that is your objective you will find improvement in some areas, but at the expense of slowness, and of continuing some faults which may be part of your natural contribution. Each single repetition of such fault serves to 'build-in' the fault. I urge you to play each etude (or specific fingering or other problem) with only *one* clearly identified objective. When you are satisfied move on to the next single objective, and you will find that the first one just does not get lost in the process. You will soon find that though you *can* focus on several points at once the real breakthrough comes in doing so *after* single-subject concentration. Then you gradually emcompass all.

Though most of the points discussed in this chapter have already been, or will be, discussed in other chapters I repeat them here specifically in the interests of tone quality, legato and sostenuto.

One of the most common pitfalls is in separating the motion of the fingers from the flow of the wind column. The symptom is a lapse in the continuity of sound, a break of sorts in the legato, and a tendency to 'push' or 'open up' on sounds. Ideally one must be able to move, in a legato situation, from one tone to the next without a moment of re-adjustment of either embouchure or wind flow. True there are instances when a fine player may wish to have these tiny lapses, or hesitations, but this is not the concern of the moment. Try sustaining a C^3, A^2, F^2

or E², as in Ex. 5, until the security of the wind flow is clearly established, then with your eyes on the mirror, your ears on the tonal continuity, merely lower the next adjoining finger as lightly and cleanly as possible. If done really well you will hear a very marked continuing fullness of sound. The resonances of the two sounds will appear to overlap as in Fig. 1.

Ex. 5

Think only | Think only | Think only | Think only
of LH 1 | of LH 3 | of RH 2 | of RH 3

Maintain an absolutely uninterrupted level of sound.

Fig. 1

First tone   Second tone

Fig. 2

A - Aspire to this continuity   B - Avoid this lack of continuity

Now the matter of tone quality is a markedly individual one, as it should be, since each has his own ideal. Nonetheless every tone should be resonant and well supported. In these past couple of decades there has been great emphasis on a 'dark' sound as opposed to a 'bright' one. In my experience I have found these terms used inexactly—dark, often used principally to mean well connected and without 'edge'. As any fine artist will attest, both varieties are absolutely necessary if one is to play the full gamut of the clarinet repertoire. Dark or bright, what is truly essential is the carrying quality, which must have the maximum potential. It is no trouble at all for a player whose tone is

normally resonant to withdraw support from a sound to produce, for example, a sub-tone effect; but no player who usually plays with a non-resonant sound can instantly add resonance on command of the music.

One of the exercises I have used most effectively for developing evenness of finger touch is one which I wrote some years ago and which is quoted below. Practice it *slowly* with plenty of thinking time on each note. Before you move on to the next note, consider the efficiency of your last move and make such adjustments as are necessary to improve the next. Even when you begin to play it more quickly you must keep in mind that the finger motions remain the same for all speeds; all that varies is the time spent on each note. Notice that I have it in a ternary rhythm so that the accent is at some time on each note.

Ex. 6

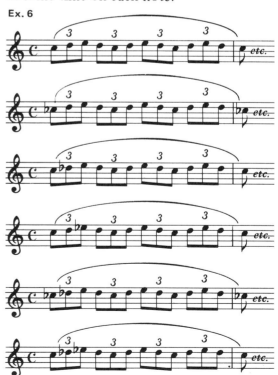

Now follow the exact same procedure using sharps instead of flats. Then proceed with a combination of sharps and flats as exercise #7.

Ex. 7

Afterward follow the same procedure with any three successive notes over the entire clarinet range. I suggest studying and practicing each set of three notes for a number of days, until you feel that all the qualities you want are present.

All of these main elements of playing must be *identified* individually, *dealt* with individually, and *mastered* individually before combining them. This takes a considerable effort of concentration and self-analysis, but the rewards are great. I think it axiomatic that if anyone is studying and practicing (particularly the latter) to make *everything* better, far less will happen than when focussing on one specific problem. Obviously as one's expertise develops it is possible to keep more subjects under surveillance—my emphasis here is on the earlier stages. This is when it is absolutely necessary to identify each of the controls separately before combining them. Only the fine quality of the individual components will allow the 'manufacture' of a complete technique with its many ramifications, because phrasing depends on your ability to exercise each of these controls separately. Then you are free to make music.

Chapter 5:
TEMPO—SOME NOTES ON ITS INNER MYSTERIES

The word 'tempo' is over-burdened with opinions—and under-tenanted by universally accepted procedures. However, that it is subject to so much individual interpretation is one of its greatest strengths.

The easy way out of decision-making in the matter of tempo is to turn instantly to a metronome. Having a metronome marking indicated by the composer, one is hopeful of having found the truth. Lacking this one can adopt a metronome speed conventionally related to the composer's verbal indication, for example MM 120 ±, if he wrote 'allegro.' Neither reliably produces the composer's wanted mood; the seemingly precise first method is sometimes unbelievably inaccurate. I recall dozens of rehearsals in which strict adherence to some world-famous composer's metronomic indications only made them splutter that the music did not 'sound right.' I recall even more instances when the conductor disregarded the metronomic indications thus making the music sound as *he* felt it—the composer meanwhile wreathed in smiles because the music *did* 'sound right.'

Different tempo feelings are achieved by playing music with different kinds of inflections. For me the most important markings are the composer's words, rather than his numerical indications. The 'Allegro con spirito' would have a very different meaning (and feeling) than 'Allegro amabile.' It is imperative that the modifying word(s) be given full consideration as these describe the musical effect that is the composer's. Adherence to a numerical MM standard may—or may not—coincide with the intended effect.

A really expert player can, for example, give an illusion and feeling of movement by the character of his articulation, pulsing, and tonal inflection. A less capable player, not having those controls, can give the feeling of movement only by playing faster—and inevitably creating all kinds of technical problems for himself. This is why I believe that the strictest attention should be given to tone production—its clarity of enunciation and delivery, its edginess or fogginess of start, its incisiveness, its legato, its color (bright or brilliant to dark), its accentuation, its articulation, indeed *any* controls which help to give the intended feeling of tempo. When arbitrary adherence to a stated metronome tempo takes you beyond your ability to exercise all of these controls, your less controlled sounds become less effective. What really matters is that you attain the mood and feeling indicated by the composer!

Now let us consider the words commonly used today in relation to tempo, with definitions drawn from the dictionary as well as common musical usage.

grave	—solemn (very, very slow), heavy, weighty, serious
largo	—broad (very slow), wide
adagio	—quite slow—slowly
lento	—slow, loose, relaxed
andante	—a moderate walking pace
andantino	—the original meaning is 'going not quite so fast', but it has been corrupted into meaning slightly faster, *or* slightly slower. You can determine the intention by the character of the music, or the words of the composer.
moderato	—moderate
allegretto	—moderately fast
allegro	—fast, cheerful, merry, gay
vivace	—lively, quick, brisk, bright

presto   —very fast
prestissimo —very, very fast

There is no universal agreement as to the order. This is amusingly shown by a currently popular textbook which has gone through many printings. In one printing (1963) the order is largo, grave, lento, adagio, andante, etc. In the next, seven years later, the order becomes grave, adagio, lento, andante, etc. Quantz, in the early 18th century, listed the order as lento, adagio assai, adagio, grave, affettuoso, spirituoso, cantabile, arioso, andantino, andante and allegro. It is a clear case of having to know your composer, or at least the milieu in which he worked. The greatest ambiguity is with the slower tempi. Without knowing the source of the music you are to play, I would suggest relying only on the character of the music, rather than trying to guess at the intended order of speeds.

The first modifications of each of these tempo markings are the suffixes: 'issimo' (to make stronger or more) and '–ino' or '–etto' (to make weaker or less). Important: notice that 'ada*gissimo*' would be slower than adagio, and 'prest*issimo*' would be faster than presto. Andantino could be either slower or faster, as I indicated above. 'Larghetto' would be less broad than largo, and 'allegretto' would be less fast than allegro. Consider the *actual* meaning of the *basic* word in deciding what the effect of the suffix would be.

Most of the commonly modifying words and phrases—'piu' meaning more, 'meno' less, 'non troppo' not too much, etc.—are easy to interpret. But some of the more individual modifying words are subtle enough to warrant discussion. I cannot resist illustrating this point with the King-Of-All-Modifying-Word-Makers, François Couperin. A random sample of his grada-

tions (translated from his native French) might include graciously, majestically, tenderly, very gaily, nonchalantly, languishing, naively, imperiously, firmly serious, amorously and tender badinage. Try setting your metronome to these!

The best way to illustrate the importance of modifying words is to cite specific examples, and naturally I will use clarinet repertoire.

Brahms–*Sonata in E♭ major,* Opus 120, #2

1. 'Allegro amabile.' The amabile (amiable) connotes a more relaxed, broader, and perhaps very slightly slower tempo.
2. 'Appassionato, ma non troppo allegro.' This poses a curious problem. And an interesting question is raised by the new Wiener Urtext Edition. In their notes they seem to say that Brahms changed the tempo markings of this movement on the engraver's copy from 'Allegro, ma non troppo allegro' to 'Allegro appassionato.' But then they have proceeded to print it with the 'Appassionato, ma non troppo allegro' in the clarinet and alternate viola parts, and as 'Allegro appassionato' in the piano part! I have not yet had the opportunity to track this down with the editors, but nonetheless it clearly shows that Brahms did not think that one marking meant the same as the other, since he took the trouble to change the engraver's copy. One thing I feel sure about—he did not expect the clarinet and piano to be playing from differently marked parts.
3. 'Andante con moto.' With the usual ebb and flow of tempi following the character of each variation.
4. 'Finale' (played segue) marked 'Allegro.' The 'non troppo' which was added subsequently was deleted later

in the score. It does seem to indicate that at some point he did not want a hasty allegro.

Brahms–*Sonata in F minor,* Opus 120, #1

1. 'Allegro appassionato.' Notice that this was the original marking of the second movement of the E♭ sonata. When he wanted a driving allegro, passionately played, he said so. The coda–'Sostenuto ed espressivo'–obviously yields some of the motion and drive in order to achieve the sostenuto and espressivo.
2. 'Andante un poco Adagio.' This is the most misunderstood movement. *Andante* paces the quarter note values (denominator) and *Adagio* is the modifier toward slowness–and only a little (un poco) at that.
3. 'Allegretto grazioso.' A 'normal' allegretto tempo, well articulated as evidence by the 'grazioso' marking–which would bring about graceful, somewhat dance-like movement.
4. 'Vivace.' Clearly a true vivace–everything the word implies.

Brahms–*Quintet in B minor,* Opus 115

1. 'Allegro.' This later changes to 'quasi sostenuto' then returns to the original allegro, marked 'a tempo.'
2. 'Adagio.' The middle section is 'Piu Lento' with possibly increasing speed and tension in measure 78 but relaxing at measure 87 so that measure 88, the recapitulation, will be at the same speed and mood as the beginning. Notice that the recapitulation is *not* marked as to tempo, yet it simply has to be at the same speed as the opening of the movement.
3. 'Andantino,' followed by a 'Presto non assai, ma con sentimento.' This movement is frequently played by simply looking at the word 'Presto'

and ignoring the very clear modifying statements.

4. 'Con moto.' Each variation finds its own slightly different tempo. The coda, marked 'Un poco meno mosso,' takes the tempo of the first movement, perhaps slightly relaxed.

Mozart–*Trio in E♭ major* (Kegelstatt), K 498–is, as regards tempi, a bone of contention between players. The three movements are marked Andante, Menuetto, and Allegretto. Because the first movement is in 6/8 meter, and because the themes also lend themselves to playing with two pulses in a measure, the movement is often so played. This produces a trio with three quickish movements, something one would hardly expect from Mozart. If you heed the rule of thumb that the denominator of the time signature is the measuring stick for tempo, and couple it with Mozart's word 'Andante,' you will arrive at a tempo in which the grupetti (written out as 64th notes by Mozart) can be lyrically played. An absolutely fascinating article has recently appeared– *"Mozart's Trio, K 498"* by Dennis G. Giokas in the International Clarinet Society's journal *The Clarinet*–which for me sets this matter finally to rest. By a most ingenious examination of the relationships of all the thematic material therein, Giokas arrives at a beautiful, logical solution–a trio properly balanced as to tempi, and with each theme sounding its best. The ♩. of the first movement equals the ♩. of the second movement, and the ♩ of the third movement. He uses a MM marking of 44 to the ♩. of the first movement (equivalent to an ♪ at 132), a MM marking of 44 to the ♩. in the second (equal to ♪ at 132), and a marking of 66 to a ♩ in the third (equal to ♪ at 132). You will see that the eighth note speed of the first movement equals the quarters of the second and third movements. If you have been in the habit of playing the first movement with two rather quick pulses to the measure, you will be uncomfortable until you bring yourself to play the melodies of this movement more broadly and lyrically, as would suit a 6/8 movement in six pulses.

Incidentally, this is a good moment for a digression to correct what I believe was a copyist's oversight in preparing the parts of this trio. Or maybe Mozart's oversight! The Menuet begins cleanly on a melody and after twelve measures, repeats. Then it goes on to a second melody, a slight tonal variant of the first, introduced by three up-beat leading notes (Example 1).

Ex. 1

I believe that this probably was a separate '1st and 2nd ending' situation which in printing was compacted into a single repetition, therefore unintentionally producing the three up-beat notes for the repeat of the first theme. I believe that the first melody was intended always as a head-on entry, and the second (measure 13) always had the up-beats. This, of course, necessitates adding the three up-beats at the repetition of this second phrase (measure 41 returning to measure 13). If any further proof be needed, look at measure 114—there again are the three up-beat notes in their proper relation to that second theme (Example 2).

Ex. 2

In short, you have the best chance of re-creating the mood and atmosphere of the composer's intentions, since your every effort will be bent in those directions, if you don't struggle to adhere to a numerically indicated tempo.

Mozart–*Quintet in A major* (clarinet and strings)—KV 581. There is one problem in this quintet—the Larghetto. In this instance it is the diminution of Largo, therefore a little quicker. Add to this the fact that the denominator of the time signature is in quarters, plus the continuous moving eighths of the three upper strings, and you have an easy flowing movement with three pulses per measure. As to the *variance* in the variations of the last movement: rather than indicate new tempi for each (which then tend to depart too much in one direction or another) I use the two symbols ⎯⎯⎯⟶ and ⟵⎯⎯⎯⎯ to indicate moving the tempo *slightly* forward or backward.

Chapter 6:
METER AND RHYTHM

Our first step should be to sort out these two words—meter and rhythm. Whereas in the eighteenth and nineteenth centuries they were often used synonymously, the increasing complexity of our century's writing makes it helpful to have a clearer distinction in our minds. Meter, the first term, is the easier to articulate—it generally being used to mean fixed time patterns in music. Rhythm, on the other hand, is much more complex in definition. Its meaning, coming from the Greek word for 'flow' is best understood by me as meaning 'pulsing,' a living, audible and felt sensation. In a practical way one can say it is a means by which most music can come truly alive. A continuum of sound without some sense of pulsing could more easily be understood as sound coloring, rather than music in its more usual complete meaning. However we must not overlook certain compositions, or at least sections of such, where color atmosphere prevails. Nor, some of today's music where no discernible rhythmic flow is intended.

The interrelationship between these two words is a complex one, dealt with variously by many authorities. For my own use I keep the metric definition in its simplest form—fixed patterns in music in which we interpolate a variety of rhythmic patterns or pulsed feelings. Speaking as a teacher and interpretive musician, this gives me an immediately understood terminology—and this last is an absolute must in music teaching.

The simplest meter is obviously one with two components, a strong and a weak sound—born undoubtedly out of the the 'two-ness' of our legs and arms, and

their subsequent use. In music writing it is indicated by a simple numeral as:

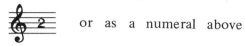 or as a numeral above

another as in Example 1.

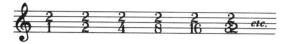

Denominators larger than 32 are rarely, if ever used, and serve no practical purpose. Sometimes a note value (i.e. ♩.) is used as a denominator. It is important to recall that the denominator indicates the note value which is used as a 'beat' or pulse to which a metronome indication, or composer's descriptive instructions are tied, or at least related. The numerator indicates the number of such units (values) there are between bar lines, and the number can be various as in Example 2.

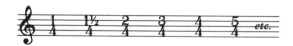

I have seen music with numerators as high as 20, but this is rare though theoretically possible. As a practical matter when you are dealing with large numerators you may find that they need to be subdivided into component groups, such as a 7/4 measure being either a 4/4 plus 3/4 or vice versa. This usually serves to indicate a principal pulse on the first group's initial beat and the secondary one on the first tone of the second group. The reason for the choice of a numerator is easily understood by consulting the music itself, but the choice of a numeral for the denominator is mostly psychological—the most usual being 2, 4, 8 or 16.

The presence of meter indications gives the first sense of flow to the music, but beyond this first sensing there is an infinite array of possibilities. It is here that we are really dealing with rhythm. It is here that the infiniteness of variety, and the most complex subtleties of pulsing are felt. Indications for rhythmic pulsing, beyond those indicated by the simple meter terminology, include accent or stress marks written above or below the note; articulation or other phrasing marks; and the musical content itself, i.e., the presence of more or weighter tones or chords on certain 'beats' of a measure. The net effect is a superimposition of a rhythmic pattern over the more simple metric pattern of the time signature. Composers often retain a convenient time signature, though the music may go through moments, or periods, of pulsing other than that indicated by the time signature, sometimes at cross purposes, and sometimes merely elaborating the basic meter. As you see, the metric signs thus indicate a basic pattern or pulsing without inhibiting the use of more complex rhythmic indications.

More and more contemporary music is written without bar lines as metric indications, and of course without the conventional time signatures. In these instances pulsing has been sometimes indicated by numerals over notes where metric stresses were to be given (in effect momentary time-signatures, since this method is frequently used when metric accents change often), and sometimes by the bracketing and manner of grouping the notes themselves. In his *Sonata #2*, for clarinet and piano, Hugo Kauder uses short vertical lines (|) above the wanted pulsings. This, together with his note-bracketing, makes for a very clear and unambiguous guide to his intent, and allows for continuous easy change if so desired. No doubt a search through the literature would unearth many other methods, but they are beyond the scope of this chapter.

All of the above has been academic, and of general knowledge. I offer it here only as a prelude to calling attention to various metric and rhythmic examples in the clarinet literature evident in various degrees, yet sometimes overlooked.

Paul Hindemith was a notable example of pulse changing, sometimes by meter changes, and again by either phrasing or notation indications. In Example 3, his *Sonata for clarinet and piano,* he establishes a meter of 3/4 at the start of the first movement. Each of these measures remains constant except for individual measures which are marked appropriately, and when two such measures come in succession he indicates the meter for both.

Ex. 3

Further along in the same movement he uses other means: notation in the clarinet part, where the clarinet has to play four tones each absolutely equal to the other, and pulsed as in a 4/4 measure.

The basically established pulse is three beats to a measure (in the middle section appearing as 9/8 in the piano part). At number 7 both instruments have a 2/4 measure indication and immediately return to the basic three-beat pulse, after which the clarinet has to play four equal tones, essentially a 4/4 measure pulsed as such, against the piano's continuing two pulses (Example 4).

Ex. 4

Incidently, at number 5 in the same movement (Example 5) it should be noticed that the clarinet continues in 3/4 (though the piano changes to 9/8) with individual beats being written in 9/8 meter.

Ex. 5

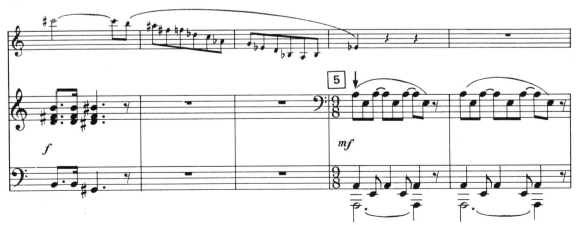

During my Tanglewood years, when playing and discussing this Sonata (Hindemith was for a number of years also a member of the faculty) I asked him about his preferred method of indicating pulsing. He said simply that he used a number of means, and each was such as to be self-evident to any musician capable of playing the piece in question. Almost invariably he intermixed binary and ternary indications in 2/4 (6/8) and 3/4 (9/8) meters. And truly they are very obvious. He was an extraordinarily fluent composer, and he used whichever method seemed best at the moment. His lifetime as a performing musician gave him an outlook more practical than most composers.

Brahms, of an earlier generation and following nineteenth century usage, indicated notational and phrasing directions to bring about pulse changes. In his *Sonata in E♭*, Opus 120, #2, in the second movement, measure 126 (Example 6), his phrasing marks show his desire to have three 2/4 measures. The quarter-note value remains constant.

Ex. 6

In the fourth movement of the same sonata (Example 7) he uses phrase markings in the right hand and notation in the left to indicate the desired pulsing in four.

Ex. 7

In the first movement of his first clarinet sonata notice the breadth of feeling brought into play by the introducing of his 3/2 phrasing (or three 2/4 measures, if you will) to bring three inflections (pulsings) equi-distant from each other and extending over a two-measure span (Example 8).

Ex. 8

Another excellent example of pulsing by phrasing indications which countermand the instructions of the time signature occurs in the third movement of the same sonata beginning at measure 75 (Example 9). Here again he is absolutely clear.

Beginning with measure 75 he indicates phrasing inflections on each of the first four measures, but he distinctly wants a 6/4 measure made of measures 79 and 80, in contrast with the clearly enunciated 3/4 pulsation of measures 75 through 78.

Ex. 9

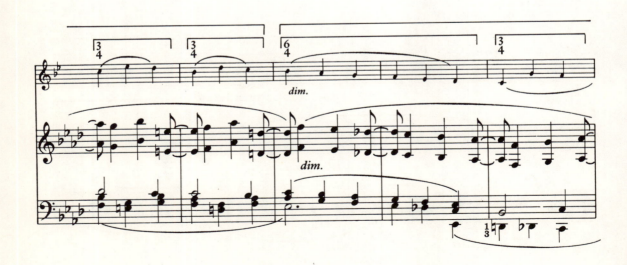

An excellent example of Hindemith's phrasing and pulsing is in the first movement of his clarinet sonata at measure 16 where the clarinet continues in 2/2 meter and the piano plays a 3/4 against it, with ♪ = ♪ (Example 10).

Ex. 10

Notice in the fifth measure after number 16 how he merely doubles the piano movement from 3/4 to 3/8, a practice which baroque composers sometimes used in fugal writing.

A more important example, because it very much affects the feeling for the whole phrase, is in the last movement of Brahms first clarinet sonata (Example 11). At measure 42—for the first four measures the right hand of the piano, and for the next four measures the clarinet plus the right hand of the piano, are playing a broad melody which has three pulses to the measure rather than the time signature indication of two. Thus this produces a broad, sweeping melody which is a beautiful contrast to the charming, active 'alla breve,' two-beat pulsation of the first theme. In the cited measures the remaining voices remain with two beats to the measure. It is not difficult to do; it gives the melody its own proper feeling, and acts as a wonderful contrast to the abrupt change of manner of the leggiero which begins in measure 54.

The performing aspects are simple. In measure 42 the pianist counts triplets (2x3 ♪), and in measure 43 merely changes this to 3x2 ♪ , with the counting units (triplet ♪) remaining the same. The clarinet continues to count 2x3 ♪ until measure 46 when he changes to 3x2 ♪ . At measure 47 both change to a broad triplet ♪ (♩♩♩). *The value of the triplet must remain exactly the same throughout.* This may sound complicated to read, but in actual performance it is easy to do and it gives each part of the music its own character.

As a final example there is the closing page of Brahms' E♭ *clarinet sonata,* which always bothers young students, and many professionals. Yet if one follows Brahms' very specific notation the result is musically most convincing (Example 12). The problems commence in measure 135. The solution is simple—count quarters in a 2/4 pattern until the end of measure 139. There count quarters and subdivide them into sixteenths. Count the last eighth value of measure 140 as two sixteenths, and the next three sixteenths as three sixteenths. Then for the piano solo merely count five times 3/16. The clarinet entrance after carefully counting 5x3/16 is on a downbeat of an eighth note, and this entrance can be made with great rhythmic security and poise. It is well to play this slowly several times until the counting is absolutely clear. The phrasing sounds exactly as Brahms indicated it, using the notational habits of his time.

Ex. 12

42

Beginning with Bartók and Stravinsky, or thereabouts, many new subtleties and problems of rhythmic representation arose. Those of you who have studied and played the Stravinsky 'Sacre du Printemps' recall that the major complexities in performance of the last few pages in the score arise because of the rhythmic cross-over against the metric designations. I have never known a conductor who did not have some problems with these pages— including Stravinsky. Yet they were written within the convention of the time (the same to which Brahms and others of the Romantic Period subscribed). With the great hurly-burly of that orchestration (Sacre) it is difficult to maintain an equilibrium against the rhythms which are combatting the metric indications. At least one major conductor has re-scored those pages, making the metric accents (therefore conductorial beats) agree with the rhythmic pulsations of the music flow. I'll wager he had a cleaner and more accurate performance.

Probably the most difficult to discern in these rhythmic vs. metric designations are the ones where the composer has given no additional clue beyond the notes themselves. A very simple example of this is in the second movement of Hindemith's clarinet sonata. Beginning in the fifth measure after 22 (second measure of the example) he has a 7-beat melody. His feeling was that obviously any good player would recognize it as that, therefore giving a slight inflection or stronger pulse on the first of each seven beats (Example 13).

Ex. 13

Another passage occurs further along in the same movement at three measures before number 24. With ♩ = ♩ no problems remain when you pulse it in 3/4.

And besides no problems you will be doing exactly what Hindemith wanted (Example 14).

Ex. 14

I have cited examples from these three works of the nineteenth and first half of the twentieth centuries. Today the sky is the limit—if you do not believe it consult any of our avant guard scholarly music journals, such as *Perspectives of New Music*. However I am confining this chapter to the periods and examples of music which most players, except the particularly adventurous, have to play. Above all I suggest that your rhythmic emphasis must sound logical, it must have 'flow,' however percussive and accented the music. Even when you hear the strident, sharply accented rhythms of Stravinsky's *'l'Histoire du Soldat'* or Copland's *'Salon Mexico'* you will, if the performance is a good one, feel the cumulative rhythmic flow. You must stress the sounds so that the phrase makes musical sense.

PART II
MATERIALS

Chapter 7:
REEDS

Reeds! I have never in all my life talked with any clarinet player who did not mention them sooner or later—usually sooner. This only focuses attention to the fact that unless you have a playable reed you have nothing. It is simply the heart of clarinet playing. The presence of a good reed will enliven your spirits, allow you to play at your best—your tone, tuning, and general sound emission being your most satisfactory. Occasionally (or perhaps I should say rarely) an optimum reed comes along—and then the world is really your oyster. Tone-quality, tuning, nuance control, staccato, et al, are at their best. This kind of reed, if it comes your way at all, will probably be at its peak when you have no concerts!

The clarinet is a *reed* wind instrument. Notice that the word 'reed' precedes 'instrument.' Take this to mean that a reed should always be a major consideration, since your instrument should be fairly constant. Just about every kind of remark has been made about reeds, mostly in frustration. I have never known a professional clarinettist who does not remember reeds as they were (then) being better than they are (now).

Tradition has it that reeds have been made out of whalebone, ebonite, ivory, silver, various woods, and of course, cane. Only recently has the field of synthetics produced any serious competitor to cane.

This I will describe later in this chapter. The variety of cane in general use is called Arundo donax. Remember that a cane reed was once a living substance. However, by the time you get it the growing part of its life is over. Its only improvement as a material for your use can come about by seasoning, and from the moment you start to play on it the path of its life is downhill, though generally the best playing time is after two or three days of use.

So much has been written about cane reeds that I will not bore you with more, but as a basis for your thinking I want to call attention to various writings which every serious clarinettist should read (see Appendix 2).

In all this reading list you will find some contradictory attitudes, but the variety will only serve to clarify your thinking, and get you to try each approach. Certainly the sum of these books brings together about all that has been meaningfully said about cane reeds. Each player should insist upon training himself to make his own reeds—not with the idea of continuing to do so, but only that he be intimately aware of all the technical problems involved.

One very important fact to bear in mind is the difference of approach of each player. I have never really known any two players who felt exactly alike about reeds. Each somehow had evolved a process and a standard with which he could live. The reason I have suggested a number of books is that you may have a variety of directions from which you can chart your own reed-making and trimming course. One thing is certain—no one can do it for you, except as a kind of general demonstration. In the final analysis the 'tailoring' must be done by you.

Even the tools will vary with individuals. For me it is sufficient to have a superlative, absolutely straight-bladed knife with a very slightly rounded end, a plastic transparent block 3″ by 1 3/4″ by 7/8″ on which to work, two or three grades of fine abrasive paper, pieces of a Kraft heavy duty paper bag (to use as a polisher and sealer after you have the reed as you like it), a straight-edged good quality six-inch stainless steel ruler, a strong light to look against, and a very high quality reed trimmer. I have never seen a better one than a 'Cordier' with a set screw. It is a lifetime investment (mine dates from 1931) and before buying you should test it by a preliminary cut or two to be sure it matches the curve of your mouthpiece. This trimmer allows the very careful positioning of the reed, and the set screw allows a controlled backing off after the cut is made, so that the reed tip is not in any danger of fraying.

One general introductory remark—do not start trying to make or re-make reeds until you are reasonably proficient and have a solid control of your tone. You must have reached the point where the variance in the tone quality resulting from the changes you are making in the reed will be easily heard, and where you will know that it is not a momentary change in *your* sonority.

Longevity—I have known one player (a superlative one with a major post in a major symphony) who normally used reeds as long as six months. The last months were hard going for him, and it used to take quite a bit of time in the morning for him to make peace with his reed and to get it and himself into a comfortable playing condition. His major trouble was that in changing to a new reed he would find himself so 'wed' to the old one that the change became exceedingly difficult. Indeed, I learned many new expletives from him! In my own experience, and for most of the players with whom I have been associated, it seems that one to two weeks of hard use is best. This has the advantage (with cane reeds) of keeping your embouchure more receptive to the change required for a new one.

Buying and storing—I do believe in buying reeds ahead when you run into a likely supply. Put them into a really dry situation, on a flat (glass, preferably) with a slight weight on them, perhaps another piece of heavy glass, or a really flat board. My practice was to have a drawer with a stack of 15″ x 18″ sheets of glass piled one above the other, with reeds in each layer. This allowed air circulation.

One especially important process not sufficiently stressed in the texts named earlier is sealing and impregnation of reeds. I have seen all manner of reed seals and impregnation, but the ideal for me is to rub the tapered part of a reed with my forefinger, it having been 'oiled' against the side of my nose, afterwards carefully rubbing the reed with heavy-weight Kraft paper. Seal the trimmed side as well as the flat side. Incidentally I suggest never bothering even to try a reed until sure that it is truly flat on the under side, having earlier ascertained that your mouthpiece is *really* flat on its facing. Check these with a straight-edge against the light, both across and lengthwise.

Container—any reedholder which will hold the reed flat against a truly flat surface is fine. Some of the best I have seen are adapted in some home-made fashion, using a piece of heavy plate glass and a wide piece of elastic material. The container should not be airtight.

Cane reeds are always going to be cane reeds—the substance will always be approximately the same. During the nineteen-twenties and thirties many attempts were made to extend the period of reed use by coating or impregnating them. All attempts were seeking to preserve the qualities already present before processing. None really succeeded, and attempts continue even into these days, though in a rather desultory manner.

All of the foregoing presupposes that we are going on with cane reeds forever. I for one do not believe this. The answer must lie with synthetics. Because the formula for these new materials can be varied ad infinitum it stands to reason that someone, somewhere, will persevere and produce reeds with more stable qualities than cane. Indeed I can offer actual evidence of this progress.

Along with everyday acceptance of synthetic materials, there has been a great deal of experimentation with them in connection with reeds. My own experience began in the early thirties in conjunction with a leading laboratory. Yet until some time ago I felt that no one had produced a practical replacement for cane reeds, and only because it had not been possible to find a means for building-in the longitudinal strength and springiness which is a prime requisite for a sound generator in the form of a reed. Early attempts produced reeds lacking the springiness necessary to withstand extended vibrational life.

In this half century the idea of binding a mass of fibres of synthetic material, arranged the long way of a reed, was advanced—thus simulating the grain of cane. It was possible to maintain the same external physical proportions, thus requiring no change in the embouchure of the player.

For several years while I was with the Boston Symphony I played on such reeds—hundreds of rehearsals, concerts, recording sessions, broadcasts, and many lecture demonstrations. Despite the drawbacks no one ever knew I was playing a synthetic reed until I told them, and even then some were so unbelieving that I had

to show them. I continued for many years after I retired from the orchestra, and then changed because much of the chamber music repertoire, which I was then playing demanded extremely high range facility.

It is currently possible to produce synthetic reeds:

a. in a form identical to those of cane.
b. with fibres which have equal or more resiliency than those of cane.
c. with longer life, due to non-absorption of saliva—no wetting and drying. Because of playing a reed longer one can be far more accustomed to its idiosyncracies, thus making playing with greater sensitivity possible. There is new mental security, the greatest boon of all. One can be certain that the reed played at a rehearsal will be available for the concert.
d. which need not be wet beforehand. They play at once. Mine was left on my crystal mouthpiece at all times, except for weekly cleaning. This meant that the reed could more accurately retain its fit to the mouthpiece, thus making for more efficient blowing.
e. which does not splinter. In fact they will play even if the tip is split. While this last does not matter to a professional, it does matter very much to the harassed teacher whose young pupils are less than careful.
f. whose savings in time are unbelievable. Think how much time you spend preparing reeds?
g. which have far less tendency to whistle. Indeed I found occasional ones which would refuse to do so.
h. which make it unnecessary to keep a great backlog of selected reeds. It is enough to know that you have one more in case of emergency.
i. which can be handled just like cane

reeds—scraping, sanding, trimming, etc. This last had to be done with scissors. I found no reed-cutter which would work well with this material. This was not a drawback, because using a curved manicure scissors and an old reed as a template made the process easy.

j. whose cost annually is but a small percentage of what you pay for cane reeds.

The drawbacks are few, but sufficient to keep these synthetics from being the final answer for the finest symphony and solo playing. In my experience:

a. they did not respond quickly enough to allow for playing quick passages requiring extremely rapid tonguing.

b. it was difficult to play tones above the high G^3.

c. they had a somewhat abrasive feeling to the lip.

However there is absolutely no doubt in my mind that constant refinement will produce a wholly acceptable, stable synthetic reed, suitable for every kind of playing at any level. Even now they are completely practical for anyone not playing in the 'outer space' of the clarinet's top range. Recall my own years of use during which cane had to be used in only a few isolated instances. They are wonderful for the bass and alto clarinets, with no reservations whatsoever. The future looks bright.

Chapter 8:
LIGATURES

The question of ligatures seems to be in the forefront of every clarinettist's attention these days. The past twenty-five years have seen such a proliferation of improvements on the old type which succeeded the string-winding of yesteryear, that it is no wonder that players are confused by claims and counterclaims. Many have talked or written about this subject, so perhaps a few observations are in order.

First let me say that the remarks I am making are only valid for a careful player. Even though the better ligatures would make a difference with any player, it does not really matter with the beginner, or with any player who does not want to make the 'last effort.' Other shortcomings and faults would cancel out any possible benefits of the new ligature.

Before discussing the ligatures themselves let us first see what the proper function of this piece of equipment is. It is merely to hold the two flat surfaces of the mouthpiece and the reed together, and not to inhibit the vibration of the reed. As a starting point, see that the table on your mouthpiece is absolutely flat. This is not only important—it is vital. Equip yourself with a fine quality 6" stainless steel rule with a *really* straight edge. Hold this edge against your mouthpiece table in each direction. Then similarly check your reed. Many players use the time-honored test of suction from the bottom of the mouthpiece (with the reed in position), thinking that if the reed closed against the facing all was well. This test only means that the reed is held against the facing during the suction

period, it does not prove that the facing is equal on both sides, nor does it prove that the table is flat. It is possible for the reed edges to be pulled into full contact with the table by pressure of the ligature. You can test this after ten minutes of playing by removing the ligature without disturbing the position of the reed, and then pulling the reed straight away from the mouthpiece in the direction of the arrow in the illustration below. If you find water on the table you can be sure that either the surface of the reed or the table of the mouthpiece is not really flat. This will make your reed seem hard to blow (not the same as when it is too stiff), and it will lack clarity.

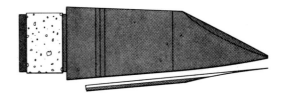

Generally I test a reed for flatness even before playing it, because I know that even if it appears to play reasonably well the ease of blowing and clarity of sound will improve if it is truly flat. To flatten a reed use a fine piece of polished plate glass, or your plastic reed-trimming block of a convenient size (inexpensive—since you can buy this from remnant stock), some fine aluminum oxide paper, and some double-coated Scotch tape #665.

Put the glass near the edge of a desk or table, attach the tape to the top of the reed, essentially for the whole length, so you can hold it securely with your fingers spread over most of its length (but not the tip). Place a strip of the aluminum oxide paper over the glass, tucking it under at each end and move the reed over it in a longitudinal direction only. Let the tip of the reed project beyond the end of the paper and glass so that none of the tip is thinned. When the reed is really flat you can fairly consider the subject of ligatures.

The ligature's holding power should be no more than absolutely necessary; otherwise the reed will be inhibited in its vibration. Though we all joke about the string-winding of the old-timers it still is one of the most effective means of holding a reed properly. It is slower to manage than a modern ligature, at least for those of us who do not use it daily. I suspect that many a conductor of the past has had nervous moments when he watched a clarinettist unwind the string from his mouthpiece just before an important solo, adjust his reed, and rewind the string, all in the space of a few measures!

The conventional ligature with the two top screws on the lower side works well, but it has the disadvantage of damaging the reed if tightened too much, and also it puts too much solid material against the reed. Nonetheless it is probably the best type for beginners, and in general use, because one can easily see its position when putting it on the mouthpiece. I normally train my pupils to rest the top of the ligature on the top of the mouthpiece, thus keeping it as far away from the reed as possible, then sliding it on. There is no danger to the reed in this way.

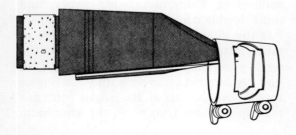

Among the variants, the first are those which are conventional, except that the screws are designed to be on top of the mouthpiece. Since most people are right-handed the set-screws are threaded to be operated from the right. This kind works very well, especially if there is a large opening on the surface which is in contact with the top of the reed. If there is not a large opening the reed will be somewhat prevented from maximum vibration. This is, I think, the best compromise in ligatures.

Other ligatures fall more or less into one category; they are designed to have as little contact with the reed as possible. Some have two raised rails which bear on the edges of the reed, others go a little further and have only four contact points at the extreme corners of the contact area. If your mouthpiece is really flat, and your reed also, all of these free the reed considerably. The effect is particularly noticeable to the player, though a perceptive and trained listener can also detect the difference. Keep in mind that if you, the player, feel more comfortable you will play better in general, even though there may not be much, if any, apparent difference to the listener. Use anything which makes you feel better about your playing!

The last kind I have seen combine all the major features of the above—plus the fact that they are made of a plastic material. I tried two for a while and found that though they seemed to work well they did not last. The plastic threads stripped very easily and made me uncomfortable, because I did not know just when they were going to strip. Now some have metal threads.

Some years ago there was introduced a unique type which merely slipped on and adjusted itself to apply only the gentlest pressure. It was most nearly like the old string ligature of the past. The construction was of very thin metal, so perforated that it was very springy indeed. One had to be careful when changing the mouthpiece from one clarinet to the other. There are now several types of 'strap' ligatures which seem very successful. One of the most practical (and least costly) is made of two adhering pieces of velcro used as a slip-on ring (ligature). Another is made of a synthetic and cord, with only the cord coming into contact with the reed.

Summing it all up I feel strongly that what matters most, really most, is the flatness of the table of your mouthpiece and of the bottom of your reed. Once you have determined *that*, you are ready to play—without blaming the ligature!

Chapter 9:
LIP GUARD

Curious how a problem seems to surface everywhere at once! I have recently had at least a dozen teachers and players come to me with the problem of badly aligned teeth in relation to clarinet playing. In these days of fine orthodontic work we see fewer irregular teeth than in former years, but keep in mind that some of us living today were born in former years!

First, let us see where we are. Though the majority of players in America use a 'single lip' embouchure, my remarks will apply equally well to those using the 'double lip'. No matter how well under control your embouchure, and no matter how even your teeth (lower ones especially), I am sure that there have been moments after extended playing (not necessarily excessive, but at least more than usual) when you have found your lower lip cut through. Besides being painful, it obviously causes some lack of control, and much loss of endurance. The same is equally true of the upper lip, though generally those players using the 'double lip' embouchure play under more evenly distributed time situations, and therefore build up a sufficient callus to withstand the necessary amount of playing. What answers have I seen to this problem? And which of the answers do I recommend?

Solutions offered and used by many players include some form of cap over the teeth. The cap can be made of:

1. Material like Visqueen (a plastic sheeting material available at your hardware store).

2. Paper, hopefully not too absorbent, yet sufficiently soft to adapt to the teeth.
3. Two or three pieces of gauze folded over.
4. Silver or aluminum foil.
5. The central part of a small Band-Aid (without the adhesive ends).
6. A stainless steel form.
7. A plastic form of one kind or another.

These solutions have been of varying degrees of effectiveness. Except for the last two, all appear to be stop-gaps only.

What is the best approach to the problem? First and foremost is the need for regular practice periods. These build up enough callus to withstand the lip vibration and tooth cutting action. But for those who have uneven teeth, the regular practice alone will not suffice. Some protection for the lips is sorely (no pun intended) needed. The protector must round off the tooth surface being applied against the lip. It must stay in place while you play. It must not absorb so much moisture that it loses its shape and form-fitting adherence to the teeth. It must have very little, indeed minimum, bulk. It must not interfere with talking (else how will you be able to tell others how really to play that passage!). It must not move when you are clearing your mouth of saliva. It must not move when you use your tongue to commence notes. It must not move in sympathy with any lip motion. It must not look like an extraneous something. Quite a lot of 'musts'!

Plastic materials of the Visqueen type do not adhere well enough to the teeth. Gauze materials vary in efficiency depending on the tightness of the weave, and they tend to bunch. The combination of gauze and tape (Band-Aid) is too unyielding. Paper disintegrates. Stainless steel can be well formed by an orthodontist (a sympathetic one), but the feel of it is too unlike that of the teeth. It does not feel warm in the mouth, and it is not sufficiently springy to settle into place in some instances of badly aligned teeth. However, when in place, and if well formed, it can be small enough to work well.

I have found a plastic substance to be the very best—indeed absolutely satisfactory—solution. This can be either an acrylic or vinyl plastic. I have two which were made for me in 1944. One I have used constantly. The second is merely an insurance back-up. My #1 has worn superbly through thousands of concerts. It allows me to talk freely without a lisp of any sort (I have often given lectures of one to two hours with it in place because I was to play at the end of the talk). It cannot be discerned unless one is peering into your mouth (obviously another clarinet player wondering how you solved the problem). Its color is like the teeth. It instantly assumes mouth temperature. It does not shift position. And it remains in daily use even now—after 35 years. I paid $18.00 (1944 dollars!) for the two of them, and judging by the service rendered thus far I would guess it to be a lifetime investment. I have never used the second one.

Details to watch for when you have one made:

1. It must be small as possible and still cover the tops of the eight central lower teeth.
2. It must not be built upward any more than absolutely necessary to cover whichever tooth projects upward most.
3. It must offer an even horizontal surface, though following the curve of the teeth to the sides of the mouth.
4. Its bulk must be as small as possible. My own is so comfortable that on

occasions I have forgotten to take it out and discovered it only at the next mealtime when I started to eat!

5. It is best colored exactly like your teeth, thus saving innumerable hours of explaining to your doting audience what that thing is in your mouth.
6. It must hook well into place and feel as solid as the teeth. In effect it is just a normal removable denture. I clean mine with a toothbrush and powder, and keep it in a small plastic container right next to my mouthpiece.
7. It should extend downwards almost to the gum in front, barely hook over the tops of the teeth, and snap into place.

I am surprised that more people do not use one. There is absolutely no difference in the sound with or without this cap. Most people to whom I have talked, and who need help, expressed an urgency, but do not know just where to turn to have them made. Your family orthodontist is your best bet, providing he understands the problem. I took my clarinet to my orthodontist and played for him (free!) so he could observe exactly what was needed. One of my teeth was badly out of line, because of crowding by the back teeth. The cap solved the problem perfectly. These days, when I play only sporadically, it is proving more valuable than ever. I would hate to think of playing without it, since endurance would be so reduced. After using it for a week, you will forget that you ever played without it.

I am surprised that more has not been said and written about this subject, but on reflection presume that each person thought it a private matter, not necessarily shared by others. Yet I would hazard a guess that one-fourth to one-third of all clarinet players have felt the need for some help in this direction. And the help is so easy to come by!

PART III
CONTROLS

Chapter 10:
TUNING (some rules and ironclad maybes)

I've heard quite acceptable players who really did not control their dynamic ranges well. Others who did not phrase well. Still others who played with less than perfect rhythm, whose dexterity left a good deal to be desired, or whose articulation was not refined. And finally some whose sounds were not of the best. These shortcomings were constant, yet each of the players involved had managed, by virtue of other qualities, to achieve a degree of success. Indeed some of the players in our major symphony orchestras are less capable in one or another of these areas. But show me one player who has really made the grade while consistently playing out of tune! Let me examine some aspects of what is more often than not a painful subject: the practical problems of tuning in ensemble performance.

However *good* a player is, no matter now *great* a sound, no matter how *rapidly* he can play, no matter his *superb musicianship*—no one wants to play with him if he is not playing well in tune. Here are two aids for those who play B♭ and A clarinets in the same concert, or for that matter any two woodwinds. The former is especially helpful for players who have to transport instruments in very cold weather, then suddenly play them in tune in an orchestra.

Advice No. 1 is certainly to allow ample time for the clarinets to warm *naturally*. I used to bring my instrument case into the hall in which we were to play, open it, and then proceed to catch up on the news, or read a book for half an hour. Then the clarinets were ready, and so was I. It was very relaxing.

Advice No. 2. If you will look in the catalogues of various sporting or camping goods houses you will find a variety of hand warmers. These are small, safe, inexpensive and can be carried unobtrusively in a case. Result—you arrive with pre-warmed instruments. However, even with pre-warmed clarinets you have the problem of keeping them warm during the performance. I have seen many ingenious solutions, but the best and simplest was the little bin used by each member of the Amsterdam Concertgebouw to protect instruments from draughts after they had been warmed.

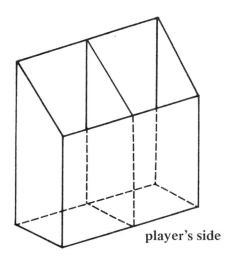

player's side

This bin is of very simple wood construction and it should either be weighted at the bottom, or have an extending platform under it, to keep it from tipping.

The tapered upper side should be high enough, and not more, to allow you to grasp the clarinet by its barrel. Clarinet pegs could be set into the floor.

Incidentally, an aside, I recommend that you change clarinets a short time before any important solo or other important passage. It is worth the little amount of transposing, and it will make you more popular with your woodwind colleagues by easing the tuning problems. After all, they continue to play on single (and warm) instruments.

All too often, players who suspect an instrument of being flat, quickly turn to shortening the barrel. On questioning I have found that the complaints were usually registered by other woodwind players whose judgment was made largely as a result of *initial* sounds made when an instrument was first played. Never judge an instrument that has not been properly warmed. Reject all the hasty, early remarks of flute and oboe players, but heed their *later* remarks.

Remember that a barrel length has been arrived at by careful acoustical analysis, and you should for all general intents and purposes accept it as being correct. If you really *do* need a shorter barrel, get a new one of the length you wish, preferably from the manufacturer of your clarinet. They usually vary from 65 to 68mm, occasionally 64, with 66mm being most usual. Be sure to supply him with the serial number of your clarinet, since models differ in dimensions. Keep your old one as a known point of reference.

The subject of mouthpieces is somewhat more complex. While there are a number of excellent custom mouthpiece makers, I generally recommend use of a mouthpiece made by the maker of your instrument. If there are occasions when you want to avail yourself of a 'custom' model, be sure that the maker warrants it to be compatible with your *model* of clarinet (not just *make*). And remember that no matter how well the new mouthpiece 'blows' or sounds, it is no good at all unless it tunes well.

First—and foremost—a repetition of the ironclad rule for playing in any kind of ensemble: tuning is a relative, not an absolute quality. Many hard feelings have been aired because of the failure to realize this. When your instrument enters into a musical passage you must, of necessity, be guided by the pitch extant at the moment of entrance. Assuming, of course, that this pitch is acceptable, the listener has for that moment accepted it as definitive, and measures your entrance by its terms. Therefore it behooves you to be sufficiently elastic and responsive to fit your pitch with it. This calls for a 'good ear' and a sensitive control of your instrument.

If the pitch is much below or above what it should be you can fuss about it at rehearsals, hoping to induce others to adjust, but at the concert you yourself must adjust. When it comes to playing in tune with another instrument you must remember that it is cooperation which makes for good tuning. Cooperation by both. I believe that each should make a 51 percent contribution to the total effort. Thus, if my arithmetic is right, two people really trying will achieve the desired 100 percent!

Even really fine orchestras 'bend' the tuning to accommodate some dominant factor. Playing in a flat, dark key for a period of time will bring the overall playing pitch down. A longish bit with a dominating, and perhaps sharp, piccolo or muted trumpet, will make the entire ensemble tend in that direction. Even so, the net *effect* is one of being in tune, because the listener, unaware of the change (as indeed are also many of the players—they adjust by instinct alone) moves his reference pitch up or down as required at the moment. Expert string players are adept at this. I have seen a fine violist look up in surprise at the finger position he had assumed in playing the last note and say "Gosh, it sounded all right when I was playing with the group—but look where my finger is!"

Attitudes about pitch vary depending upon circumstances. First let me write about origins of pitch concepts. Certainly in these electronic days many, many people use electronic tuners—a most unimpeachable source. This is fine. But their mere presence in your studio does not, of itself, make for playing in correct pitch. How often have I seen a player check his pitch against a tuner, and then turn around and play a completely different pitch in his group. He just had not trained his ears, did not have good pitch memory, and was doing it the lazy man's way—depending on outside help. This will never work.

While it is true that you do or do not have a 'good ear,' it is also true that you can develop your *comparative* pitch sense. While looking at a Stroboconn, play an accurate 'A.' Now close your eyes and try to play it again. While holding the note and *retaining the pitch of this second note as of its start,* open your eyes and look at the discs. You will probably find that you are a few hundredths of a semitone off. If this is the case, what you ought to have uppermost in your mind is the memory of the true pitch. You should learn to *hear* this true pitch before you play it. It is a matter of developing pitch memory, and is especially valuable for carrying the memory of your own prior pitch. This is far more difficult than merely fitting your note with other simultaneous sounds.

How often have you heard a poor

player adjust his 'A' to the standard 'A' by changing his embouchure or otherwise adjusting himself? This is the worst possible thing to do. The 'A' may now be in tune, but how about the other notes? How about the 'A' itself if he plays it once more and his memory does not serve well? By altering his 'A,' he has changed its relation to the rest of the notes on the instrument and no longer has an evenly tuned scale (assuming he had one to begin with). My advice is to play the best-centered, best-sounding, most resonant 'A' you can—with *normal* embouchure. *Then* check it for pitch; if your tuning is not right, *do not adjust yourself!* Adjust your instrument. Pull or push your barrel and again play the note, using your optimum quality of tone, etc. Continue adjusting your instrument until you jibe with the established pitch. Then you will be able to play over your entire range with ease, because you start with a normal embouchure, and the 'A' is better related to the other notes on your instrument. This also diminishes the tendency to overlook consistency of tone color. If you have a very good instrument the chances are that it will sound best in tune when you play with a consistent tone color.

It was this very quality which brought me to the invention of the Mazzeo mechanism.* Because players constantly had to 'assist' the throat B♭ into true pitch and better resonance it led to embouchure distortions and false tonal relationships with other notes. With my B♭ it is possible to play throughout this normally troublesome register without any 'favoring.' The many, many thousands of Mazzeo charinets which are in use all over the country are an eloquent testimony to this evenness of color and resonance, to say nothing of better tuning.

* See Chapter 19.

Incidentally the written B♮ on the Boehm clarinet is not the best tuning note —it lacks the centered quality such as is present on the next note, C. The B♮ on the basic Mazzeo clarinet (because of its bell design), or on a full Boehm (because here it is not a 'bell' tone), is easier to tune to, because of its more resonant quality. Except in an orchestra, I recomment tuning with the written C for the clarinet.

However you go about it, *never* try tuning your instrument until it is really warmed up. The tuning of woodwinds, the clarinet especially, is particularly difficult because the lower part of the instrument is never as warm as the upper. Reeds contribute their share of tuning problems, since some sound sharper or flatter than others. Did you ever try to get a player to throw away a reed which played beautifully, but which made the instrument sound too sharp or flat?

Many players are unable to dissociate tone color from tuning. They will accept the pitch of an oboe because it sounds more dogmatic and give way before it, but will fight a flute to the death. Brass mutes may introduce pitch changes, and by the nature of the beast, the dominant brass instrument dictates the pitch. A player on the lower octave will invariably give way to the fellow playing the upper, in the same way that two players playing in unison (not quite!) find the flat one out of tune. The one who is sharp seems somehow more dominant. I recall that during my many years in the Boston Symphony, Dr. Koussevitzky never once failed to accuse the flatter of two instruments as being 'out of tune,' though I am sure that there must have been many occasions when the sharper instrument was really at fault. It became an orchestra joke—if you were flat, you were out of tune—if you were sharp, you were the soloist!

Another illusion of hearing—many players, especially younger ones, do not take sufficiently into account how much clarinet tuning can change when going from very loud sounds to soft ones, or vice versa. Years ago, as a boy, I discovered a graphic test for this. Together with a cooperative flute player friend we practiced long tones in unison (anyhow we called it unison). Taking as large breaths as possible we proceeded to play each note to the extent of our lung capacities, starting very softly, increasing gradually to our loudest, and then again gradually to our softest sounds. As you know, the clarinet tends to sound flatter as one plays louder, and the flute sharper. Thus our out-of-tune tendencies were in opposite directions. Playing constantly in tune called for enormous controls, and brought the point very clearly home to us.

Beginners, throughout the earlier stages of playing, tend to change pitch by adopting a slightly different embouchure the moment after the tongue ceases to be involved. Thus at the moment of attack (better called the release) the sound is slightly flatter than it will be a moment later when the tongue is no longer involved. Young players often sound tuning notes and then change as the note is sustained.

So much for the clarinettist. Now for the clarinet. First and always (since the clarinet essentially cannot be changed in pitch), be sure to use the little insert rings when pulling out your barrel. Otherwise the gap between the inside of the barrel bore and the upper tenon will make your throat notes too flat. If you need to pull more than the width of a barrel ring I suggest the following:

1. Tune the bell tone, or third space C^2, by pulling out the barrel as much as

necessary. This will only give you a general indication of how much your instrument is off pitch. If it is more than the thickness of the ring on your barrel, I feel sorry for you. Any adjustment beyond that calls for one thing more—changing your standards.

2. Carefully tune your open G by adjusting the barrel precisely. This may change your third space C^2.
3. Tune the low C^1 by pulling apart the middle joint (impossible to do if you have an articulated G# mechanism).
4. Tune the bell note (or C^2) by pulling out the bell.

Thus you will have distributed the correction (discovered in No. 1 above) over the entire instrument. Many players fail to take into account the simple mathematical relationships that make this tuning method so effective. A B♭ clarinet is 26½ ±" long. The bell note requires the entire length of the instrument. When you pull out your barrel, let us say ¼", you lower the pitch by a certain amount. You have changed the length of the instrument from 26½" to 26¾". Now take open G. The first vent hole for it is about 9¼" from the tip of the mouthpiece. When you have pulled the barrel out ¼" you have changed that dimension to 9½". As you see, the ratios are very different. Since ¼" is a far more significant part of 9¾" than it is of 26¾", it will be far more effective as a flattening influence for the 9¾" length.

What this all boils down to is that you do not so much play with your instrument—but with your ears.

Chapter 11:
LEGATO

Funny thing—how interest in a certain aspect of clarinet playing seems to surface simultaneously in so many quarters at once! Recently many players have written me about finger action, indeed they seemed to be preoccupied with the subject. I discussed fingering principally in chapters 1 and 4, and rather than quote here suggest that you re-read that material at this point, since it is very pertinent. However what these clarinettists were *really* after was legato sound, and clean manipulation from tone to tone, especially in quick passages.

Let us think a little about the first point, and the second will almost take care of itself. There seem to be two contrasting theories as to how to play legato well. I believe in yet a third principle. The first group feel that the transition from tone to tone should be accomplished by a crisp, very abrupt popping sound as the finger closes the hole. The other school moves a finger so slowly and unobtrusively that before the clarinet knows it the finger is covering the hole. There are virtues in both methods.

Putting aside the actual sound of the 'pop,' the first method has the virtue of very quick finger motion—the acme of efficiency, or at least speed. The aim of reducing the 'travel time' to zero is ideal. The second has the virtue of sometimes making a very smooth legato (especially between notes involving the first three

fingers of each hand), but it does not work as well when manipulating keys. The second method usually achieves this at the expense of a clean, uniform finger-action which should operate the same *all* the time. It is slightly at fault, or at least not as cleanly efficient, when operating in rapid passages. Each method has, of course, it proponents and staunch supporters. These include some of our better players.

However the very finest legato (and most nearly immaculate technique) I have found is among those players who create their legato with the breath. The more resolute, firm, and unyielding the breath—whatever the nuance—the better the legato. First, reliance should be on the wind stream, since it is a 'wind' instrument we are playing, not a 'finger' instrument. The piano is an example of a 'finger' instrument. An initial shortcoming is that not enough young players pre-hear the note they are moving towards. It is imperative to do so. For a really beautiful legato on the clarinet it is necessary to change the throat dimensions, generally smaller towards the higher notes, and to build a beautiful wind 'bridge' between tones. You cannot form the next tone as you move towards it—it is then too late. Since we are trying to *reduce* the travel time between tones to zero—or as close to that as we can—the density of the air column required for the coming tone *must* be prepared before leaving the last tone. The mental tuning of the coming tone *must* be precise. You don't land on it and *then* adjust the pitch. By a careful pre-evaluation of the pitch standard you will make truly meticulous wind column adjustments, with a consequent beautiful legato.

All of the above presupposes that you are playing at or near the peak of pitch of each tone. The quality then will be best in terms of resonance, true clarinet color, and uniformity of pitch. As a matter of fact it will also work if you are *not* playing at the peak of pitch, but then it will make a greater demand on your voicing each tone into its particular groove, and your tone will be duller. Gustave Langenus, one of the finest clarinettists we ever had, wrote what I consider one of the best exercises for developing a good legato. It consisted of nothing more than intervals of thirteenths played thus:

Ex. 1

$$fff > ppp \quad fff > ppp \quad fff > ppp$$

Like all good etudes it isn't the notes, but what you do with them. It is imperative that you have a fine, resonant forte on the low note; it is important that you complete the diminuendo before you move to the next note; it is *imperative* that the diminuendo not be accompanied by *any* lessening of resonance or change of pitch or timbre. The last is the catch—and the point. Proceed upwards in A major, taking each note of that scale and playing it together with its 13th. It is meaningless unless you are truly conscientious about the tone quality, especially at the soft end of the spectrum. Remember that it takes more diaphragm pressure when you are playing softly. The soft tone must begin as though born directly out of the preceding loud one.

Now, having established certain desiderata for the legato, let us move back to the part the fingers play. Let me say again that each finger should move up or down with equal quickness, whether in a slow passage or a rapid one. This is a difficult concept for some people to accept. It will help to understand it if I say that in a quick passage the fingers move more *frequently,* or in quicker succession. You merely live less long on each tone when you are playing a fast passage. On a piano the touch is *always* downward when commencing a tone, but the clarinet must give forth each tone with equal clarity whether your finger is going up or down. This is why the lowering and raising of each finger should be uniform as to speed and simplicity. There is no difference in the speed of motion whether your finger is going down or up. The motion of 'up' should equal the motion of 'down;' the finger should have a precise, succinct motion. There need be no 'follow through' motion as with the arms in golf. It should move from where it is to where it is going and *not beyond*—whether you are going down or up. You are not moving *into* the wood—also don't make a huge quarter-arc with your finger when it goes up. Do make the most deft possible motion—without moving any joint except that at the base of the finger.

This kind of motion, when used with a truly steady wind delivery, will create no 'pop,' and if made by an 'alert' rather than a 'muscular' finger will not only *avoid* disturbing the legato, but will simplify the transition. You will have the first tone, then the second tone, with *no* transitional sound in the travel time between tones. You can play your clarinet like what it is—a wind instrument. And your tuning will be better.

One other factor in legato playing which is often disregarded is the long phrase line. If your mind accepts the idea of an objective *beyond* each next note you will find that your sound has more continuity, there is a better joining of tones, there is a much greater uniformity of tone quality, and your phrasing will sound infinitely more cohesive and musical. Consider the following phrase from the *Eroica Symphony* of Beethoven:

Ex. 2

You will often hear this phrase chewed to pieces, with each note breath-pushed. This destroys all its grandeur of line and it becomes a juicy, gypsy-type melody. How much better if one thinks of the breath as unyielding, both in crescendo *and* diminuendo, until the final resolution—indeed not *until* it, but *through* it to silence. Controls should not be relaxed until the silence beyond the last tone. If you succeed in producing a continually forward-moving air column (and why not?) then you can let your fingers do their own job better, and with greater succinctness of motion. You will be able to think of singing instead of fingering. What we most want is to sing—but with a clarinet tone.

Chapter 12:
THE ARTS OF TONGUING

One of the things I have learned in my life, especially because of my travels, is that there are so very many ways of playing a clarinet, and in the matter of tonguing many seem correct. I have heard clarinet players in many lands with no real sameness in their techniques of playing except that practically all of them did use the tongue in starting sounds—I say 'practically' because one player I heard in England did all of his tonguing without the tongue! By a system of short puffs of wind he was able to play surprisingly fast passages, and believe me, they sounded quite well, though lacking the incisiveness and speed of attack characteristic of the more usual way. Yet I have heard this same lack of sharpness from players who did use their tongues. Therefore I want to examine this subject on a more wide and comprehensive basis, then, if possible, reduce the *modus operandi* to a somewhat simple straightforward statement.

One of the most worrisome aspects of playing, to most clarinettists, is the 'staccato.' The problem arises somewhat from the definition of the word—which most players interpret as meaning 'short.' This is really not correct. If you will look in a catalogue listing Italian orchestral music you will see the word *'partitura'* (meaning divider, or division of parts, i.e., score) and *'parti staccati'* (meaning separate parts). There is your real meaning—separate, separating. The *amount* of separation is another matter. Our adjective 'articulate,' meaning segmented, gives the same general sense. Do not confuse this with the verb 'articulate' meaning enunciate—or unite by joints (as for example various combinations of tongued and slurred notes). I mean separation.

It is easiest to think about this correctly if you consider the word 'staccato' in the light of analogy with bowing on a stringed instrument, or touch on a keyboard instrument. With them, by means of a bow or finger you determine not only the degree of impact in starting a sound but also its length, manner of completion, and the amount of space between sounds. Exactly the same result can be obtained by the use of the tongue on the clarinet reed.

Before stopping a tone in order to have a 'staccato' effect, let us concern ourselves with starting it. What we are after is a means of inducing the reed to begin its vibrations, so that it in turn will force the air column into vibration. When you ask the average player about this he will at once talk about methods of bringing the tongue to the reed. Actually it is the *removal* of the tongue from the reed which determines the cleanliness of the start of the sound. The forward motion is really a preliminary one. Even as it goes forward one's controls should be directed to the ensuing rearward motion. A surprising lightness becomes possible. Many players find themselves playing with a thick start to their tones mostly because their tongues remain too long in contact with the reed.

One point of no agreement is in deciding which part of the tongue to use. Though generally, in the United States at least, most players touch the reed just below its tip with a forward motion of the tongue, striking with the part just back of its tip, this is by no means a universal practice.

I have known players with longer tongues who used a side motion. Altogether there has been an enormous amount of gobbledegook about the use of the tongue.

Putting this aside in favor of descriptions by players who seemed to know what they were doing, I am prepared to say that I have heard tonguing where the player said the reed was activated by the heel of the tongue, by its point on the tip of the reed, and various intermediate positions. Some struck the roof of the mouth (something which the heel of the tongue does do in double-tonguing). In each case the results were not only somewhat satisfactory but also just about indistinguishable from each other. With all this variety you will readily see that what has really mattered was the cleverness of each player in adapting to his own resources.

I believe that most players (successful ones) strike the reed just under the tip, with the tongue just back of its tip. There is a great difference of opinion as to the precise syllable to be pronounced by the tongue; concensus seems to be that the pronunciation of 'tu' as in French induces less distortion of the normal tongue use and gives a cleaner emission of tone. Keep in mind that, as in everything connected with clarinet playing, the more you are able to maintain normal position of any part of the body, the more successful you will be, since abnormal posture automatically requires more effort—hence more time to master it. Therefore the tongue when not actually in motion should be in your own individual normal 'at ease' position in the bottom of your mouth.

One factor very much affected by the starting motion of the tongue is that of saliva. It is inevitable that when you bring your tongue forward a certain amount of saliva will pass onto the reed. This can be somewhat counteracted by clearing the mouth of saliva and, by suction with the lips, clearing the reed before the first sound and at every opportunity where there are pauses in the music. This is absolutely necessary, else the tone will have an undersirable buzziness.

I am surprised at the numbers of young players heard in schools throughout the country who pay absolutely no attention to clarity of sound. Actually the suction process is very easy to make a matter of habit, and once the habit is acquired it will be a thoughtless, instinctive action. The really lucky people are those who play with reeds against the upper lip! For them saliva flow is no problem, and even in extended passages involving much use of the tongue their saliva will merely flow along what most of us normally refer to as the roof of the mouthpiece. When I first heard him, one of our finest clarinettists played in this fashion and sounded absolutely wonderful. In these last years he has turned his mouthpiece to our conventional way—but only because his former habit attracted too much attention. In Latin countries, especially, you will see very fine players still using the reed-up method. They claim that they can tongue more quickly, and judging by results I have heard, they seem to be right. The tongue then strikes the tip of the reed.

Before continuing the discussion of tongue motion I must say something about embouchure and blowing, even though I treat each of these subjects more fully in other chapters. Many players in commencing discussion and use of the tongue have failed to take into account that the embouchure should be well formed *and remain that way while tonguing*. Further, the jaw should not drop with each tongue stroke. You should not be forced to reform the embouchure after each tonguing motion. The action of the breath is of paramount importance. If the action of the tongue in starting the reed vibrating is not concurrent with an explosive entry of wind into the aperture of the mouthpiece, you will have inefficient sound emission. The sound when starting should at once be full and round, not one which gradually opens out to a fullness. Naturally, as your playing becomes more refined there will be infinite subtle variations of this, ranging from the most gentle (with no tongue use!) to the most abrupt (by means of sharp tongue strokes). At the moment of tonguing, the deeply inhaled breath should be in a state of tenseness, as if you were about to undertake some substantial muscular effort. I have found that a good way to make players conscious of this was to ask them to play a long note with an intense sound and then to interrupt it by bringing the tongue back to the reed *but continuously blowing even though the blowing was against a closed circuit.* Then the tongue was pulled backward and the tone was allowed to come into being. The alternation was continued in this manner:

Ex. 1

T   T—T   T—T   T—T   T—T   T—

Where the line connects two T's, the tongue remains on the reed and blowing is continued. When there is no solid line the tongue is in normal rest position. It is important that the blowing be continued during the silence else you will perhaps find yourself drifting toward that general relaxing of embouchure and throat muscles which allows pitch changes at the beginnings and ends of notes. Use a mirror to watch both the embouchure and throat. Do not play at the end of your breath—

always have a full reservoir, your sound will be the better for this backing.

Having understood and played the example in the preceding paragraph you should then start playing single notes in the middle range, with medium volume, paying attention at first only to the start of the sounds—not the ends. It is good practice at this stage to imagine something of this shape for your sound length:

Ex. 2

The end of the sound is brought about by merely ceasing to blow—*but with lungs, throat and embouchure remaining in a tensed position.* Don't inhale. Don't relax. If you do, all of the starting operation (embouchure, throat, etc) will have to be reactivated for the next sound.

This tensing will seem awkward at first. Try to visualize it by imagining a cut of hard sausage in an automatic slicing machine. As each cut is made the meat remains in position and is then moved forward under the blade for a new cut. It does not back up each time in order to go forward again. So must it be with the breath. The first sounds should be straightforward and of reasonable volume. Do not try at this stage for subtleties. See only that you have an honest, forthright tone emission. Once you have cleanly mastered simple starts of your tones you can begin varying their quality. Since this is a subtlety which need not concern us at this moment, we can now consider the ending of sounds.

There are two ways of ending sounds to have a staccato effect. The first is merely the stopping of the breath as described above. This kind of sound ending is used most of the time, especially in music of gentle character such as Schubert's *Ballet Music* from *Rosamunde*:

Ex. 3

Here you would not tolerate crisp endings to the B flats, they must be lightly released. The same is true in such a passage as the *Till* motif in *Till Eulenspiegel's Merry Pranks:*

Ex. 4

This theme should be played in a light impish way. However near the end of the piece where it is repeated when Till is brought to trial, you will see a most effective use: from ending a note as described above and then gradually becoming more abrupt so that in the final statement, when Till is suffering his worst moments of apprehension, the staccato effect is best produced with abrupt tongue stoppage. The first of the three following statements is lackadaisical, the second somewhat alerted, and the third frenetically apprehensive. Stopping

Ex. 5

of the tone by bringing the tongue back to the reed must be accompanied by thoughtful attention to the continuation of blowing as described earlier in this article. Generally speaking, most players use this latter method and can play tongued tones more quickly this way. Normally the ending of tones should (when done with tongue action) be as imperceptible as possible, but there are all manner of exceptions where you may wish a harder, more obvious stroke of the tongue on the return, as for example the very last measures of the *Till* quotation above, or more grotesque effects.

All of these tongue manipulations have only one purpose—to allow the starting and closing of a tone in whatever manner you choose. It is the tone you are really after, the tongue is only a modifying factor.

Because fine clarinet (or any instrument) teaching is undoubtedly best on a one-to-one basis it is probably inevitable that meanings and identifications of the precise motions necessary to make a clean emission of sounds (attack!) have become somewhat twisted, due to the lack of really precise knowledge of the tongue and throat motions on the part of the teacher. This information is usually absorbed at the habit-forming time of life, therefore it is also probably inevitable that we find many entrenched positions and attitudes regarding tonal emission—tonguing. Fortunately, as I have said in other chapters, modern science will bring this all to a happy clarity soon.

Chapter 13:
TONGUING (The Subject Which Never Ends)

Some years ago when I appeared at the National Clarinet Clinic in Denver I had one desperate older person approach me to talk about—you guessed it—tonguing. He wailed that he had also talked with all of the other eight or ten teachers and had been utterly baffled by the variety of their prescriptions. One tongued with the tip of the tongue, another an eighth of an inch back, another a quarter of an inch back, with the 'heel' of the tongue, underneath the tip of the reed, against the teeth. You name it.

In the past, each clarinet teacher had of necessity to give advice on tonguing in terms of self-analysis, and of his impressions of results as he heard them in others. There were no eye-witnesses to the actual motion of the tongue—only 'ear-witnesses.' Consequently there has never been a true theory of tonguing based on accurate observation.

Now, thanks to wonderful new cameras which make possible photography within the mouth, plus various other measuring devices coming on the scene via the medical profession, we have the possibility of really definitive, visual answers. Particularly so since we also now have a dedicated body of clarinet-scholars, themselves fine performers, who are teaching in our universities. They have the know-how to couple their expertise with the newly

available instruments. The next answers should be definitive.

Meanwhile, my reason for pursuing the subject further at this time is the delight I had recently in reading an article written by one of my 'grandpupils.' Deborah Abbott was a student of one of my University of California, Santa Cruz graduates, Margaret Thornhill. Her article is so human, so right in its expression, that I can do no better than to offer it to you whole. I do suggest that before reading it you re-read the two immediately preceding chapters. You will then better appreciate her most delightful, understandable approach.

RULE TONGUE:
Tips for Slips of the Trade
by *Deborah Abbott*

In the middle of a soggy winter, the subject of tonguing suggests a summer analogy. The tongue in summer is occupied with the seasonal perfection of ice-cream-cone swabbing. On a warm afternoon, in order to keep the body of cream firm and intact, quick, neat, well-timed strokes of the tongue are necessary. Despite the heat, the mind must be alert to changes in the consistency or texture of the cream, and must guide and determine the tongue's sensitivity to the cone. With skill, only the slightest expense of effort is needed to enjoy the parlor sweet: the cone remains in perfect shape, bears the grainy texture of the tongue's impression, and is savored, the memory of the well-mastered cone against the momentary flavor.

It is with the nonchalance of the ice-cream-cone consumer that the clarinettist must approach the art of tonguing. Indeed, classification of the action as an 'Art' and specifically one of 'tonguing' tends to overemphasize the matter and can serve to intimidate the beginning clarinettist. After years of meals have been chewed and swallowed, and infinite syllables have been uttered, the tongue's actions have slipped into automatic response; the tongue has become, until the desire to master the art of tonguing, unconsciously employed. To reintroduce the long forgotten tongue to the clarinettist without rendering it massive, awkward, and insensitive, it is recommended that the subject be broached casually, as the simple solution to problems the pupil may have had in distinguishing cleanly between sound and silence in his phrasing, delivering precise initiation and finishing of notes, or achieving the *staccato*. Because the tongue is by no means the major element of the 'art of tonguing' it is perhaps more important to emphasize other ingredients of the art initially. One finds that mastery of breath, embouchure, and jaw eliminates the major obstacles to the well-tongued performance.

Vast technical distinctions from the slur, with which the student is undoubtedly comfortable already, should not be made. The elements of tonguing should be introduced as supplements to elements employed in the slur; in this way the learning of tonguing may be seen as a building process: likenesses, not contrasts, between the two techniques should be stressed.

In order that the tongued passage be of high quality, concentration on breath steadiness should be emphasized, if it has not already been in previous instruction. The tongued note will sound choppy (if it sounds at all) when the breath flow is not constant and breath support is weak. Since support behind the tongued note does not differ from that behind the slur, it is beneficial preparation to tonguing that *legato* passages be assigned, and that attention is given to wind.

The player should be made conscious of the factors which give his breath strength; muscles in the diaphragm and abdomen combine to expand the chest during inhalation—so that a full supply of air can be taken in—and then compress tensely, in a measured exhalation into the instrument. The pupil should be encouraged to maintain a full reservoir of air and to keep this supply in constant preparation to be emitted during rests. When the wind is allowed to sag (fall back into the lungs) the subsequent sound suffers from the time and effort required to re-gather the breath.

This principle may be demonstrated with the 'curly blow out' party favor shown below (1). Unless the favor is supported with a consistent, full breath (3) the end will collapse and retract, forming the deflated 'curl' (2). Without a sustained breath support the clarinet tone likewise curls, or loses its body. A good exercise to discourage 'sagging' is for the pupil to play a series of whole or half notes, letting the tongue finish each, and after the note for the tongue to remain on the reed, the student continuing to blow in the silence. This should demonstrate that the accuracy of tongued response depends on the breath.

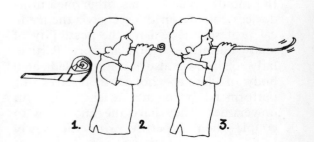

1.   2.   3.

Contributions of the mouth, lips, and jaw to the perfectly tongued note must be considered passive or inactive. As with the slur, a tensed, steadied embouchure is required in the absence of lip or jaw movement. Strict command of these will result in beautiful control of the sound produced. Once again, relaxation between notes only necessitates in time and energy being wasted to reform the tensed embouchure.

When composure has been gained with the breath, mouth, and jaws, the action of the tongue may be presented to the student. Because the dimensions of tongues vary from one player to another (and yet share similarities of effect) it must be kept in mind that each person will necessarily develop a somewhat singular manner of tonguing—in effect, the contact point between reed and tongue will differ according to the individual.

The student must give attention to the reed in order to understand its role in tonguing. Air blown at and past the reed sets the moving air stream into vibration: this accounts for the sound. Therefore, brief contact of the tongue to the reed initiates the vibration cleanly; prolonged contact produces a hesitation of sound; a long contact stops the vibration completely until the tongue is removed and air is once again allowed to flow.

Since reed vibration is maximum near the tip of the reed, it is usually recommended that the tonguing occur there. The portion of the tongue used will vary according to the length of the tongue: players with long tongues may feel more comfortable using the mid-tongue, with the tip anchored at the base of the lower teeth; those with normal or short tongues will usually find the area just behind the tip most convenient. Although minimal contact between tongue and reed is optimum, the tongue should not become

stiff or taut to achieve this end. The tip or contact point should be tense, yet flexible. It alone should be in motion: the remainder of the tongue needs to be still so as not to alter the contour of the mouth cavity and hence the nature of the sound.

Fractional contact can best be achieved when one regards the tongue action as rearward. Sound is emitted when the tongue is *withdrawn* from the reed: sound stoppage is the result of the forward tongue movement. The action is a slight brushing of the reed, a quick retreat. It is the retreat which is to be emphasized if the most brief contact is to be achieved. By concentrating on the compressed contact point the student can actually disregard the great bulk of the tongue, and develop real sensitivity. It is often helpful for the student to shape his tongue in imitation of the syllable 'tu' pronounced in French.

When the student has achieved the correct tonguing effect on long tones (i.e., when keenness of attack has developed) he may attempt repeated notes. This rapid tonguing needs to be pictured as tiny interruptions in a continuous air stream. The conclusion of one note and the initiation of the next must be fused into one action.

For accuracy in a rapid succession of tongued notes, tongue and wind must be moving absolutely parallel: when the tongue begins to move, the wind must simultaneously flow into the instrument. If a problem arises with synchronization of the tongue and fingers in active sequences, it may be helpful for the student (if his fingers are slow) to imagine his fingers actually working faster than his tongue, and in the opposite case, for the student to consider his tongue working at a more rapid rate than his fingers.

It is essential for the student to differentiate mentally between the slur and the tongued passage. Because the only distinction is the minuscule separation between the tongued notes, the student may have difficulties actually separating the two. If he isn't acutely aware of the silence of a fractional second between notes, he may become lazy, and his tongued notes will inevitably be sloppy. In order to bring to focus the perception of time, the following quotation may be useful.

> Perception of movement would be absolutely the same in a universe which disappeared from existence utterly and was recreated in a succession of different stationary forms sufficiently frequently. A cat running across the floor, or a bird flying, would look precisely the same if it were annihilated and recreated fifty times a second.*

The goal in tonguing is to fill the fraction of a second between notes with awareness. The listener needs to hear the tongue produce a succession of sound and silence as he would magnify the second and see the bird being annihilated and recreated fifty times. The listener hears the absence of tongue, the slur, as the constancy of sound, as he would enlarge the second and see the bird, in a single existence, fly across the sky.

* Lord Brain, *Perception: A Triologue*, Brain, 1965, p. 702.

Chapter 14:
STACCATO

Many players spend a disproportionate amount of time studying the staccato control, as opposed to the legato. Many do not understand that the real basis of good staccato playing is in legato, and is not confined to the action of the tongue. Why?

Because it is such an important subject, allow me to re-state a definition given earlier. By definition, staccato means 'separate' (verb). Separate what? In our case, it is a tone and its successor, even if it is a rest. But you cannot separate sound unless it is continuous before the separation, and *after* it! The more continuous— the more dense and resonant the tone quality—the greater will be your control, either staccato or legato. You will have 'the something' in your tone which is in effect more tangible. When you add to this the absolutely instant speaking of sounds, plus a deft tongue action, you have all that is necessary for beautiful staccato execution.

This foundation will allow all manner of staccato controls necessary for really sensitive playing. But before discussing these staccato controls, let me back up a little and present some thoughts on legato as the basis of good sound.

Somewhere in my writings I am certain to have said something about the *absolute need* for separating or divorcing *each* element of control during study and practice sessions. Such procedure is a must if you want to make steadier and more rapid progress, because it is so much more efficient. It is all too easy to approach a passage with everything in mind at once— a hodge-podge of advice, and a lack of centralized focus. The more things you try to accomplish simultaneously, the less you will really accomplish.

Let me cite a familiar analogy. When you ride a bike it is somehow a 'total' experience. You have to keep upright, to steer, to continue pedalling, etc. But try riding with no hands on the handlebars, and right away you will notice a greater, more obvious consciousness of your foot action—of the driving force which is carrying you forward. Study and practice each passage with only one thing in mind at a time. If you have played it a few times with quality of sound as your principal focus, you will find when you move on to the next objective—continuity of sound—that you will not so easily allow yourself to lose any of the quality achieved in the earlier part of your practice session. And so on as you come to each new point of emphasis. Once gained, a point is seldom lost.

Good tonal concept is easier to come by than ever before, what with all the fine records available and fine players among the many teachers. But keep in mind that your best teacher, and therefore most frequent and best example is *you*. It is you who will be with yourself throughout life, and who will give judgment every time you produce a sound, adjust a reed, etc. How do you go about using yourself as a good example? I'll tell you, if you will keep in mind that my basic subject remains 'legato.'

First, when you are studying and practicing, do not arbitrarily go through a ritual of playing long tones ad nauseum. It is very easy when practicing long tones to fall into a state of suspension of thought. The long tones seem hypnotic. You land on a tone, get it going, and then find yourself thinking about something else. Don't believe it? Try a long session of long tones and count the times extraneous thoughts intrude. An orderly sequence of long tones from your lowest to your highest, played with infinite patience, will not give you the best results. Far from it. Remember that any time you play *a* tone *it* at once becomes the example by which you judge the *next* tone. For instance, low E on a clarinet is by no means the best sound on the instrument. Because it is generally not cleanly resonant, you will find yourself perhaps adjusting the pitch and sound with your lips, instead of playing with the most beautiful 'centered' tone and getting the most out of the natural timbre of the instrument. What is really better is to start with tones that need absolutely no adjustment and which give off the most beautiful sounds—for example:

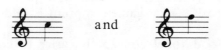

Play these with every possible effort to make them truly optimum in quality, then proceed to notes which are only a little less good, trying all the while to match them to your best tones for examples of quality. Come back often to your two 'example' tones. Try to have your study sessions in a room where the acoustical effect is as normal as possible—

don't take refuge in a tiled bathroom and think what a great tone you have!

One very important aspect of tone quality which many people do not take enough into account is that if you lack a clean release or 'emission' (usually incorrectly called 'attack') of sound you are corrupting the overall tonal impression. Imagine in slow motion a sound which originally lasted one second. The clumsiness of the tongue action can occupy a considerable fraction of the total sound, and the clumsiness is the first impression the listener gets. Listen most carefully to the quality of your sound at the *instant* of hearing the tone. Don't produce a tone which reaches its zenith of quality only after the first 20 percent of its life. It must be pure from the very outset. This discipline alone makes for better tongue control and staccato manipulation (I'm tempted to say linguipulation!). If your tongue's clumsiness detracts from optimum tone quality for about 20 percent of a 1-second note, think what it does to a tone lasting only 1/10 of a second. All you hear is tongue action and no really good tone. Try this very objectively. Remember that a short tone is merely a *short* length of a *long* tone—and that every instant of each tone must be equally good.

Now having reviewed my idea of a good tonal concept, we come back to the thoughts voiced by many players. These really hinge mostly on the fact that there does not seem to be a good concept of the *continuity* and *persistence* of quality in a sound.

Let me illustrate by returning to the bicycle analogy. In these days of '10-speed' bikes we are all aware of the effect of gears. The principle is simple: by adjusting the relationship between the crank wheel (operated by your feet) and the gears (which operate the rear drive wheel) you cause more or less revolutions of the wheel in relation to your foot action.

Now a good bike rider will tell you that the most efficient technique is in finding the cadence which allows you to keep your foot pedalling at a constant rate. No matter what the grade, you merely adjust the gears so that the speed of your foot action does not change. It is the *constancy* of physical action which makes for efficiency. Now how does all this apply to tone quality and legato?

Let us for the moment put aside the idea of 'coloring' your sound, and concern ourselves only with producing an ideal basic sound—the sound you live with most, the sound you most want to hear. Without your instrument, and pursing your lips, go through the breath motions necessary to play a phrase; utter no sounds except breath sounds. You will find yourself becoming acutely aware, perhaps for the first time, of how much a part your throat and tongue play in making legato transitions, especially over wide intervals. Take a piece of very light typewriting paper and hold it from the top, and broadside in front of your mouth, so that when you blow, the paper moves away from you. If you blow (as for a passage in one dynamic indication), the paper should reach a position and *stay* there regardless of the intervals you are blowing.

This is visual proof that your blowing (like the cyclist's pedalling) is consistent. Your mind should be at work on the internal wind motion every moment while the sound is being produced.

The very act of producing different levels of dynamics brings more control factors into play. Hence you will understand my emphasis on diaphragm support in pianissimo passages. Remember that soft tones take relatively more diaphragm support than loud ones. Be conscious of the *continuing* density of your air stream —particularly between tones of different pitches. There is your legato.

It will help matters considerably if you do this in front of a good-sized mirror so that you can see that there is no excessive manipulation of the lip or cheek muscles. Also it will help very much indeed if you record this on your tape machine and listen really carefully to it. Try this enough times so that you are truly conscious of blowing as a separate, powerful, and constant effort. Then when you apply it to an instrument, you will find it easier to concentrate on the blowing aspect, as separated from the fingers, etc. It is the continuance of the stream of tone—the thread of sound— unbroken and unyielding, which must be in the forefront of your mind until the years make it as automatic as riding a bike.

In chapter 10 I spoke of 'pre-hearing' the pitch of each next tone. For fine legato playing it is essential that you pre-hear, since each tone has its own resonance and speaking factors. When you land on a tone, be aware whether or not it is of your optimum quality *at its very outset*. Do not correct a tonal deficiency in the sound after it has been started. Like jumping across a brook, do all your evaluating as to distance, quality of the terrain at the take-off point, etc., *before* you leap, not while you are in mid-air! Do not be forced to do any scrambling or adjusting once you have landed. Come down squarely and solidly. So it is with tones—you must land on each succeeding one with full tonal confidence.

Imagine your tone a solid substance. No amount of finger manipulation should make a dent in the substance, nor should there be a 'dent' in the tone, whether sustained simple tone, or legato between tones. Play the clarinet from the inside (the tone) to the outside (the fingers).

In order to make *differences* in sounds —which obviously we need to do in order to play as expressively as the music demands—it is first necessary to make two tones really identical in quality; then it is no problem at all to make them different when the occasion demands.

Chapter 15:
STYLE IN STACCATO

'To be' or 'not to be.' Is it or isn't it? Slurred or tongued? Alas, that is the usual approach by wind players to the idea of staccato, a word that has somehow come to mean 'short tone' and thus to have lost many subtleties implied by its true meaning. The word itself is, of course, Italian and it comes from the verb 'staccare' meaning 'to detach.' Thus in performance detachment affects the adjacent tones.

Charles Munch, the eminent conductor, used to say—"Silence can be the most wonderful moment in music." When you think of the awesome effects he made in his performances of such works as the Berlioz *Fantastic Symphony* you can easily understand this. (There probably lives not one music teacher who at moments during lessons has not felt the need for some of this silence!) Silences are so effective that their durations should be scrupulously adhered to. In Mozart's music especially, we should be careful never to neglect the timing of the silences. Thus—why, how much, and when are the questions wind players ought to ask about staccato. They are answered by other instructions of the composer or by musical taste generally. First and foremost

are the general stylistic instructions of the composer at the start of a movement. The following notes in the Brahms *Second Symphony* would probably be played in an elongated, sustained fashion (given only the tempo instruction) if it were not for the word 'grazioso' at the start of the movement. This clearly states the need for lightness and a slight lift between tones, rather than a continuous substantial sound.

Ex. 1

Adagio non troppo, ma grazioso

p dolce

Before getting into the details of staccato, I would like to discuss for a moment the matter of the word 'rest.' When used in connection with music symbols the word appears to have the effect of inducing rest, including resting of the mind. This removes the mental discipline required to regulate the exact amount of silence. Furthermore if during the silence one does not continue the momentum and spirit of the immediately preceding music the entrance *after* the silence will not be in tempo or mood with the preceding music. Play something in a spirited fashion. When you come to the silences (rests) count the silence in the same spirited manner and you will find that your entrance will be correct as to timing, tempo and style. Try it again and let your mind relax, meanwhile counting beats somewhat lethargically, and you will find it more difficult to enter in step and mood.

The actual spaces between tones, and the manner of the tongue strokes at the beginning and perhaps at the end of tones, largely determine the character of the space between tones. Since 'staccato' has no absolute meaning as to length it is well to consider the following thoughts:

1. It is necessary to keep firmly in mind the idea of the long phrase line so as to avoid being bogged down or preoccupied with staccato or articulation signs en route.
2. Staccato effect must take into account the room or hall acoustics as well as the listeners' distance from the sound —especially so with repeated tones.
3. Staccato effect must take into account the style and mood of the music.
4. Evaluate the staccato effect very carefully when any articulation pattern is involved. Care must be taken to play *through* the final tone under a slur. The amount of time the tongue takes to commence the following tone must not apparently detract from the final tone under the preceding slur.
5. Articulation must be more clearly enunciated in any situation where there is considerable reverberation. The actual silences during any articulation patterns are a 'staccato' effect.
6. Do not confuse 'staccato' and 'spiccato.' The latter means 'marked' and 'conspicuous.' In practice 'spiccato' has now come to mean a shorter tone than 'staccato.' It is made more marked and conspicuous by particularly shortening and accenting it.

Please notice that my definition of 'staccato' and the symbols I set forth later are those commonly accepted today, thus avoiding Baroque and other specialized practices; also that I am most concerned with the clarinet and other woodwinds. A few guiding definitions or attitudes will help you to understand my treatment of staccato symbols.

1. Staccato and articulation symbols can be above or below the affected notes. Sometimes these indications are stated only at the beginning of the section throughout which they are to apply.
2. The common dot used as a staccato indication is taken most generally to mean shortening the tone by about ¼ to ½ its length.
3. On every conventional instrument, except the organ and other instruments where sound is electronically produced, each stress is followed by a diminuendo or decay of sound (unless consciously sustained). Great subtleties are possible with string and wind instruments in this matter of decay.
4. The tone before a syncopation or accent is often shorter, partially because the effort of making the accent creates space.
5. Sharpness of staccato effect can be increased by differences in accentuation.
6. Despite all definitions, staccato and articulation symbols over a single (or group of) note(s) are still in some state of confusion, generally settled by the arbiter of the moment (conductor, leader, etc).
7. Attention should be paid to a short, round separation of the tones as opposed to a sharp abruptness, unless the latter is intended.

Here it is well to take notice of the fact that most woodwind players play 'staccato' tones by starting and stopping the tones with the tongue. It is almost ludicrous to present a short tone by emulating the 'tut' sound described by Thomas Mace in the 17th century. This was done by clapping the next striking finger upon the string already sounded, giving a spirited end to the tone. It was intended to be somewhat amusing. In Chapter 12, I explained why I recommend using the tongue-stop method only infrequently, breath control being a much more subtle and effective means. The following drawings seek to picture tonal decay, as opposed to abrupt stoppage (as in 'tut' referred to above).

A much misused example is the following meant as and which should more accurately be written as and played with a light use of the tongue. Written in the first manner it is most often played by wind players as a complete legato to the second tone, and the second tone is then shortened. These examples are also usually played in the same way.

 and

Another frequent inaccuracy is:

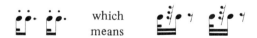 which means

but generally is played as:

Articulation, by virtue of its silences, must take its place in our thinking about staccato. It is a process in phrasing by which we change the continuity of sounds by small, almost imperceptible silences. Thus endless variances between full legato and continuous staccato effect are

possible. It is generally indicated by a curved line (slur):

or a 'legato' indication at the start of the section. Sometimes this kind of curved line is used to indicate full phrase length, but it is better for that purpose to use the brackets:

preferred by Schoenberg and others. It is important to remember that the silences resulting from articulation are not synonymous with staccato, though the two functions may coincide.

Articulation slurs are commonly short, seldom extending over more than seven or eight notes. Unlike true legato slurs they cut off the last tones to some extent (alas, how many wind players *always* shorten the last tone under an articulation slur!). When an articulation slur is over two or three notes of generally equal length, it is usually intended that there be an accent or emphasis on the first tone. This is particularly so if the first tone is off the beat. A legato sign over two or more slur marks indicates the shortest possible separation between the lower slurs, or the lightest possible tonguing.

Appoggiaturas and acciaccaturas are best dealt with as a separate subject; I mention them here only because of spacing implications in performance. An appoggiatura is a 'leaning tone' and therefore emphasized. It assumes the principal pulse, taking its time value from the tone it precedes and to which it is connected. Sometimes there is a slight lifting or hesitancy before it, in order to give it added melodic emphasis and importance. An 'acciaccatura' is a 'cut' tone, now meant as either on or directly before the note to which it is connected. The character of the music, if demanding more rhythmic emphasis, almost demands a bit of silence before it.

Now to specific symbols. Most earlier music used symbols whose interpretation had been based on string and keyboard usage, and of course that varied with the period. Our current manner of playing will be dealt with later in this chapter. Those which we wind players have inherited are often misused. To correct this, I find it helpful to illustrate their tone lengths and releases by suggesting a visual image of bowing a string instrument. The following symbols are the most common, either singly or in combination. Notice that the 'rest' indications separate tones of a phrase, as well as phrases themselves, or sections of music.

(also 'staccato' or 'stacc.' at beginning of passage)

In the following examples (2 and 3) notice the gradation on each line. Though the manner of playing each type will vary according to the indications, the tones generally increase in length as you go to the right on each line.

Ex. 2

above or below a note—generally means a crisp shortening, and is normally used in strongly rhythmic or marcato music.

the common dot is used to mean many things—generally a shortening by ¼ to ½ of the printed note value. It is found in all styles of music and in all moods—from soft and light all the way to vigorous statements, each demanding appropriate tongue action to portray the desired musical feeling.

is a tone slightly less than the full written length, with no diminuendo effect.

is slightly longer than the preceding example. I jokingly describe it as a very long dot, since it has no easily perceptible decay though it must be separated from the next tone.

Ex. 3

when there is no indication, each tone should be tongued and held with clearly enunciated spacing between the tones, and with little (or only the slightest) diminuendo effect.

this indicates barely perceptible spacing between tones, and no diminuendo effect.

indicates even less spacing than the preceding example, and with no easily perceptible separation.

All of the following are played as in Example 2, but with the addition of a normal accent on each.

Ex. 4

All of the following are also played as in Example 2, but with the addition of a shorter, harder and more abrupt accent.

Ex. 5

The tones in Examples 2 and 4 are often stopped with tongue action, if the character of the music warrants it.

I cannot lay enough stress on the need for developing attention to the composer's written advice at the start of the movement—example: grazioso, marcato, leggiero, dolce, etc. It is these indications which fundamentally dictate the direction which your tonal delivery, tongue action, and accentuation should take.

PART IV
SCALES AND OTHER STUDIES

Chapter 16:
A GUIDE TO SCALE STUDIES

What do you have to do in order to master the clarinet? The formula is very simple—in words. You have only to be able to play every note over the entire register, in every nuance, with a variety of tone colors, at any speed, with any articulation, with every kind of start and close, and with all changing gradations. Add to this whatever musical talent you have, and mix thoroughly!

After the production of single sounds is launched, the everlasting study of scales begins. Why scales? How? The answer is simply that scales (including scales in thirds, fourths, etc.) are an efficient approach to solving the formula described above. They give you just about every combination of sounds that you will want to make, whether playing Bach, Brahms, Tchaikovsky, Stockhausen, jazz or rock. The simple repetition of the notes in the scales is probably futile; one also has to include in their repetition all the control factors. By including within your daily practice all the variants required you extend your controls—and your musical vocabulary—increasingly in all directions.

To do this efficiently, it is best to practice only those versions of scales which are most productive, giving results quickly in a *carefully graduated procedure*. In my life I have examined just about every available published set of scales for the clarinet. At this point I am willing to say that seven of them are more productive and comprehensive than any others I have seen. Study of them will give you better and more complete results in the shortest time. After listing them I will examine each for you and explain my reasons for the choices. Please note that I always mean to refer to scales as including those in all intervals (thirds, fourths, etc.).

1. Klosé—*Méthode*
2. Jeanjean—*'Vade-Mecum' du Clarinettiste*
3. Hamelin—*Gammes et Exercises*
4. Gay—*Méthode*
5. Gillet—*Exercises sur les Gammes, les Intervalles et le Staccato*
6. Stiévenard—*Practical Study of the Scales*
7. Slonimsky—*Thesaurus of Scales and Melodic Patterns*

The order is that in which I usually assign them, except that parts of the Jeanjean are studied before the Hamelin scales. As one can readily understand, the study of these scales takes years. Indeed I have scale study as part of each pupil's regular work, whatever his level.

The scales in the Klosé are those at the beginning of the second part of his method. They are to be studied after the student has a reasonable facility and can play over most of the clarinet. Their great virtue at this point in a student's life is that they are succinct—giving in the shortest space and playing time each combination of fingerings needed in the ordinary scales. They are to be played in a regular fashion—emphasis at this point being on *sameness* of tone quality, evenness of rhythm, and a well-sustained legato. Variety later.

The value of these scales will be considerably increased if you change all the minor ones from the melodic to the harmonic form. By doing this you gain the benefit of the practice of the step-and-a-half interval between each 6th and 7th step. In the melodic pattern you are merely repeating what turns up elsewhere in the scales. For instance the melodic scale of A minor:

Ex. 1

All of these intervals occur either in C major or in A major. By placing a natural before each F and a sharp before each G you have a harmonic minor scale with the interval F–G♯ . This occurs nowhere else, and since the harmonic is more difficult you have the opportunity of practicing it more regularly.

The next point of interest is that the required range is excellent for this stage of playing, the highest note being

The sequence of the scales is a common one, going from the major to the related minor, then to the subdominant of the original major, and so on. However Klosé has one interesting abbreviation which is important in view of the daily scale exercise pattern which should be set up. His sequence of scales is:

C - a - F - d - B♭ - g - E♭ - c - A♭ - f - D♭ - b♭ -

G♭ - e♭ - B - g♯ - E - c♯ - A - f♯ - D - b - G - e - C

Now look at the full set of scales in all flat and sharp keys:

C	F	B♭	E♭	A♭	D♭	G♭	C♭
a	d	g	c	f	b♭	e♭	a♭

G	D	A	E	B	F♯	C♯
e	b	f♯	c♯	g♯	d♯	a♯

Instead of 30 scales you have (by enharmonic notation) all of the same finger motions in Klosé's 24. If you examine these closely you will see that each scale of the full set occurs in the Klosé version, either in the same or an enharmonic form.

One other point which is important at this stage is that each scale is oriented to its tonic, thus setting up good diatonic imagery in the player's concepts. They should be practiced with a healthy mezzo forte nuance, with great evenness of sound and rhythm. Once they are under good control, then variants of articulation patterns should be introduced. Pay especial attention to the scales in thirds. They are among the most valuable since they start the life-long attention needed for the legato of wide intervals. The Klosé scales are begun as early in the student's career as he can play comfortably up to the high D and E♭ . Even when he has progressed to other more demanding scale versions, the Klosé will remain as a good 'warm-up' set to start each day's practicing—*after* some long tones to stablize the embouchure.

Before commencing with the Hamelin scales I like to work with the first three sections of the Jeanjean studies. At this point the student has a sufficient acquaintance with the notation for scales that he can more efficiently concentrate on the cleanliness of finger motions. This is of fundamental importance in making for equality, and what I call neutrality, of all finger motions. Each fingering must be equally mastered—each must be supple—each must have no 'personality' of its own. Obviously each tone has its own character—I am addressing the dynamic, resonance, and evenness factors.

These Jeanjean studies are studied and practiced in a turtle-like tempo, first with the metronome at 40 for each two sixteenth notes, then when fingerings are clean this can be increased to 80 for each two sixteenths. These are of enormous help in orienting one's listening to the moment of pad or finger contact with the wood, rather than the start of the finger motion. Consider only the *effective* moment of each pad or finger-hole covering—*not* the moment of finger contact with the lever or ring. It is the 'moment of truth' (actual sound of the new tone) which counts.

The first section is devoted to special trills where generally only one or two fingers are involved. Every aspect of each individual finger motion is under scrutiny, and cures can be very specific. A mirror is most useful. Play with eyes closed, so that your concentration on the motions will be complete.

The second section is devoted to left-hand motions. Here again is an area of study where you can set lifelong habits. Alternations are both binary and ternary—thus tending away from habit-forming accents on certain tones. The third section concerns itself with right-hand work. Again the concentration is on the cleanliness of finger motions. It is imperative at this stage that no *hand* motions be tolerated. The fingers should move independently. After all we should *finger* a clarinet, not *hand* it!

As you will see further along, I like to keep certain subjects in perspective for a long time. In the case of these Jeanjean studies I assign three per lesson (one of each of the above types), thus a continual attention on this aspect of technique. When completed we move along to the Hamelin scales.

These are extremely valuable and the student should not move through them too quickly. Indeed my usual habit is to assign only two of these scales each week, plus all his other materials in the same keys. By two I mean not only the original version (page 2 of the studies) but also the version with rhythmic variations (page 11), the ones for thirds (page 15), and the arpeggios (page 24). Thus, for example, a student will work for one week in C major and A minor in all of these forms.

Ex. 2

You will recall that in my comments about the Klosé scales I stressed their adherence to tonality by beginning and ending each scale on its tonic. Here in the Hamelin in the first form we begin to break away from tonal orientation, thus acquiring a freedom which is absolutely essential to mastery of the instrument—especially with today's atonal, polytonal, and what-have-you music. Though Hamelin starts his scales on the keynote and extends them over as much of the range as this allows from tonic to tonic, he repeats the scales on different fulcrums. This is critically important. Notice that in the first form the accents are on the first, fourth, seventh, tenth steps, etc. On the repetition they are on the third, sixth, ninth, twelfth steps, etc., and on the last repetition the second, fifth, eighth, eleventh steps, etc. Thus each step is at some time accented and you begin to acquire the sense of accenting away from the tonal base. At the end of this he then states the whole scale over most of the range of the clarinet, regardless of key-note start.

Ex. 3

You have moved a substantial step forward from Klosé.

A major problem in playing subdivisions of beats (or rhythmic patterns) is the distribution of notes within each beat. At this stage of development it is relatively easy for a student to play scales with four notes to the beat, or five, or six, etc. It is *not* so easy when several of these rhythmic subdivisions are in close juxtaposition with each other. This is why the ability to define and establish each pattern *instantly* must be carefully developed. *It is the placing of the second note in each beat which is critical.* Needless (I hope, needless!) to say, I firmly believe that study and practice sessions be with a metronome—*and also without*—it being necessary to establish a firm rhythmic motivation by the player in order to avoid becoming a 'metronome-hanger-on.' In my *Musings from Mazzeo* I once wrote that a player should never follow a conductor. If this were done, reflexes being what they are, your playing would be late. *You* must initiate a pulsation in

anticipation of his motion. Then synchronization is actually achieved. In this section, devoted to rhythmic exercises on major and minor scales, there is the beginning of very precise placing of all elements within a beat.

MM 40= ♪ (note: ♪ *not* ♩)

Ex. 4

The section on chromatic scales has them occurring as triplets, and in groups of four and five notes to the pulse. I extend these by adding groups of six, seven, eight, nine and ten at the appropriate places. Play them very slowly MM 40= ♩ , increasing gradually to MM 72. Especial attention must be paid to the placing of the tones within a beat (remember above, the placing of the second tone?). Have in mind the clear concept that each *up*-finger motion must be as clearly and firmly made as each *down*-finger motion; then the playing of chromatic scales becomes completely controlled. Make a very clean rhythmic distinction when you place the second tone of each new note value. The metronome is constant for all groupings of tones.

Ex. 5

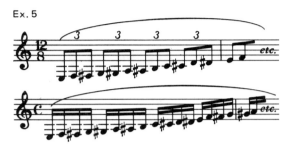

and also in groups of 5,6,7,8,9 and 10 to the beat

The section on velocity and arpeggios extends the practice of intervals in thirds, and also brings a good deal of attention to smooth upward interval slurs over the entire range of the instrument up to high A, the final and most demanding being:

Ex. 6

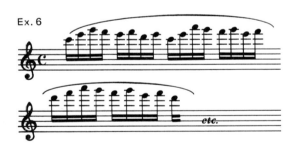

This section concludes with a progressive sequence of the same pattern going through all keys, and is an excellent resumé.

Next there is concentration on arpeggios —each upward as an arpeggio in the written key and on its tonic, and downward as an arpeggio on the dominant seventh of that key. These should be practiced in all keys.

Ex. 7

Play indicated upper groups, following immediately with lower—*carefully keeping 16th note lengths the same*. Only the beat speed changes.

At the end of the volume Hamelin has a study for evenness in trills in which he uses the rhythmic juxtaposition idea described earlier in this text. These trill studies should be studied and practiced between *every* two tones of *every* scale. I extend this study by including groups of five and seven in the appropriate measures. Again—remember, *up*-fingering must equal *down*-fingering in firmness.

At this point the pupil should have a considerable command of the entire range of the clarinet and is then ready for the next version of scales, which continues the broadening of his technical command of the instrument. This step encourages the increasing sophistication in technique so necessary for the mastery of the most complex forms of music being written today. The scales throughout the *Méthode* by Eugene Gay are excellent study materials for this step, and they will be discussed fully in Chapter 17. However a little description at this point will allow you to understand their place in the sequence of scale studies I outlined at the start.

Gay's control exercises and approaches are various. Normally one is expected to devote each day's practice period to working only with the scale material in one key, and continuing throughout the week, or until the teacher feels it right to move on to the next key. He begins with long tones to be played with a slow crescendo—and an even longer and slower diminuendo, the whole taking up an entire long breath. The emphasis should, of course, be on tone quality, healthy resonance, and perfect uniformity of these qualities throughout the entire note in its varying degrees of loudness. Great attention must be given to maintaining consistency of pitch. The embouchure does not change at all, rather the throat area controls the pitch by varying its aperture (smaller in the ff part and larger in the pp beginnings and endings). The exterior appearance of the throat should show no sympathetic movement accompanying the interior control.

Gay continues with a slow statement of the entire scale, tonic in orientation. This is followed by an exercise which focuses attention on small sections of the scale, gradually extending the range so that the embouchure develops accommodation. This exercise should be repeated in front of a mirror, first establishing the starting note by a long ⌢ so that the sound production becomes well settled. Then watch the finger movement very carefully. Invariably, some parts of the hand move unnecessarily, in sympathy with the motions you need. Prune all these excess motions and see that you are really moving only those fingers needed for the passage being studied. Make extremely efficient each of these required motions. Recall how many tens-of-thousands of times each motion is to be made in your life! This will help your 'time-motion study' of each fingering. Then comes a resumé of the entire scale.

Ex. 8

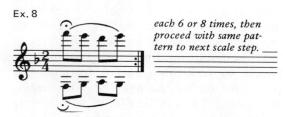

each 6 or 8 times, then proceed with same pattern to next scale step. ___

continuing with many other patterns to produce full suppleness.

This is followed by a simple statement of the scale in *mf* and lento, contrasted by repeating it *at once pp* and rapidly. Great care should be taken to see that the tone color remains the same when playing *pp*—one is apt to allow a duller sound to prevail when quickly changing to the *pp* version. Full control demands the maintenance of the same tone color and quality regardless of nuance.

Then come a number of examples including rhythmic variants, introduced so that each note is at some point given more (or less) length. The player must not repeat and repeat this exercise with any one note continually falling on either a weak or strong portion of the beat, as this would develop a tendency to *always* slight (or accent) it. Articulations are also varied and the patterns go throughout all the usual ones quite exhaustively. Even and uneven subdivisions, as well as diatonic and chromatic scales, are juxtaposed. Great attention is given to scales in thirds and to various metric patterns. Duets of excellent material by the better-known composers bring home all the points developed in the scale practice, coupled with other artistic matters of phrasing, nuance control, etc.

After this you will find the whole-tone scales based on this same tonic, and with the same treatment, plus scales chromatically in minor and major thirds, both in binary and ternary rhythms. These are very important and are especially difficult to play in succession with each other.

Settle all questions of fingerings *beforehand.* Do not leave any open questions to be resolved as you play. There should be no possible question as to the fingering of a note at the moment you reach it.

Scales in fourths, fifths, etc., follow, and finally a recapitulation which consists of original exercises in this same key involving many of the problems brought out in the scale material. All in all, this method of Gay's can serve as the backbone of study material through several years. To me it is the most carefully graduated method of all, and it is in graduation that most methods fail.

At this point some recapitulation is in order in the form of a review, or summation. For this I use the balance of the material in the Jeanjean volume. There is a review of scales which tests many things. All the scales are played in immediate sequence, together with their chords. Articulations vary from measure to measure, therefore the chief value in playing them non-stop is to insure your 'shifting gears' quickly, easily and surely. All of the common articulation patterns are used as well as some uncommon ones, and they are sufficiently random that you must keep your concentration fully focussed. Speeds vary with the individual, but it is important that they be worked up to rather a quick tempo, and of course to be played non-stop. Do not settle for less than 100 percent accuracy.

Ex. 9

At this point I usually assign the remaining two studies in this volume—the first is excellent for developing cleanliness and speed in staccato, and the second is a melodic one of considerable beauty, but also considerably difficult.

The most sophisticated and productive of all scale studies are those of Fernand Gillet, the celebrated oboist—who, after a distinguished record as an aviator in World War I, came to spend the major part of his life as principal oboist of the Boston Symphony Orchestra and as instructor at the New England Conservatory. He wrote these studies specifically for the clarinet.

In my lifetime of association with some of the greatest players I can safely say that no one better understood how to bring a passage under complete control in the most efficient time-saving way. His technique consisted chiefly in using his head first—and then the instrument. First I will describe his *Exercises Sur Les Gammes, Les Intervalles Et Le Staccato.* The underlying principle is that you

must be able to control every tone on your instrument to the extent that you can place it in any part of a passage, accented or unaccented, with any coloring, with any articulation, and with any nuance. Remember my previously stated formula? Instead of the time-worn method by which you work your way through the various key signatures, generally tonally based, he builds his studies on all the binary and ternary positions, using *all* tonalities on each, and all manner of intervals, nuances, and articulations. All the rhythmic studies emanate from control of tones in pairs and in threes. The clearest way for me to explain his process is to set forth one position as an example.

Imagine a loose page with various articulation patterns, giving examples for use with all binary and ternary positions. Place this on the left of your music stand and superimpose the articulations given on the loose page upon any scale you are studying.

Take the first binary position, play the

entire scale in the key you have selected, legato as well as detached (Example 10).

Ex. 10 — First binary position

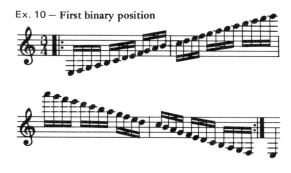

Next play the A section of Example 11 both legato and detached, keeping in mind the need for homogeneity of sound (equal resonance, loudness, and of course well-related tuning of all intervals).

Ex. 11

Then play the rhythmic variant at B (all legato) before returning to the A section. Finally, return to the basic scale (Example 10), again both legato and detached, *mentally superimposing the note pattern of the A and B forms* so that these particular tones receive maximum attention and

control. Pay particular attention always to make a fine legato, especially when playing the wider intervals. When you are satisfied that these tones are as you would like them, proceed to Example 12.

Ex. 12

In this the attention is on the first and fourth of each group of four 16ths. Following the same routine, play the matching pattern from the loose page (Example 13).

Ex. 13

Keep your thoughts particularly focused on the first and fourth tones of each group. Maintain the sameness of tonal quality, etc., in each of these tones under scrutiny. When you are happy about the overall homogeneous quality, return to the basic scale (Example 10) *but* keeping the tones of Example 12 mentally super-imposed, as well as using the two articulations of Example 13.

If you conscientiously follow the same procedure for Example 14 through 20, with the matching work-articulation sheet beside each, you will be amazed at the results, when finally you come to the summary scale (Example 21). By having at some moment given *each* tone prime attention, you will have achieved an unbelievable evenness of sonority over the entire range and, needless to say, of finger manipulation.

Then Gillet moves on to the same routine for the second binary position, identical to the first except that it is started on the next higher step (Example 22).

The third and fourth binary positions are treated with the same critical approach (Example 23).

These are followed by the three ternary positions (Example 24).

Ex. 24

Ex. 25

The ideal is to practice in one key signature throughout the seven binary and ternary positions for an hour or so each day for about a week, or until you are satisfied with the results.

While this explanation may seen long, you will find that it does not take very long to study and practice the exercises. Wonderful results are obtainable far more quickly than ever imagined. The final objective is the playing of the entire scale so that no idiosyncracy of fingering, or unevenness of tone, will identify *which* scale is being played. At some time, of course, these exercises should be practiced in all keys, using these same forms as the skeleton.

After having worked your way through all the keys in a matter of months, commence the same procedure with chromatic scales, intervals from thirds to seventeenths diatonically, and chromatic invervals from major seconds through major sixteenths. You will find yourself facing an unbelievable array of intervals, and the sounds thereof will do much to 'stretch' your hearing capabilities. Note, for instance, Example 25.

Throughout my life I have found that on occasions when I was preparing some particular material for concerts it was far more productive to work with some of these exercises in *the key of the piece being studied* than to practice the piece itself. In an hour or so I would acquire an easy familiarity with all the manipulations in that key signature. It is a superlative shortcut to positive technical mastery.

Staccato studies involve much work with rhythms juxtaposed against tonguing patterns so that the tonguing pattern often opposes the natural interval movement. This develops independence of tonguing, rhythmic orientation, and finger action (Example 26). Notice that Gillet uses both first and second positions for starting, so that you are not always 'balanced' on the same starting point. *Of course* one must go through the same routine with chromatics. Only when you actually do these fully will you realize how many variations of articulation patterns there are (and how awkward are some!) when coupled with note movements.

Do not feel that you must establish a massive routine of practicing *all* of these every day—or even every week. Approach the whole matter selectively. Because your object is to master the instrument, work on those areas of your playing which need reinforcing, in those positions and keys which seem most unnatural, but *always* over the entire range of the instrument. Do not restrict yourself to any one register for very long. Prescribe the key and position which you feel needs most attention and stay with them for whole practice periods. If you are already a fine player (you must be a pretty good one to approach these scales profitably)—I repeat—seek out areas related to what you are preparing for performance. You will find yourself 'easier' in any given key or signature if you have prepared via the Gillet method.

When you have achieved freedom in all keys and modes of articulation, and with all intervals, you will then be ready for the final volume of Gillet's series for the clarinet *Exercises Pour La Technique Supérieure De La Clarinette*. This remarkable summation of his studies for wind instruments can serve well as a basis for daily practice periods throughout the career of any artist.

The first of its twenty-one sections, in groupings of four, five, and six notes, follows the general pattern of his earlier volume just described. These new studies make more demands on the embouchure, and on sophistication of articulations.

Beginning with Section III he begins to work assiduously and with much freedom in changing tonalities. For example, a scale section which is to be studied and practiced (chiefly legato) until fluent (Example 26)

Ex. 26

is changed one measure at a time so that one half of the material being studied is in a new key. This is done by working the section between 𝄆   𝄇 as the second step (Example 27).

Ex. 27

Begin 8va lower

Thus one develops freedom and fluency, both mental and physical, in quickly changing tonalities, avoiding the mental lethargy and finger laziness which can come with constant repetition in one key. It is extraordinarily productive.

The next several sections have a number of variations of the earlier material, then move into a superb section devoted to broken arpeggios and intervals *up* to tenths, including chromatic ones, and of course with many articulations. All of these are of the greatest value in developing tuning and voicing. They demand 'prehearing' each tone. I suggest that these be studied mostly in the legato form.

I have found that the greatest value in all the Gillet studies lies in having them constantly at hand on my music stand. Whenever new problems arise in repertoire being prepared, it is easy to turn to Gillet and find some related study. Their enormous variety enables one to improve any facility by practicing fresh material each day, yet pursuing the wanted principle. It is the most comprehensive work on the technical and tonal control of the clarinet.

One question can be asked at this point. Is each pupil assigned the full sequence of the entire contents of each of the volumes discussed in this chapter? No. The Klosé, Hamelin, Gay, and Jeanjean material is studied in full. Depending on the individual, we study enough of each author's types to establish a full understanding of the necessary work. Then each pupil can pursue these throughout all the key signatures. I keep the subject of scales alive throughout the entire period of each pupil's study with me. This I do by having scale assignments each week, thus keeping a focus on the subject for a very long time. The other factor of major importance is to instill a feeling for the use of these scale studies as preparation and support of any studying of *any* material. Thus, when facing particular passages or problems in any repertoire, at any time of life, it is well to precede that preparation by substantial review of any of these scale forms I mention, in the key(s) of your immediate problems. This has the virtue of making you a momentary virtuoso in the chosen key(s)!

The next material I use, in the sequence I prefer, is the scale volume of Emile Stiévenard. These bring forth problems which no other volume has. Further, I extend this work by my own particular way of studying comparative note values, and pulsing. The scales themselves are set forth in a wide variety of articulations. I increase this variety of dynamic markings so as to extend that vocabulary, taking very great pains to see that tone color does not automatically change with dynamic range. It makes for a constant awareness of the full range of the steps of loudness. *Volume and tone color must be kept as separate controls.*

With the idea of being able to maintain an absolutely steady tempo despite metric variations, I ask pupils consciously to seek the common denominator between each two lines. Thus the individual note values as played will be exactly related to the given tempo, and it will be pulsed properly. I further complicate matters by doubling, or halving, the tempi of certain lines—thus introducing matters of staccato tonguing speed, range, and rhythmic poise which are needed to arrive at a point of sophisticated controls. These are changed for each new key, and indeed I change them to suit the particular needs of each pupil. A metronome is to be used liberally. Do not be misled by thinking of 40=1 pulse as being slow. These introduced new pulsings will test your agility.

Ex. 28

ı = principal pulse—set to metronome
　　ı =40—*unchanging tempo*
ı = subdivisions of principal pulses
* note: doubling of time signature values
** note: halving of time

signature values

It is important to keep a strong pulse sense in these last measures, thus, in effect rehearsing the 'common denominator' subdivision

Ex. 29

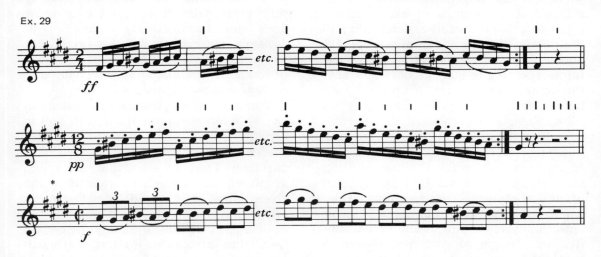

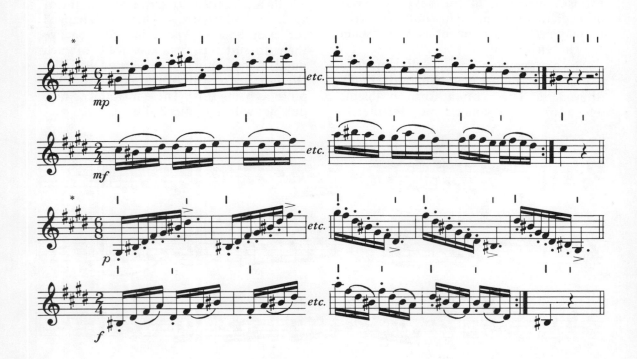

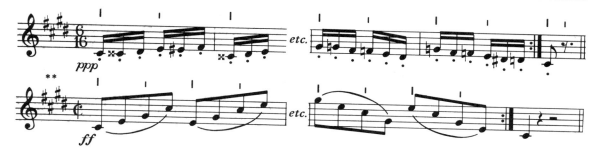

And now for the final material for scales—the *Thesaurus of Scales and Melodic Patterns* by Nicolas Slonimsky, the remarkable musicologist, author of many important books on music—*Lexicon of Musical Invective, Music Since 1900,* etc., who also edited the fifth edition of Baker's *Biographical Dictionary of Musicians* and other reference material. Here you will find the final sophistication and freedom. There are all manner of technical definitions: Phrygian Polytetrachord, Sesquiquinquetone (interval of a major seventh), Ultrapolation, Infra-Inter-Ultrapolation, etc. Do not be dismayed! You may even wish to develop your theoretical knowledge to the point where all these terms mean something! For my part I have been interested only in their value in developing that final freedom from the clichés of ordinary clarinet technique. For this the first four-fifths of the book are invaluable. Although the scales are not written especially for the clarinet (indeed some have a two-hand version for keyboard), one can adapt them to the range available.

Despite the fact that I recommend them principally as a final step in scale mastery, I warmly urge you teachers to choose appropriate ranges of notes and tempi and use some of these with students at *all* levels of playing. Apart from the controls which develop, the chief value is the freeing of the pupil from finger clichés which are a result of usual chordal and scale writing for the clarinet. I have found that pupils who have worked on these are less bothered and timid about reading modern atonal music. Their sense of orientation is not based alone on the simple 'square' statements of scales and chords.

For instance take an interpolation of one note in an equal division of an octave into two parts (Example 30). Have you are faced with three problems, the simplest of which is the reading. The others are the voicing of the intervals, and the evenness of the fingering between the chromatic and wide interval movement. Looking at it will make you think it will be easy—but try it! Remember not to let up on your standards of tuning and tone homogeneity.

Ex. 30

Slonimsky continues with interpolations of two notes (Example 31).

Ex. 31

and of three and four notes (Example 32). As is obvious the next steps would bring a true chromatic scale. Home again!

Ex. 32

Symmetric interpolation of notes (insertion of notes at equal intervals from respective pivotal points, resulting in invertible progressions) is used in Example 33. It is surprising how quickly one can grasp the pattern.

Ex. 33

With infrapolation of notes we come on old friends by a fancy name (Example 34). These are patterns which are often met within the music of the 19th century.

Again the problem is regularizing the chromatics and wider intervals with each other. Do not think of these as 'finger exercises' alone. They must be considered as tonal development material.

Ex. 34

While moving through progressions in which the octave(s) are divided into many parts, we come to the equal division of one octave into six parts—an old friend indeed, the whole tone scale. Why this division (six) has been so much more widely used than four, or some other, is not the subject of this article. The last fifth or so of the book does not concern our present discussion.

Summing up: the study of scales is the surest, most economical way to develop mastery of the entire instrument. As you develop all controls, you are also encompassing an unbelievable array of note patterns and intervals. If you can conquer these—you can play anything which is possible for the clarinet. Your ability to read will be developed as no other means makes possible.

Chapter 17:
EUGENE GAY'S CLARINET METHOD

Now that I have begun my second half-century of teaching clarinet and chamber music, I find myself more than ever reflecting on the various approaches to instrumental instruction. I have had ample time to witness cause and effect—cause, in that I have known many of the principal teachers in most clarinet-playing countries, and have been aware of their methods; effect, as revealed in the careers of their pupils. Although the temptation to examine materials used by others in the teaching fraternity is great, for the moment, I will confine myself to the one basic method which I consider best of all—in fact in many ways, the ideal model for most instrumental methods. Before describing it, allow me to give you a rationale for my approach.

The materials are these:
- a pupil—more or less talented, with a variety of personal bias, strengths and weaknesses.
- a teacher—ditto.
- a clarinet—hopefully the best possible AND with a fine mouthpiece-reed set-up.
- a pencil, pad and music.
- a metronome—preferably a fine electronic one.
- a music stand with attached mirror.
- a basic method—that of Eugene Gay.

The object:
To become able to play every tone over the entire register of the clarinet, in every nuance, at any speed, with any articulation, with every kind of start and close, and with all changing gradations.

Now how are we going to do this? Answer: to bring the pupil the experience of gradually becoming acquainted with all idiosyncracies of playing the instrument—by careful guidance. This involves his personal work inclinations, natural motor controls, rhythmic aptitudes, musically poetic impulse, and general aesthetic awareness.

Because these vary widely from pupil to pupil, no one standardized text or procedure is adequate. This is why I continually evaluate the pupil's potential and receptivity *at that moment*. There is no point (only harm or waste) in passing on knowledge which he cannot assimilate *right then*. Therefore your probe must be working always. In the interest of preserving or lifting confidence or morale, there is much to gain by not confronting a student with a step he can not fully comprehend or execute at that moment. The object is to help him see precisely that step which is possible. I cast aside all the claptrap described as 'secrets,' 'plain drubbing,' 'sugar-coating,' etc.— and leave only clear analysis and precise direction.

Learning to play an instrument is like building a brick wall. You have to lay the first course of bricks first (and *firmly*), then proceed to the other courses in sequence. If any of you have ever had the privilege of watching a fine craftsman build a stonewall, preferably the dry ones prevalent in New England (note: I mean dry stone walls, not dry stone masons!) you will fully appreciate my statements about prescribing for the pupil. The craftsman will often just contemplate the wall he is constructing (and not necessarily the place he worked on last), then examine the stones he has assembled and spread out. After much deliberation and 'eye-matching' he will pick up a stone that fits perfectly. No rush—just deliberateness. So with advice about playing an instrument. Select and solve the problem before the pupil is allowed to 'practice' it.

Your judgement must tell you the moment to concentrate on this, or that, or the other thing—regardless of the book-sequence. I seldom use anything more than a generally similar choice of texts for different pupils—and over the years I have found that this brings great rewards in the development of their controls. Generally I try to have them leave after a lesson armed with one to three major points of emphasis for the next week's study-practice, despite the fact that many other points may have been touched upon. They are able to accomplish more when they focus on fewer points. As I have said many times: there is no point 'practicing' something you cannot play reasonably well. Think first; take time for *evaluation.* Unless all components required to make the passage truly correct are under control, you should not repeat (practice) it. You will progress faster. After all, practice merely means *making a habit of doing something*—something you do well, or something you do badly!

A common hindrance to efficient practice is our American habit of studying always with an instrument. Consider that when you are trying to solve and execute a rhythmic complexity you do not need the added handicap of an instrument in your hands. How much better to isolate your rhythmic problem by tapping it out with your fingers, or singing (however bad your voice). Thus you can concentrate on the specific problem unhampered by fingering correctly, playing in tune, playing with a good tone, etc. And you save your physical strength, including lips. Likewise with phrasing—unless you have a clear concept of how you mean to phrase a passage, and can sing it to suit your ideas (again with that bad voice), there is no point trying it only with your instrument. And you can use this approach at any time—a real time-saver from your instrument sessions. Solfeggio is the answer. Then when you come to play the passage on your instrument, you will find that with the prior problem solved you are free to concentrate on the purely instrumental controls—tone, tuning, fingering, etc. There is no use 'assembling' a passage unless each component is correct of itself. If they all are, the finished product will be excellent.

One of the weaknesses of most clarinet methods is that they are too tonally oriented. How many times I have heard players stumble over a passage only because it was not rooted sufficiently to the tonic—it did not 'lie' well under the fingers. I believe it is essential that players learn to manipulate their instruments in all keys throughout the entire range, or in no key!

The foundation for all the study materials I use with my pupils is the '*Méthode*' for clarinet by Eugene Gay. I believe I have examined virtually every method for the clarinet presently available here or in the principal countries of Europe, and none is as methodical as the

Gay, nor as comprehensive in all aspects of development. But for me it has the additional merits of diagnosing the specific technical problems most troublesome to each individual pupil, and of prescribing exercises that solve those problems efficiently. In short it is an ideal foundation for the flexible approach to study I have just described. This is why I use it as a backbone to the rest of the teaching material which I select to meet the needs of each pupil.

My first example illustrates Gay's diagnostic technique (Example 1):

Ex. 1

All of the following should also be played both in quarters and eighths.

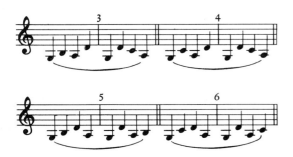

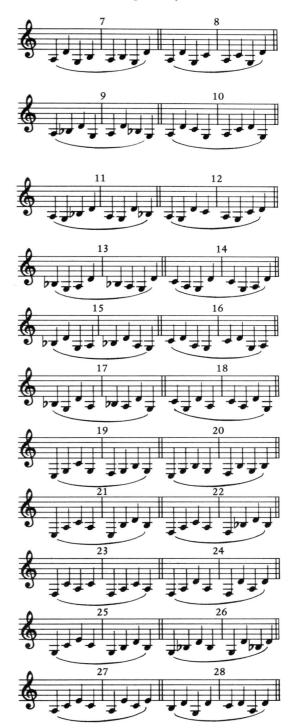

At first glance this will seem needlessly repetitious. But you will find it invaluable in searching out the needs and idiosyncracies of each pupil. Then you know how and where to work. The main problem at this point is coordination of hands. The pupil himself will recognize which of these tiny numbered units needs attention—the goal, of course, being the ability to play each of them equally fluently and with absolutely equal finger confidence. Gay stresses proper and efficient embouchure, even calling for substantial rest after each note at the beginning. Initial sounds call for no finger change, but when he introduces movements of single fingers he carefully illustrates a continuous single note above, to focus on the idea of a continuous embouchure and wind perseverance, despite finger motion. The studies become more complete with the introduction of new notes, tonal gradation, intervals, etc.—but all in a very elementary way. He makes no real issue of tonguing until the end of the first section of Volume 1, where he introduces a graded series of tongued interval studies which bring to light the individualities of response of the notes in various registers. These introductory sections avoid 'sugar coating.' If younger pupils miss it, there are any number of small study books which should be carefully selected to supplement each stage of the work done in Gay.

Now begin the most interesting parts—the carefully examined problems which each key signature brings to light. First, in C major he outlines the intervals which will probably give the most trouble:

Ex. 2

At the start, practice these intervals for evenness.

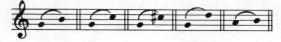

and then proceeds with a carefully graded series of studies which increase in length and interval size until a complete 2-octave scale is available to be mastered with considerable suppleness. Very important to note here is his constant advice to remove the mouthpiece from the mouth between each small section so as to have the experience of reforming the embouchure position. It is amazing how effective this is in building endurance as well as purity of sound, and all so simply effected.

Next he establishes a few precepts of sound—one: how inevitably the note *after* a rest sounds accented in relation to the silence before the note, which, if you do not intend this as an accented note, must be counteracted.

Ex. 3

Note well the relationships of the shorter notes (♪) to the long ♩ values which follow them. Mark well the lengths of the ♩ so that the necessary accent will mark the tempo strongly.

Then he has a series of finger movements which continue until the 2-octave span has been completed. Important: he uses ¼ time signature to give visual stimulus thus assisting in arriving at an audible rhythmic equality. This is fairly easy to do in a slow tempo—but try it at a fast clip and see if you can avoid falling into patterns of four or more pulses.

Ex. 4

Tempo according to the ability of the player. Accent tempo with foot beat. Repeat same exercise without repeat marks, playing it all segue.

Notice the emphasis on establishing well the first note; only when the sound is properly sonorous does one proceed upward in scale fashion, with constantly expanding range, with pauses between segments for embouchure analysis and reassurance, and finally playing the whole in unbroken sequence. Obviously, it is not enough merely to repeat the exercise; careful analytical attention must constantly be kept.

By this time he has already introduced one other important practice, that of asking that a passage be played at first slowly, with great attention to the equality of sound (in *mf*), and then abruptly changing to a pianissimo and playing at twice the speed—always with great attention to equality of finger action and the matching of tone quality.

Ex. 5 ♩ = 120

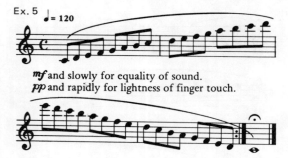

mf and slowly for equality of sound.
pp and rapidly for lightness of finger touch.

I use this type of exercise to establish the clear understanding that resonance must be equal from one version to the other when played without pause, thus clearly separating control of sound level (nuance) from sound color. One of the greatest single shortcomings in most playing I hear is that the sound is allowed to become dull in soft passages. Naturally I am not speaking of situations when the composer requests (or the player wishes) it—but only of being *able* to go from one level to another without change of color.

To develop great suppleness and absolute evenness, Gay has a number of studies with varying rhythmic emphasis, all leading up to the final playing with great evenness of tone color, volume, density, tuning, fingering and touch.

Ex. 6

Think. The study of detached tones (staccato) (being harmful to the tone quality) should be practiced after the legato version. Lento—the sound well sustained.

Particularly awkward intervals are studied thus:

Ex. 7

Play these as in Ex. 1.

In dealing with widely different demands he uses examples like this, calling for sameness of quality in tuning, density and color, regardless of the nuance:

Ex. 8

Sustain well the sound, all tones with the same strength.

A variant of Example 7 is Example 9, where he follows the same procedure but with wider intervals, in this case 4ths. The exercises themselves, of almost imperceptibly increasing difficulty and sophistication, are interspersed with duets by some of our best composers, exemplifying the problems of the moment.

Ex. 9

1st time **mf** and lento—for ease and equality of sound
2nd time **pp** and more rapidly for lightness of finger touch.

Notice how he approaches and beautifully solves one of the mannerisms which young people fall into—and which many players carry into later life—slighting the last note before the end of a legato mark.

Ex. 10

Tongue well the first tone. Carry the sound well to the down-beat without shortening the value of the up-beat. Give clear tongue enunciation to the 2 detached tones. Maintain the same method of work (carrying the sound to the 2nd 8th in each measure). Relax, the mind and fingers must mark well each 1st beat.

He 'sneaks' up on you—first the crescendo is towards where pupils normally make an accent (start of measure), then with the exact same tonal distribution he induces you to consciously elongate the second note, and finally, having lived with that, you come to the actual performance of what you are really after, only now you hear it properly. So simple, but so eloquent.

He inserts a test for the pupil at this point:

Ex. 11 - 1st time *mf* and slowly, for ease and equality of sound. 2nd time *pp* and move rapidly for lightness of finger touch.

Can he play this (a) with ease (b) in tune (c) with full equality of sound intensity (d) with full equality of sound volume (e) rhythmically even, and (f) with equal finger 'touch'? It should sound so well that one would not hear any individual peculiarities of any one of the notes or fingers. *It will be only as good as your standard of listening,* and that which you have given the pupil.

The approach to chromatics is generally the same—working within a small range, and gradually expanding into two full octaves. Here he introduces articulation variety, in a condensed form, saving many pages of space while developing the pupil's mental and muscular acceptance and mastery of each pattern. Here it is up to the teacher to learn which ones are the easiest for the pupil. The intention is not that one should practice *each* scale in *each* articulation pattern, but rather that each be studied until it is fluent. This will vary from pupil to pupil. In general he approaches a problem from all angles, to probe for the weak example needing development, so that all come to a neutral likeness in a fully controlled final example (last lines):

Ex. 12

Do not be misled by the apparent simplicity of the examples I am quoting; these will later occur in all keys, at *all* positions on the instrument.

He introduces the idea of minor thirds in sequence, later juxtaposed with major thirds in sequence to bring you to a fine point of expertise. As a test, see if you can play Example 13 with absolute homogeneity at both speeds and with the stipulations of Example 5 given earlier:

Ex. 13

Repeat, but in major thirds etc.

* Note: the above two examples are written-out versions of Mr. Gay's condensed form.

In Example 14 it should be reasonably impossible for a fine musician (but not a clarinettist) to distinguish dynamic and tonal differences, except by pitch. An experienced clarinet teacher automatically identifies the peculiarities of each tone in relation to the particular instrument, and only with concentration can he make his listening 'neutrally based.' Here, as everywhere, I make it a practice (once a pupil can use the full range of the clarinet) to expand Mr. Gay's version by starting at the lowest possible tone of the instrument and proceeding to the top. After all, you have to learn to play in each key throughout the entire range. Attention must be paid to the development of suppleness, and for gaining courage in playing long unbroken passages. For this he does the following in whole tone sequence and in all the keys.

Ex. 14 Lento

mf sostenuto

1.
6 or 8 times

2.
6 or 8 times

for each ending.

3.
6 or 8 times

Note that each time you repeat the scale you go to one step higher until finally you play the whole unbroken scale *in one breath* with every note from the 3rd step upward serving as an apex—a total of 208 tones in one breath (or more—depending on your turning point at the top). There are even more when you do similar chromatics, or in playing three octaves. Superb exercises in concentration!

I use a variety of material to establish absolute rhythmic certainty in difficult mixed rhythms and meters (a principal one is my own adaptation of the Stiévenard scales). This is how Gay introduces this whole area of study:

Ex. 15

In each case see that the metronome is *meticulously set.* Normally I allow the pupil to commence playing one form, then at random while he is playing, I suggest shifting in the next measure to one of the other forms. This forces him to make an immediate appraisal and adjustment.

All of the foregoing occur in all key signatures (you are by now aware that all of my quotes have, for the sake of clarity of visualization, been in easy key signatures). Actually, he uses compact symbols to represent much of this; if Gay's book had been fully written out it would be several times as long (and far more expensive). Notice that his concept of scales includes scales in all intervals, seconds, thirds, etc. It goes without saying that the exercises and duets, become more sophisticated as one goes along, and there are suitable explanations of trill fingerings, mordents, gruppetti, appoggiaturi, etc.

A fine example of his not making exercises which follow the 'clichés' or 'inclination' of the clarinet is this next, in which he takes the progression to its logical conclusion—regardless of the clarinet—and thus bringing quickly to light sequences which might otherwise occur elsewhere only in piecemeal fashion.

Ex. 16

Note also the aptness of his choice of duets when in the F♯ minor section he has the following Campagnoli posing fine problems for the left hand:

Ex. 17

116

ger movements only—most of us are right-handed, or at least live in a world which is mostly right-handed. Listen carefully (even among the best players) and if there is any finger unevenness, it will usually be in the left hand. Now consider that the keys, rings, etc., are for all practical purposes equipped with springs of equal tension—and the A♭ and A throat keys are relatively small to the hand. Now allow me an analogy to illustrate this point. Go to your kitchen and open (with the right hand) a drawer which is a little hard to pull out (every kitchen has at least one sticky drawer!). Note the strength you use. Now do the same with the left hand and notice that it seems to take more effort. However, consider that the drawer has not changed between the two pullings. What happened was that you had to exert more effort to counter the weakness or ineptness of the left hand. Consequently I have found it wise (in the early stages when pupils' lifelong habits are being set up) to have them think of using the left hand with slightly more vigor or emphasis. Try to be aware of the *contact* moment of finger-wood (on ring or open positions), and pad-wood on key or lever use. *That* is the feeling to be equalized.

In reading Gay's text do not be confused by such as the following.

Ex. 18

Which reminds me—the left hand . . . concerning myself for the moment with fin-

If you are ascending the scale with stems upward (ascending 3rds) descend with stems downward. Otherwise you will have a mixture of patterns.

To conclude, he has a number of solo movements, some from Bach flute sonatas (I wish there were more), others by Mozart, Weber and Schumann. Personally I prefer to study solo pieces from the regular parts with piano score so the pupil can learn the architecture and proportions of all the parts.

Since nothing in this world is perfect, you may ask me what I do not like about the Gay Method.

1. Would prefer it bound in four or six volumes instead of present two.
2. Would prefer to have it in English for U.S. use. This seems to be the greatest single drawback to its extended use here.
3. Though the editing is in general very good, many little slips have been discovered in the years it has been in print.
4. There should be more use of odd and mixed meters (5/8, 7/8, various combinations thereof such as 3/4 + 7/8, etc.) to prepare for playing contemporary music.
5. The ranges of all scales and pattern studies should be written thoughout the entire compass of the instrument, regardless of the key signature and tonic orientation.
6. There should be some atonal material.
7. It would be helpful to have extensive selected listings of supportive studies from all publishers. This would assist in the more extensive use of the method itself.

But considering that the book was published in 1932, it has withstood the test of time unusally well. I doff my beret and salute Mr. Gay for the finest basic method of them all. If you combine it with Keith Stein's *The Art of Clarinet Playing* you will have an excellent foundation for your clarinet instructional library.

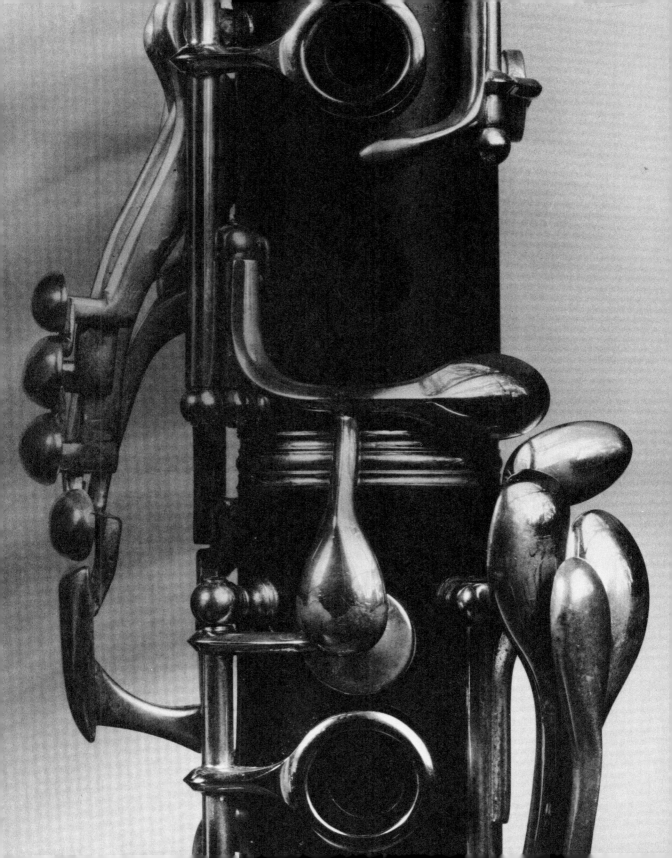

PART V
MECHANISM—INSTRUMENTS

In the absence of a universally used terminology for fingering identification, I have devised one that at least has the merit of simplicity. Keys and levers 1, 3, 5, 8, 9, 10, 14 and the one marked X in the chart are used in this following explanation. Thumb hole and register key are assumed open or closed as needed. Rings are 1L, 2L, 3L (hole or ring), 1R, 2R and 3R.

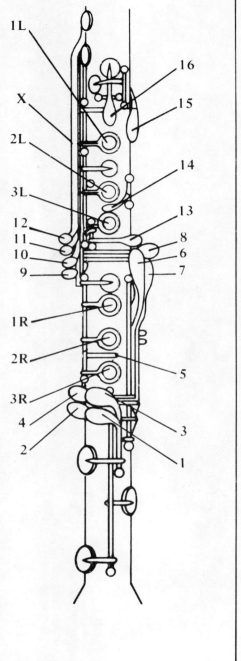

My terminology for:

$E\flat^1/B\flat^2$ fingerings	keys, levers and rings used
R	1L, 2L and 9
L	1L, 2L and 14
1/1	1L and 1R
1/1+2	1L, 1R and 2R
1/1+3	1L, 1R and 3R
1/1+5	1L and 1R and #5
1/2	1L and 2R
1/3	1L and 3R
1/3+k	1L, 3R and #3
F^1	1L and 3L (only on clarinets with 3rd L ring)
F^2	1L, 3L and #13
F^3	2L, 3L and #13
Bis	L1 and X (both played by 1L finger)
pp	1L, 3L, 1R, 2R, 3R and #1

Chapter 18:
$E\flat^1/B\flat^2$*

Good fingering depends, far more than most people think, on a substantial and solid tone. Such a tone is the *necessary* basis, otherwise any slight deficiences in finger manipulation will be magnified. To this end I want to write a few words about stability and security in tone production before going on to the fingering problems in themselves.

Your clarinet is best played with your ears. Everything else must be subservient to them. And the ears should be attuned to the bell-end of the clarinet, rather than the mouthpiece-end. When you have analyzed a problem, and applied your solution, be sure to continue to listen, because (a) you may not have completely nor properly analyzed the problem; (b) other factors may vary the results of your prior solution. Your ears should be turned off only *after* the music has ceased.

One fault I hear, especially among young players, is that of 'scooping' a tone—that is, starting it below the pitch on which it ultimately settles. Sometimes they also drop the pitch at the end of the tone.

This is caused by the embouchure not being in its final position before the moment of the tone's inception, and by relaxing it before the end of the tone. Let me illustrate this with a visual example. We are going to make a movie of a person. The name of the movie is 'A—In Tune' or 'At Attention.' Our *in tune* has become *at attention*. We start the movie camera, the person comes to attention, holds it the required length of time, and relaxes again. The movie camera then stops. When we look at the movie, we see the following:

* NOTE: To avoid repetition in the text I will speak only of $B\flat^2$, understanding that it also applies to $E\flat^1$ unless otherwise described. Though I have used tremolos or trills as most of the examples, it is understood that I mean any rapid passages involving the particular notes given. *Key and ring identifications as per the chart at the head of this section.*

Fig. 1—We do not want to see the A & C sections. Our interest is only in B.

The point: your embouchure should be in its ultimate tensed position *before* you initiate any sound—there should be absolutely no movement of your embouchure as the sound commences, nor as it continues, nor indeed until *after* it has ceased. You may think it enough to 'feel' this, but believe me a mirror will be a real eye-opener. In fact, a mirror is an absolute must for proper embouchure analysis. Attach one to your music stand so that a glance out of the corner of your eye will show you what is happening.

Of all the fingering problems I have heard discussed, the clarinet fraternity seems most indecisive about the efficient uses of the available choices for the $E\flat^1$/ $B\flat^2$. Somehow many seem to fasten on to the exclusive use of the R forefinger (my lever 9), learn to play it with some freedom, and then find themselves unable to use efficiently all of the other choices.

Consider the player (in a major symphony orchestra) who played the cadenza of the second movement of Rimsky-Korsakov's *Scheherezade* with the 1/1 fingering for $B\flat^2$ (note: see my terminology for fingerings in the fingering chart in this chapter). *That* would have been some recording to hear, if ever it had been made! Or the leading studio player on a New York radio station who, because he felt it to be in the way, had the L key removed and the tone hole plugged. Or the advanced (?) student—from a well-known conservatory—who would not believe there was any other fingering than the R one. Come to think of it, the subject is not just in order—it is urgent!

I'll begin with a statement of my general philosophy regarding alternate fingerings. It is a simple one, perhaps best illustrated by personal experience. A player would come and play for me. Noting that he never used the L Eb/Bb lever, I called it to his attention, explained the reasons for its use, and suggested becoming acquainted with it during the coming week. When the week was over the player would come back, still not using the L fingering, but explaining that he could do it better with the R. I asked how many times he had used the R fingering in his life. Answer: "probably tens of thousands of times." The L?—"half a dozen times in the past week." At this point one has not earned the privilege of choice until having become adept with *both* fingerings. This may involve a good deal of woodshedding, but it is an eye-opener. Keep in mind that each of us has a greater facility with certain fingers, perhaps related to left or right-handedness, or to prior specialized use. The important point with a new fingering is to use it enough to remove all 'strangeness' of feeling. *Then* you can be your own best judge.

When all fingering motions have become automatic, then in any given passage tuning and tone quality must be taken into account *first*. If the passage is a slow one, use the best-sounding fingering, no matter how awkward the manipulation; if fast, use the most fluent-sounding one.

Ex. 1—*Verdi-Aida (excerpt)*

Brahms-Clar. Quintet
Adagio

Above all recognize that fingering habits must be automatic.

R(9) This is the most-used fingering. It is also the most mis-used! Ideally (and that means making the most efficient use of all possibilities for these notes) this fingering is used when the note either before or after the Bb² does not require the first finger R manipulation of its ring. Like all good rules this one has exceptions. Normal use:

Ex. 2

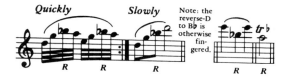

It is possible to become quite expert with these movements in the following examples, especially example (a), if slow and not too soft. Generally I allow the matter of legato to be the deciding factor in the choice. If the notes are detached, then by all means 1/1.

Ex. 3

L(14) This I use in all scale passages where the 3rd finger L does not next go (or come from) the 3rd hole covering, and in all chromatic scales. This Eb/ Bb lever is best played with the tip of the LH 3rd finger touching the lever close to its own rod. There will be more immediate response, a shorter 'throw,' a cleaner tone, and better tuning—and all because your 3rd finger is not partially over the 3rd tone hole. After all, the indicated fingering does not call for partially covering the 3rd finger tone hole. Incidentally, this is particularly important for the D♯ since tone tends to be low in pitch on most clarinets.

Ex. 4

Since these first two uses are the most common and important fingerings for these notes, allow me to dwell on a superb example of a combined use of them. This came to my mind when I was listening to an old but beautiful recording of Rimsky-Korsakov's *Scheherezade* played by one of our best orchestras. The playing was inspired and dramatic, but the clarinettist 'barely made' the cadenza in the second movement. I tape-recorded it, reduced the speed to ¼ of the original, and confirmed what I suspected. The G^2s were almost entirely missing in substance. Mind you, this passage can go very quickly— especially with dynamic conductors who conduct the entire cadenza (and who seem to be eager to get to the after-concert party). Over the years I have heard numberless players perform this, but none of them with the ease of Gaston Hamelin. His execution was impeccable, for clarity and evenness as well as speed. And he did it by a simple formula. Because these were scale-type passages, he used the L for B♭ (since it was not involved with G before or after the B♭) *except where the B♭ was on a pulse*. Then he used the R. When you practice this until the fingers move easily, you will find that there is almost a ballet-like movement and rhythm to your music and actions, and the passage glides almost effortlessly under your fingers. If on your clarinet the long-held B♭'s are better in tone and tune on the R, then by all means use that.

Ex. 5

I use this also for legato passages down from D^3 coming from a 1R (finger-in-use) position.

Ex. 7

If the passage (a) were extremely fast, I would use R, but this would not be good for players with particularly long fingers. It is surprising how easy it is to make a beautiful legato from Bb^2 to G^2 or A^2, though not quite as easy to do the reverse.

This is a valuable fingering—with certain restrictions to its use. Chief among these is the tuning, which varies in different clarinets. Normally the Bb^2 is the standard by which manufacturers arrange the tone-holes. But not all manufacturers are agreed on how best to tune the 12ths generally—with the result that the Eb^1 is often too sharp and pinched in quality. If so, the 1/1 fingering can be used only for very rapid passages where tuning is a lesser consideration than fluency. This fingering is ideal for the *Overture* to *Orpheus in the Underworld* by Offenbach. Try making comfortably long breaks where I have indicated, and do not run away from the first few notes of each arpeggio.

Ex. 6

These work beautifully on many clarinets. They darken, fatten and help tune the Eb^1. They make it a better blend with its neighbors, and make a better legato than the R in the following situation. Tuning varies slightly with individual instruments. Not usable in upper register.

Ex. 8

I use this for facility, sometimes for better legato, and occasionally as a leading tone.

Ex. 9

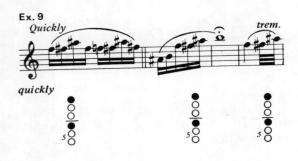

Quickly

quickly

Note: only L2+3 need to move for above tones.

(same) slowly

This is used mostly to make a leading tone sharper in the keys of B major or minor (lower register E major or minor), and for rapid manipulation of passages involving middle fingering F♯.

Ex. 10

Slowly

pp L   R   ½

Quickly

pp

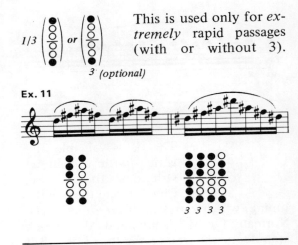

This is used only for *extremely* rapid passages (with or without 3).

3 *(optional)*

Ex. 11

3 3 3 3

F¹

(Only on clarinets with 3rd L ring)—A very advantageous fingering, but with serious drawbacks. Its uses are obvious in the examples below. The problems are that this E♭/B♭ is seldom either truly in tune, or of a tone to match its neighbors. Even more important is the fact that the E/B naturals become uncomfortably sharp, and one loses a comfortable high F♯³ (middle L ring). When the 3rd ring is present it becomes too flat and insecure, though it may be improved by adding lever 5 pressed near its fulcrum. The disadvantages are so great that after using clarinets with this mechanism for over 20 years I changed in the early '60s in favor of instruments without the 3rd L ring. However some players have instruments which they prefer in spite of these points, and for them the mechanical advantages are great. There are no adjustment problems.

Ex. 12

Quickly

F¹   F¹   F¹   F¹

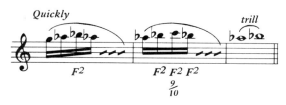

F2 13

This valuable fingering is, alas, one about which most players do not know, although it has been available for some 50 years. It exists on a model of the Mazzeo clarinet, could be added to *any* Boehm clarinet in a few minutes by a competent instrument worker, doesn't change any other fingering whatsoever, *cannot* get out of adjustment, and makes many difficult passages ridiculously easy. It is excellently in tune on most clarinets, particularly in the low register. It consists only of a little piece of metal 1/4″ x 1/8″ soldered onto the C♯/G♯ arm so that when 13 is pressed it takes down the L2 ring.

Ex. 13

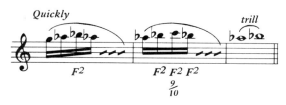

Quickly

trill

F2   *F2 F2 F2*
                $\frac{9}{10}$

F³ 13

Very useful for tremolos, but too sharp— do not raise fully the 1st L finger.

Ex. 14

tr

13

Bis

Most clarinets do not have this, and it is rarely needed (but when you do . . .!) Indeed it is

not needed at all if you have a 3rd L ring. It is a little too sharp and I use it only for tremolo. You can also do this (uncomfortably) by extending the 1st L finger to take down the pad between the 1st two rings.

Ex. 15

tr

1L
Bis

pp

1

This one is rarely needed, but oh so handy then!

Ex. 16

pppp

I strongly urge the study of Jeanjean's 'Vade-Mecum' etudes (at *very* slow tempi!)—using each of these fingerings in the appropriate situations, and staying with them until *each* is comfortable. Remember your motor-controls must become automatically responsive. Fix well in your mind the reasons for each, so that when you are confronted with a problem the best solution is automatic. After all, when performing you have enough else to think about—tone quality, tuning, phrasing, ensemble, etc.—without having to consider fingering.

Chapter 19:
SOME NOTES ON AUXILIARY KEYS AND OTHER SPECIAL FINGERING PROBLEMS

Throughout my career I have received questions from teachers and players related to the so-called extra keys on clarinets, some of which have been in use for more than a half-century. Most players settle on one model and develop a strong bias towards it—a laudable idea, since it removes much indecision. My comments are intended for players who are curious but do not have access to the various types of auxiliary mechanisms, or who have not made a final choice. My own experience equips me particularly well, since as a result of my natural curiosity I have, in some fifty-six years of clarinet playing, spent considerable time with most available types.

I began with a wood plain Boehm (17 keys and 6 rings), went on to a wood full Boehm (20 keys and 7 rings), then to a pair of beautifully made metal 17–6 Boehms. During my student years I experimentally played a wood Albert system for three months, and over the years have critically examined and played many varieties of Albert and Oehler system clarinets. In the years I studied with Gustave Langenus (one of the most sensitive clarinettists of this century, principal clarinet with the New York Symphony and later the New York Philharmonic, an ardent and renowned chamber music player, performing with the most prestigious groups, author of a method and other music for the clarinet and an extraordinary teacher), I changed to a Belgian-made clarinet which had an additional ring for the left third finger. Upon joining the Boston Symphony Orchestra in 1933 I changed back to wood 17–6 clarinets. After a few years I changed once again to full-Boehm models. While these better satisfied the demanding and often surprising requirements of symphonic playing, I also began the design of my own mechanism.

About 1960 my own design was refined enough for use in the orchestra. I then changed to a version of it which was the counterpart of the full-Boehm model. I played this type until I retired, having decided that 33 years of symphonic playing was enough. Since then my playing has consisted entirely of chamber music and solo material—all presenting problems, but no abrupt surprises as in the symphonic repertoire—I have changed to the plain model of my clarinet (17 keys, 5 rings and 1 plateau key), and in these last few years to what I whimsically call *The California Custom Clarinet*. After all, it was conceived on this California mountainside overlooking the Pacific!

Before describing the uses of the 'extra' keys, I would like to comment again on the use of *any* unfamiliar key. Many times in my life I have met players (including some proficient ones) who would try to play even such a simple key as the left Eb / Bb for a moment or two and then give up, saying "I can do it better the way I have been doing it on the right." Of course they can. They will have been playing the right hand Eb/Bb fingering for umpteen or more years, and the new one for about thirty seconds. If they would stop to analyze the motion of the fingers, they perhaps would see the advantages in certain passages, but there is no earthly reason why the new fingering should not feel strange, uncomfortable, and inefficient at first.

My own attitude is this: practice the new fingering until you can use it fluently. At that point you are in a position to choose the best for you personally. Until then you are not a proper judge. Now let us turn to the keys themselves, starting at the lower end of the instrument. All of these are found on various models of the Boehm and Boehm-Mazzeo clarinets.

Eb/Bb key
(extra)

This is an important and helpful tone.

1. It extends the range, giving composers more scope.
2. It makes the B natural

a better sound, more like the quality of the notes immediately above and below it. And it is better tuned because it is not a bell tone when the low Eb is present (no bell tone has exactly the same sound as other notes on an instrument, nor is its sound as centered).

3. It makes possible the transposing of A clarinet parts on the Bb clarinet without loss of the A clarinet's low E. I always recall with great amusement the player who, when he saw this key on my instrument, said, "Oh, you have one of those transposing keys." And I, all the while, thought I had been doing all my own transposing!

4. When you transpose A clarinet parts it allows you to play Bb [1] with the same fingering as the low Eb (plus, of course, the register key). This keeps the sound consistent with the upper-register quality you would have had on an A clarinet.

5. It makes a perfectly tuned Bb to B natural trill.

6. On the A clarinet it extends the range to low C (concert pitch).

Once mastered, transposing becomes an entirely automatic and thoughtless process. Witness my 10 years (1942–52) of transposing all of the Boston Symphony Orchestra repertoire played in that time. At first I did this as a lark—then discovered that the sensitivity and feel one developed in relation to manipulating the keys of a single instrument made playing more fluent. Tuning was easier because the instrument was always warm. Transposition was, of course, no problem—it merely became automatic. And it was easier to carry only one clarinet about! I recall occasional technical problems, but rarely any reading concerns. As regards tonal differences, these are negligible when a fine player is using today's beautifully made instruments. I know from actual experience that practically no conductors (including most of the greatest of these last 35 years) can distinguish one from the other. This was not so in the days of Brahms, when A clarinets were not as well-matched with the Bb instruments.

Transposing to one clarinet has the unbeatable advantage of an always-warm instrument. The changing of clarinets does more to disturb the tuning of a woodwind section, and hence the entire orchestra, than anything else. In the Dvorak 'cello concerto, if memory serves, the player uses one clarinet throughout the first movement, and at the start of the second commences to play a solo on the other, which is naturally cold and flat, thus imposing another pitch standard on the other players. The rest of the woodwinds are of necessity forced to alter their pitch—and not to the general good.

Generally speaking, it is easier to transpose from 'A' parts to the Bb clarinet than the reverse, but you should be able to do both. I have known of only one player who preferred to transpose to the A clarinet—Sarlitt, the famous French virtuoso. And I know of one other who did it out of necessity—a very fine New York player who built his life around wine, women and song. At one point wine got the upper hand and he had to pawn a clarinet. Unfortunately, the pawnbroker knew the differences in re-sale possibilities between Bb and A clarinets and insisted on accepting only the Bb. Our friend, in order to hold his job, learned to transpose to the A clarinet—and very fluently. His mind was made up for him!

Two comments on the low Eb: it makes the clarinet slightly heavier, but not uncomfortably so. If you have this note you are better off in having a duplicate key for the left hand.

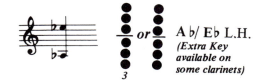

Some instruments have an alternate fingering for the left little finger. However the key position, plus the character of its action, makes it somewhat less useful than one would expect. If the passage is a quick one it is awkward to use: if slow, it is just as easy to slide, or doublefinger a note (i.e., playing the first half with one little finger and the second half with the other).

Ex. 1

On some clarinets the Ab/Eb keys also open the Db/Eb vent,

but this requires that the Ab/Eb spring be a little stiffer. This needs getting used to.

F♯/C♯

This is sometimes articulated, and anyone who has ever used it says it is a must. Personally I would not be without it. It is amazing how many good players tolerate the formerly conventional non-articulated action, which forces them to see-saw from left to right. With the articulated mechanism one fingers a D scale exactly as a C scale except that the right or left little finger is depressed on the F♯/C♯ key along with the left (or right) E/B.

Ex. 2

Many players have an extension downward added to the conventional C♯/G♯ key of the plain model, thus making this trill possible with the right first finger.

On certain clarinets the conventional C♯/G♯ key has an articulated mechanism.

This is more expensive to manufacture, but it makes possible a fuller and more open sound for these notes, and really in-tune trills for

Ex. 3

It also makes possible perfectly tuned tremolos with any right hand note below F.

Ex. 4

The little key between the right first and second fingers is enormously useful for semitone trills, especially if, as with me, your little finger is not particularly adept for trilling. This key is played with the right second finger.

This articulated mechanism has two disadvantages: it removes the possibility of

not a particularly important factor, and

for high Bb . You don't need this note often, but when you do—you do!

Eb/Bb

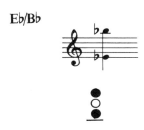

The third left hand ring is a great help. In the old days this fingering resulted in a darker and often flatter Eb/Bb^2. Nowadays it can be better tuned. However, on some instruments it is flat, pinched, or dull—and sometimes all three. In the absence of this 3rd ring, it is not too difficult to slide the left first finger forward and downward to take the adjoining pad down, thus making possible the G^2/Bb^2 tremolo (or C/Eb).

About 50 years ago this fingering possibility was introduced.

Eb/Bb^2

It is a mystery to me why this has not become universal. Presently it is available on some instruments. It changes absolutely nothing else on the clarinet, can be added to any instrument, and involves only the soldering of a small arm near the pad of the C♯/G♯ key to take down the left second ring. As you see, it makes possible a finely tuned and convenient trill from Db/Eb or Ab/Bb

Ex. 5

with the left second finger. I use it in scales because it is much smoother and more convenient than the conventional way.

Bb

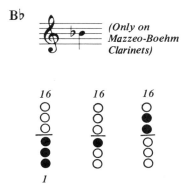

(Only on Mazzeo-Boehm Clarinets)

Heretofore this was the problem note of the clarinet because its vent hole served two dissimilar functions. On a Boehm clarinet the normal way is to play it with the left thumb and forefinger. This results in a tone less good than the others around it, and necessitates the use of the thumb—an awkward movement. I am constantly amazed at finding Boehm clarinet players who do not take advantage of the beautifully tuned and toned possibility of the right second trill key together with the conventional A key. It is usable in many slow passages. I've even known long-fingered players who used this fingering most of the time—and sounded the better for it. It opens the true Bb vent.

Back in the '30s , I played an instrument with another hole alongside the true Bb vent hole. Though manipulated with the thumb-register key, this new hole opened automatically only when the register key was used in conjunction with the A key. The result was tonally excellent. There have been, and are still available, variations on this general principle, but they suffer these disadvantages: (1) mechanism which can be complex and which often has a time lag, and (2) you are still left using the thumb too much of the time—and the thumb is by no means the cleverest or most facile part of your hand.

During the life of the clarinet there have been many attempts to arrange mechanisms which would allow playing the throat tones by other than the left hand fingers. The most notable was the design of Professor Antonio Romero, a leading clarinettist in Spain. He made an instrument which allowed the playing of

with the three fingers of the right hand, and he also wrote a method for it. The instrument did not come into general use because it involved too many cross-fingerings.

Keep in mind that as long as you are dealing essentially with the repertoire of the classic or romantic periods it does not much matter what type of clarinet you are using—Albert, Boehm or Boehm-Mazzeo. The music is essentially diatonic and every clarinettist knows how you can whiz along at tremendous speeds in F, C, or G major. The problems are very different in 20th century music, which contains awkward repeated figures, often not following a regular scale or chord pattern. And we are, after all, living in the 20th century. Hence cross fingerings become less tenable today than ever.

The Bb now available on the Mazzeo clarinet solves most of the problems.

1. It uses the true Bb vent hole.
2. It produces an optimum quality Bb .
3. It avoids the use of the left thumb.
4. It allows cleaner and quicker manipulation.
5. There is no distortion of embouchure because of 'favoring' the Bb as is normally the case when the thumb position is used. The result is a far better balanced, homogeneous scale.
6. It uses rings on the 'keyboard,' far more adept motions than the thumb can make.
7. There are many alternate fingerings—all opening the true Bb vent hole.
8. No new vent holes need to be drilled into the clarinet.
9. There are no new keys to press.

The old fingering with the thumb is still available—except that the right fingers may not be left down for G, G♯ , or A. In any case, use of right hand fingers is a stop-gap effort to tune the irregular sounds of Boehm clarinet throat tones, and no clarinets are fundamentally designed to be played with other than their normal fingerings.

A

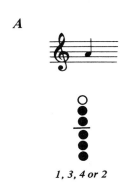

1, 3, 4 or 2

On Boehm-Mazzeo clarinets this is a fingering usable where speed is the prime consideration. No new keys are needed for tremolos such as

Ex. 6

A¹/F♯¹ HAND POSITION

Players often shift the tip of the left forefinger to play each of these notes. It is much better to play the A with the side of the first joint of the left forefinger, and the F♯ with the pad of the same forefinger. A good exercise to get the feel of these is to play the A with the fingering I have indicated, then (while still depressing the A key) press the forefinger pad on the 1st left ring. Never mind the resulting tuning, it is only to give you a feeling of proper positioning. Try the following:

Ex. 7

* While still pressing the A key.

Now reverse and do the following:

* while still pressing the 1st left ring.

These two little exercises above will show you that your left little finger will then be better poised to manipulate the 1 C♯/G♯ lever and it will more naturally fall on the E/B and F♯/C♯ levers.

D♭/A♭/F USAGES

Even players who otherwise use their fingers precisely often slip up on the above passages, producing a legato which is not truly clean. The reason: they move both fingers together, but fail to cleanly release the little finger lever soon enough. This is not effective *until the pad is fully seated*. It comes of thinking 'touch' lever rather than pad 'seating.' After all, it is the seating of the pad which is the effective moment; your thinking and timing should be sensitively adjusted to that. In going from the lower to the higher note, care must be taken not to press the little finger lever too soon.

LEGATO TO/FROM ALTISSIMO REGISTER

also reverse sequence

These slurs are better played if you will (a) take scrupulous pains to see that your embouchure doesn't shift; (b) remember that the left forefinger is making use of that tone-hole as a register key (vent). It functions best when partially covered, and this will vary with instruments (generally needs to be more covered on A clarinets). Some teachers, including myself, call this the 'half-hole' position. Recall that for *any* cross-fingering the descending finger(s) must touch the wood at the precise instant that the ascending finger(s) starts upward. Do not exchange while both fingers are in mid-air.

B^2

Most clarinets (especially B♭ s) will allow you to play this note with the following fingering:

My own is excellent. On A clarinets you will occasionally find it somewhat duller (particularly with certain reeds), but it is useful in such legato and very soft passages as:

Ex. 8

etc.

pp

C^3

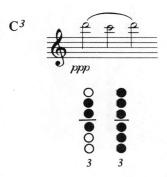

This is a little-used fingering. The C is somewhat duller than the normal one, but it is a much better blend with the D, as well as allowing a finer legato.

On A clarinets and certain B♭ clarinets #3 key is not needed for D^3.

It would be incomplete to conclude this chapter without calling attention to the amazingly clever and brilliant publication of Paul Drushler—*The Altissimo Register: A Partial Approach.* Mr. Drushler, one of our most enterprising and inquisitive clarinettist teachers is a member of the faculty of the State University of New York at Brockport. By means of some very clear elucidation, and a number of extremely clever diagrams and sketches, he has made a fine examination of the problems and fingerings of this usually problem-plagued part of the clarinet range. It behooves us to have this volume on hand at all times during study sessions. It is now a permanent resident on my music stand.

Chapter 20:
PLAYING THE *1776* CLARINET

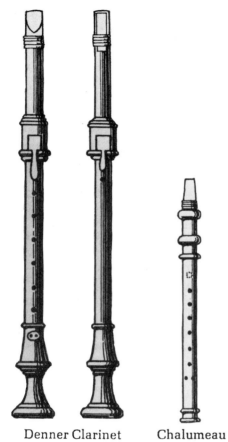

Denner Clarinet   Chalumeau

Fig. 1

Some years ago I had the rare privilege of studying the famous Mahillon Collection at the Conservatoire in Brussels. Many instruments in this collection interested me, but none more than an original Denner clarinet with two keys. I spent more than an hour with it, including playing upon it. A real thrill! Because my interest in early clarinets is substantial, I have collected a number of them, a goodly amount of music for clarinets from that period, and innumerable

reference books, journals and articles, etc., pertaining to the clarinet of the eighteenth century. Coupling all of this with yet another on-coming birthday has made me feel like the Early Clarinettist! Anyhow, recent attention to 1776 has made me focus my attention on clarinets of that period.

The idea of a single vibrating reed used with a cylindrical tube of cane reaches far back into the history of music. Perhaps Egypt was the country of origin. The reed was cut directly into the piece of cane, and only later became a separate piece of equipment. This strongly suggests that reeds have been cursed by clarinet players throughout their entire history. The earliest folk instrument of direct interest to clarinettists was the chalumeau. This was illustrated in Diderot and d'Alembert's famous *Encyclopédie* of 1767.

The instrument had seven holes, no bell or barrel, and since its compass scarcely exceeded one octave the instrument was developed in a family series of different pitches, much as the recorder family. Later one or two keys were added. Telemann, Gluck, Graupner, Dittersdorf, and Ariosti were among the many composers who wrote for it.

The clarinet apparently evolved from the chalumeau just before 1700, and for a time their histories were intertwined, sometimes confusedly. Even the first reference, that of Doppelmayr in his *Nachrichten von den Nürnberger Mathematics und Kunstlern* of 1730 is confusing, though the general understanding is that J. C. Denner *improved* the chalumeau and *invented* the clarinet. The clarinet became a clarinet at the moment that the overblown twelfths could be produced by opening a 'speaker' hole.

Denner's instruments were not all alike. The one I examined had eight open holes, one covered by a thumb, three each for the left and right hands, plus one hole for a little finger. There were also two closed holes, one above the first open hole on the top of the instrument, operated by a key pressed by the first finger of the upper hand, and one above the thumb hole, pressed by the thumb of that same hand. Because the left-hand-uppermost position was not yet fixed as a habit, the lowest hole was made in a duplicated form, side by side. Thus the player could plug one and then proceed to play with the hand-uppermost position he preferred. Somewhere during this period it was found that by reducing the diameter of these double holes an $F\sharp/C\sharp^2$ could be produced when only one of them was closed in conjunction with the holes above.

The new vent hole above the thumb hole produced A^1 when opened, and that above the first finger, when opened in conjunction with the thumb operation, produced B^1 (natural). $B\flat^1$ was presumably played with the upper key alone, possibly closing some left hand holes, and/or slackening the embouchure. The tuning of the $B\flat^1$ must have left something to be desired. Sometimes the tunings of these two holes were reversed. However, the following scale of fundamental sounds (minus the low E) was then possible, with cross-fingerings additionally making certain chromatics available. The note names are those used by the player, the pitch of the instrument dictating the actual sound produced. Open-hole names are of the tones sounded when the referred-to hole is closed. Not all two-keyed clarinets were made with this same scale.

Ex. 1

Note: the hole for the lower $B\flat$ was sometimes tuned to produce $B\natural$, in which case $B\flat$ was produced with the left 1 and 3.

The next development was to reduce the size and to move upward the tone hole above the thumb to facilitate the sounding of the twelfths. The hole on the upper side of the instrument was made to produce A^1 when opened, and $B\flat^1$ when the hole above the thumb was opened together with this A^1 hole vent.

All of the tones were then bettered, but there was no really satisfactory B^1 (natural). The solution was arrived at by lengthening the instrument and drilling a new tone hole below the F/C^2 hole. This would produce an E/B^1 when closed with the holes above, thus extending the range downward by a semitone as well as permitting a good B^1. Very recently such a clarinet, presumably made by J.C. Denner, has come to light and I had the privilege of examining it (now in the collection of the University of California at Berkeley). It has three keys, the third being a thumb key. Whether the three-keyed clarinet followed, or was developed at the same time as the two-keyed instrument is not known. The workmanship appears to be that of J. C. Denner, and not of his son Jacob. The date appears to be c.1700.

This third key is played by a thumb, and it closes the hole below the F vent, thus making possible both the low E as well as the B^1. This lengthening of the clarinet and the later designing of a long left-hand key for this E/B^1 (often credited to Jacob Denner) made practical a total range extending from low E upwards to C^3, and ingenious players could extend this somewhat upwards. Chromatics were mostly by cross-fingerings, or by cross-handing. My own experience with the Boehm-Mazzeo clarinet has shown me that the latter is infinitely easier and more secure.

Within a couple of decades after this the instrument was furnished with G♯ / D♯ and F♯/C♯ keys, thus completing the design for the classic five-keyed clarinet of the eighteenth century.

The following chart gives fingerings which were available on *some* of the early clarinets. There was no unanimity among makers.

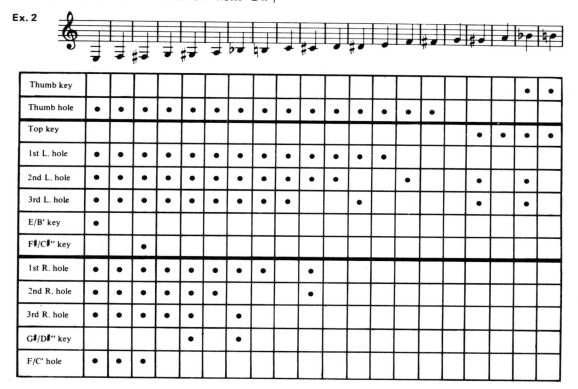

Ex. 2

Thumb key																•	•
Thumb hole	•	•	•	•	•	•	•	•	•	•	•	•	•	•			
Top key														•	•	•	•
1st L. hole	•	•	•	•	•	•	•	•	•	•	•	•	•				
2nd L. hole	•	•	•	•	•	•	•	•	•	•	•		•		•		•
3rd L. hole	•	•	•	•	•	•	•	•	•	•		•		•		•	
E/B' key	•																
F♯/C♯'' key		•															
1st R. hole	•	•	•	•	•	•	•	•		•							
2nd R. hole	•	•	•	•	•			•									
3rd R. hole	•	•	•	•	•		•										
G♯/D♯'' key				•			•										
F/C' hole	•	•	•														

Overblown 12ths—same as above plus register key (from B' to C♯'')

In 1776, that year of revolution, the Diderot *Encyclopedia, 1766 Supplement* announced that a player passing through Berlin had a six-keyed clarinet which could be played in every key signature. Diderot quotes a comment that "everyone knows how much trouble four keys were, how much more would six keys give?" We do not know whether the sixth key was the $C\sharp^1/G\sharp^2$ or the long right hand top lever which was used for the $A^1/$ B^2 trill (manufactured mostly in England). I have examples of five-, six-, and eight-keyed models in my collection. Their sound, though different from today's, is quite agreeable—but the intonation! The absence of rings puts one in such intimate contact with the wood itself that the fingers seem to move much more securely and fleetly—at least on easily fingered tones.

Five-keyed Clarinet

Fig. 2

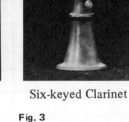

Six-keyed Clarinet

Fig. 3

It is absolutely fascinating to contemplate the repertoire (especially solo) written for the eighteenth century clarinet. There were concerti, chamber music, and various orchestra parts written by such composers as Molter, Pokorny, Stamitz (father and son), Vivaldi, Rameau, Gossec, Haydn, C.P.E. and J.C. Bach, Danzi, and of course Mozart (who was first reported to have heard it in London in 1764). The first popular virtuoso was Joseph Beer (1744–1811). Others were Fr. Tausch (1762–1817), Frederic Blasius (1758–1829), Jean Xavier Lefèvre (1763–1829), Anton Stadler (1753–1812), Michel Yost (1754–1786), and the brothers Mahon, both born about 1750. The combination of virtuosi, a substantial amount of literature,

and the continually improving manufacture made the clarinet ever more important—the legendary Mannheim Orchestra had two from 1758 onwards. In 1788 Ben Franklin recalled hearing the clarinet played in Bethlehem, Pennsylvania in 1756. This could have been possible, but it may be that his memory recalled too early a year.

Since all instruments had to be hand-crafted it is easy to understand the very beautiful workmanship on most. An early nineteenth century D clarinet in my collection, with a maker's stamp 'Stengel-Baireuth,' is a superb instrument, very well in tune, with quite extraordinary keywork, and quite easy to play.

My earliest American-made clarinet, by Graves, is also a nineteenth century instrument. As yet I have not succeeded in locating a bona fide eighteenth century clarinet manufactured in America.

Graves Clarinet

Fig. 4

Stengel Clarinet

Fig. 5

The most important writer for the clarinet in the eighteenth century was, of course, Mozart. He used it as early as 1764 (Köchel 18), and increasingly thereafter, the crowning glory being the 1786–91 period during which he composed the *Trio* (Köchel 498), *Quintet* (Köchel 581), and the *Concerto* (Kochel 622). The *Concerto* (a rewriting of the basset horn version begun in 1789) was for an instrument of his clarinettist friend, Stadler, which had keys allowing the production of four extra lower tones. That construction was not then continued, but only recently has there been a resurgence of interest in the extended range idea. Hans Rudolph Stalder, the famous Swiss clarinettist, had such an instrument made, and his performance of Mozart's *Concerto* is now available commercially in a recording by him (Schwann—Musica Mundi—VMS 807). I find it a delightful coincidence that Mozart's clarinettist, presumably the only one who was able to play the concerto as Mozart wrote it, was Sta*dle*r, and that almost two centuries later the foremost performer of the original, extended range, version is named Sta*lde*r. How I wish that Mozart had owned a good tape recorder that we might hear the two performances at one sitting!

Given this repertoire and the five- or even six-keyed clarinet, what are the specific technical problems the player must solve? In my case the first arose with the inconvenient shape of the A^1 and register keys. A real challenge was the *Trio* (Kegelstatt) of 1786. In the first movement there is this passage:

Ex. 3

Even at the moderate tempo indicated by Mozart it is not easy with the then-available key shapes. Most modern players prefer to play each measure with two main pulses, thus making a trio with three rapid movements. I, for one, do not believe he intended this—nor do I recall his doing it in any other work. If one plays the gruppetto exactly as written, on the latter half of the third 8th value, the tempo has to be moderate, else it sounds scrambled and non-melodic no matter how expertly played. With practice it is possible to do it beautifully on the early instruments at the moderate tempo.

Another problem, at eleven measures before the end of that same first movement, is:

Ex. 4

Here the C^2 has to be fingered with the R little finger, thus making a slide from C^2 to Eb^2 *and back* necessary. On modern clarinets the keys have evolved into shapes which make this possible, but on the five-keyed instruments I have seen the shape of the G♯/D♯ key and the position of the F/C^2 hole make it all but impossible to slide in both directions without a slight skip. There is a possibility (but deficient in tuning) where one can play the Eb(G♯/D♯ key) with this combination of fingers:

C hole or E/B alone (or both)

But for me the crowning problem is that of the forked Bb² in the passage beginning at the end of the eighth measure of the third repeated section of the last movement of the same trio, and again eleven measures before the end of that same movement.

Ex. 5

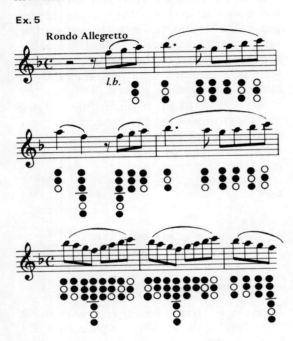

The cross-fingerings are easy enough, although the smoothness would certainly leave something to be desired; the real problem comes in their *repetition*. It is possible on any clarinet, old or new, to go at any speed in one direction or another, as long as it is in an 'agreeable' key signature. It is quite another matter when there is a question of repeated figures. In this instance, the real joker is that the C³ is fingered with the second finger of the left hand. Try this with your fingers on your desk. At least you will be spared the non-legato which your clarinet would produce.

Believe it or not, there is a solution to this problem. It is a fingering given by Lefèvre and brought to light by Hans Rudolph Stalder. Stalder, in addition to his extraordinary abilities which have made him one of the foremost clarinettists of our day, has made an entirely separate reputation as a wonderful performer on early chalumeau, clarinets and basset horns. He has demonstrated this fingering (given below) and it works beautifully (in his hands!). Obviously it demands a very considerable expertise in overblowing.

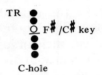

A further puzzle to me is the trill in the penultimate measure of the *Rondo* No. 4 (Köchel Anh. 229):

Ex. 6

The right Bb² key was reported not to exist until the first decade of the nineteenth century. Indeed Spohr stated that his 1808 clarinet concerto could be played only with a clarinet equipped with an Eb¹/ Bb² key for the right hand. Yet Mozart's *Rondo* was written in 1783. I can see no possible way of doing this unless one were to resort to overblowing to produce the Bb, with the fingering(s) given for the immediately prior example, the trilling being done by all three fingers of the right hand.

Another major shortcoming was the absence of the key for Ab^1, which therefore had to be played with the A^1 key plus a suitable number of left hand fingers to flatten it appropriately. Whether composers understood this shortcoming is not known, but that note is significantly missing from most clarinet parts until late in the century. This may have been due to the 'convenient' key signatures selected (for solo pieces especially) with C, G, F and Bb predominating, or because composers tended to write diatonically and not chromatically.

In his concerto, which really formed the basis for all modern clarinet writing, Mozart used the full range of chromatics, including the Ab^1. All except this last were available with cross fingerings or keys. I have succeeded in playing the concerto on an early clarinet which had the $C\sharp^1/G\sharp^2$ and Eb^1/Bb^2 keys. I can imagine it being done without these two latter keys, by fingering the $C\sharp^1/G\sharp^2$ with the L first and second plus the R first and second fingers, and the Eb^1/Bb^2 by use of the well-known fork, L first and third fingers, but it would make for laborious playing.

There has been a good deal of recent activity in the recording field with the issue of certain early works played on 'authentic' or 'early' clarinets. I suspect that most were made with at least eight-keyed clarinets. I have one of the Beethoven *Septet,* Op. 20,* performed, it is claimed, with a clarinet dated 1775. But this presumably five-keyed instrument is reported to have been made by one F. Küss of Vienna. Yet Langwill, by far our best authority, has not recorded this maker. He does have a Wolfgang Küss of Vienna, but he was not born until 1779. I should be interested in knowing if this is a bona fide five-keyed clarinet. In any event, I am very much delighted to hear

recordings of such instruments.

In closing let me say that personal experience confirms the common astonishment over the technical facility called for in those days. Indeed very few players seem to tackle the Spohr concerti even with modern clarinets. I recall only a stunningly fine recording by Gervaise de Peyer of the first concerto. Look at what Tausch asked for in his *Concerto in Eb*:

Ex. 7

plus chromatics from   Low E to C^4

To be sure the high notes must have been easier with the long mouthpiece facings of those days, but it could only have been at the expense of the gentler passages. Those players must have been real virtuosi, and having played some of this repertoire on their instruments makes me take off my beret and salute the clarinet heroes of 1776.

* Beethoven — *Septet in Eb,* Opus 20, Musical Heritage Society, New York. LP 1153.

Chapter 21:
FORWARD WITH THE BOEHM CLARINET

It is to Hyacinthe Eléanor Klosé that we owe the medal of honor for instigating work which produced the Boehm clarinet. Together with Louis-Auguste Buffet they applied again the system of movable rings which had been used without success until then, but with the success of Theobald Boehm's flute these rings came into new importance. Thus was born the first 'Boehm' clarinet, which should more correctly be called the 'Klosé' clarinet, because the movable ring idea had been around for some time before Boehm's flute manufacture. This clarinet was shown in 1839 at the Paris Exhibition, patented in 1844 and was called *clarinette à anneaux mobiles* (clarinet with movable rings). Not until 1860 was it renamed 'Boehm.' It was essentially the same as the 17-key 6-ring model of today's Boehm clarinet.

Though this instrument was an improvement over all instruments made before then it did not prevent the development of the so-called 'Albert' clarinet (also using movable rings) which later evolved into the Oehler System, widely used in Europe today—indeed played by some of the finest players there. Even in America, as late as 1950, three of our finest artists in the most important positions—Simeon Bellison (New York Philharmonic), R. Lindeman (Chicago Symphony), and Victor Polatschek (Boston Symphony) played Oehler-type clarinets.

There was a wonderful display at the 1969 National Clarinet Clinic in Denver when Professor Lee Gibson of North Texas State University played full length solos each on a Boehm clarinet and on an Oehler. The sound was, of course, different each from the other, but Gibson's virtuosity seemed equal on both—a real tribute to him.

The Boehm clarinet has continued to be improved in manufacture, particularly in the tuning of the twelfths, and numerous mechanical refinements have been made. Some of these I will describe here.

By far the most important problem has been that of the tone quality and tuning of the throat B♭. Undoubtedly more work has been done to correct these faults than for anything else on the clarinet. There have been many answers, and their history is fascinating. What is most important is—which of these answers has endured the test of time?

One solution to the B♭ enigma (its vent has to serve two dissimilar purposes, register vent and B♭ vent) was to eliminate the normal throat note fingerings in use since the earliest days of the clarinet, and to place all the action on the ring keys (Romero clarinet). This was ingenious but complex, and it never came into popular usage. A modern version similar to this has been manufactured in recent years. With all my travels and exposure to clarinet playing and teaching everywhere, I have (in the last fifteen or so years) seen it used in only one place, in amateur hands.

Another solution was a supplementary vent hole for the throat B♭, or an alternate hole for the B♭ alone—but still using the thumb register key for manipulation. This approach was shown me by a prominent manufacturer in the early thirties and appeared in the fifties in an improved form.

My own approach* to this Bb problem (actually two problems) was a very simple one: the first to correct the tuning and improve the sound, and the second to get rid of the awkward thumb manipulation. The thumb is, after all, the strongest member of our hand—and also the least adept. There exists on the normal Boehm clarinet a proper vent hole for the throat Bb (manipulated with the 2nd R trill key). I merely coupled the mechanism so that the 2nd L ring and conjoinedly the three R rings all opened the normal Bb vent. Thus the sound of Bb is now in tune and sonorous, related in quality with the A and G# immediately below it. *AND*, instead of having to put up with the awkward thumb use on the Bb, the action is now entirely on the 'keyboard' where the upper rings merely move up and down. It can be fingered more quickly and more surely, as a moment's trial will indicate, and also literally dozens of very convenient alternate possibilities are available—and ALL venting the true Bb! The normal fingering is with the A key, plus all the 3 rings of the RH and the F/C key. A performer who is thoroughly accustomed to the instrument can play with a more consistently even sonority over the throat area, and with more agile finger manipulation.

However, we must face the fact that older players, or at least players who are old enough to have played for years, simply have gotten into a busy enough time of life, have achieved a sufficient virtuosity on their Boehm clarinets, enough to satisfy their needs, so that the effort of 'changing' (however simple) is more than they want to do. But with the youngster it is different. Hundreds of teachers all over the country have told me how much better in tune, and how much more adeptly their youngsters handle their Boehm-Mazzeo clarinets than ever before with plain Boehms. The evidence is there by the thousands, and it does not remove one whit of admiration for those players who have become brilliant performers on the plain Boehm, and mean to remain with it. Many start their pupils on Boehm-Mazzeos. When the time comes that the Boehm-Mazzeo clarinet is in the public domain, and is manufactured by other manufacturers, I am certain everyone will see it in a new light, and in ever increasing usuage. After all—every normal fingering of the plain Boehm is there—none is removed, even the old Bb— you merely have a beautiful new Bb to use if you wish (see Examples).

* A complete description of the Boehm-Mazzeo clarinet will be found in my *Mazzeo Clarinet Manual.*

Ex. 1

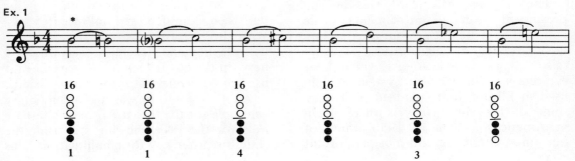

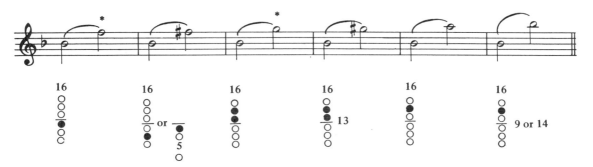

In example 1 are alternate fingering possibilities for B♭¹, though the first is the most used. The other two marked with * are next in point of frequency of use.

Ex. 2   *Excerpt from Sibelius First Symphony*
Andante ma non troppo

The principal fingering is used throughout this solo because it is the most sonorous.

Ex. 3   *Excerpt from Tchaikovsky Fourth Symphony*

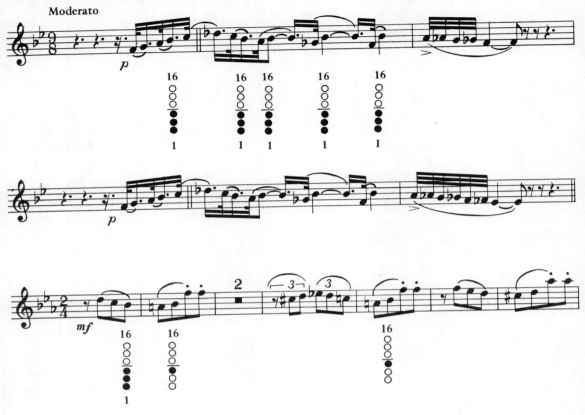

In a few years these instruments have reached a stage where many thousands are in use all over the country, by professionals and students alike. This indicates more clearly than anything else how well on their way they are toward quite general acceptance. You will find them in various symphony orchestras, indeed Cloyde Williams, the principal clarinettist of the Minnesota Orchestra (formerly called the Minneapolis Symphony) has used them since their introduction. I used them during my last half dozen years with the Boston Symphony, and ever since.

Another major step is the covered thumb hole. This serves three functions, all with no real effort beyond getting used to the 'feel' of it. On the plain Boehm the F♯ (Example 4) tends to be sharp and thin in quality. The tone hole and plateaux of the Boehm-Mazzeo tune the note perfectly and give it a heftier sound, more like its neighbors. Also (and, of course, especially with younger players) it is much more sure of manipulation; it allows an 'in-tune' E to F♯ trill (Example 5). Further—because it takes no lip manipulation, and together with the sureness of tone and tuning of the new B♭—(Example 6) it means that you develop the habit of more consistently playing without embouchure change to correct throat tones.

Ex. 4 **Ex. 5 *** **Ex. 6**

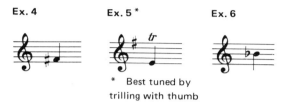

* Best tuned by trilling with thumb

A most important improvement is the articulation of the F♯/C♯ key so that you can play and E/F♯ or B/C♯ trill perfectly in tune (Example 7). Further you can play D and A major scales with the same simple finger motions which you use in the C major scale (using the R little finger on the F♯ /C♯ key). Example-8 illustrates a much better legato and quicker manipulation. The awkwardness of the passage between B and C♯ is gone forever—tuning of the trill superb—and no new keys need to be pressed. Think how easy it is now to play the solo in Ravel's *Bolero* (Example 9) with this articulated mechanism. It is as smooth as if it were in C major.

Ex. 7

Ex. 9

The bell of the Boehm-Mazzeo clarinet is without a metal ring, and without the lip of the plain Boehm. Result—a much clearer, more resonant and better tuned B[1] natural, and less weight on the right thumb, easing your right hand technique (see illustration in Chapter 22).

Another improvement is the special E♭/B♭ (Example 10) played as illustrated. This is just great. Doesn't change a single fingering of either the plain Boehm or Boehm-Mazzeo, and gets one out of all sorts of ticklish spots. The two trills (Example 11) become so simple, and the fingering is eminently useful in rapid passages, especially with reiterated use of the two notes.

Ex. 10   **Ex. 11**

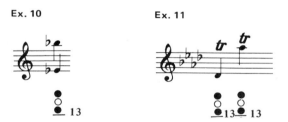

In using extra keys or positions one always has to weigh the pros and cons before adopting use for oneself. I have found determined adherents to the forked E♭/B♭ (Example 12) and equally determined

Ex. 8

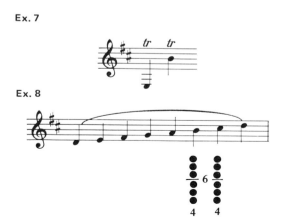

Ex. 12

non-adherents. So take your choice—what is best for you? Me, I have at one time or another belonged to each camp. My early days were without this combination (I used a plain Boehm). Then for about 20 years I used this fingering on all my clarinets of the period (full Boehm)—consequently I feel qualified to speak on both sides of the argument. Now I am back to my model 15 (no 3rd ring).

Arguments for: An infinite number of passages are easier with this fingering. No need to debate the point.

Arguments against: The presence of the 3rd L ring makes the F♯³ of Example 13 too dull and generally flat, though this differs widely between instruments. This problem can be alleviated by adding key #5 (pressed near its fulcrum). The E¹ and the B² (Example 13) are usually too sharp. However if you are fortunate enough to possess an instrument in which these have been corrected you will be much accommodated with the 3rd L ring.

Ex. 13

Articulated C♯/G♯—Ah! here's another one with divided camps. In the old days the argument used to be that the mechanism didn't always work. Now, this is simply not true—if your clarinet is properly adjusted.

The advantages? Numerous beyond mention, easier fingering, tone hole better placed.

The disadvantages? Lose the high F fingering (Example 14)—important for some players—need a longer tenon with its metal lining and greater danger of cracking, plus having the tone hole through two pieces of wood. For me the chief disadvantage is losing the high B♭ (Example 15). No other fingering quite serves the same.

Ex. 14   **Ex. 15**

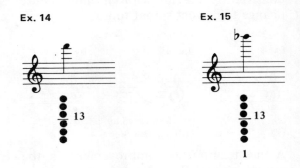

LA♭/E♭ lever is great. It has the slight disadvantage that some manufacturers move the F♯/C♯ lever a little away from the clarinet to accommodate the new lever, making the F♯/C♯ a bit unhandier for the little finger. One must be careful to see that the spring for the right hand A♭/E♭ is no stronger than necessary. These tiny inconveniences are wholly justified when you play something like this in the *Variations on a Theme of Haydn* by Brahms (Example 16).

Ex. 16

Lowest E♭ (Example 17) has many advantages (it is a must for all players in certain Mediterranean countries and in South

America). It is necessary if you want to play A clarinet parts on your B♭ clarinet. It gives you a B which more nearly matches the tone quality of its neighboring C. Very useful, though only occasionally, as a B♭. The right hand tones of this model do not feel quite as free as the model without this E♭.

Ex. 17

Summing it all up I find that "You chooses your cake and you eats it." The thing that really matters is that you remember it is *you* who will play the clarinet, and that it is *you* who must decide which of the conveniences you wish to adopt—the price being the inconveniences! You can become expert on any.

All these improvements are available on one model or another; it only remains necessary to define your needs. Have in mind that there are untold thousands using each modification of the Boehm, Boehm-Mazzeo, or the Oehler clarinets— and it is a sure thing that, at least in casual listening, one cannot distinguish. But the player can! His playing is more convincing because he believes in his instrument. Don't fall under the spell of thinking that if something has been used for 150 years it is going to be used forever without change. Ask yourself the question—what mechanical devices have not changed in 150 years?

Chapter 22:
THE FAMOUS CALIFORNIA CUSTOM CLARINET

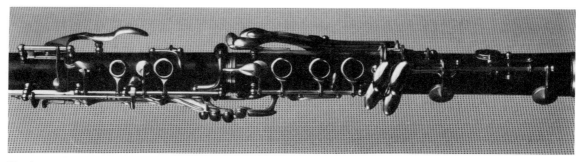

Fig. 1

The grapevine is extraordinarily efficient. Here I sit in my studio, high on a mountain overlooking the Pacific, and work and play with my clarinets. I feel secluded, yet the grapevine has a terminal (or tendril?) in my home. One result: a continuing series of letters requesting information on the new clarinet mechanism I have been building—a series of letters too numerous to respond to individually. To answer these, and to bring all interested readers up to date, I will detail the results.

In 1951 I went to London as part of a Boston Symphony tour. Besides the concerts I devoted my usual attention to museums, galleries, bookstores, instrument stores, fine restaurants—and those really wonderful Bond Street tailors. It wasn't long before I began to think of combining some of the ideals of the London tailors with some of the ideals of Mazzeo re the clarinet—i.e., humanizing the keywork.

During my 33 years with the Boston Symphony, and in the years since I retired, I have talked with, or corresponded with, thousands of players all over the world, including a very large proportion of the finest teachers. I heard of their playing comforts and discomforts, the latter being more readily identifiable as gripes. Their gripes interested me most. Without a doubt, and regardless of what make of clarinet was involved, at least two out of three of these clarinettists (more likely three out of three) had critical things to say about various individual keys and levers, as present on all clarinets.

I have set out to change all that, but my only acoustical changes were the addition of one tone hole and the re-sizing of two others so that finally (after 250 years) the throat B and C are beautifully in tune as throat tones.

Ex. 1

The key work for these notes will be described further along in this article.

I have seen players fight passages which came awkwardly under their fingers, and on questioning found that they thought this or that key too short, too low, too this, or too that. Though I have had the same experience, I still did not zero in on the idea of 'tailoring' a clarinet more specificially for the human hand in the light of over two centuries of clarinet history.

I did from time to time wish for certain personal modifications for myself, and the big opportunity came after concluding my orchestral career. With little concert playing to do, much time to think and putter, I began to develop the idea of a set of clarinets for *me*. No one else. *My* fingers. *My* hands. *No* shortcuts. *No* holds barred in thinking the problem through. *No* timetable.

I am of average height, and therefore reasoned that my size (alas not my weight) was a good starting point for building keys which might later be universally usable. I vowed that I would not be prejudiced by the shape of keys and levers made in the past.

Before I 'sell' you the result, let me clearly state that no manufacturer can even dream of offering such customized service, and very few craftsmen can cope with such a construction. Besides, you can hardly believe the expense! My mechanism, displayed here by means of photographs, cannot otherwise be seen anywhere. The only clarinets in existence incorporating this mechanism are my own personal ones. I do hope, however, that these ideas will trigger the imagination of future designers and inventors. We are nowhere near the end of the road in matters of woodwind design.

I started with my standard Boehm-Mazzeo model (see Chapter 21). Initially I had the expert help of Dennis Heaney of Santa Cruz. Dennis is a wonderful craftsman, with a very open mind, and a most cooperative disposition, but with limited time. Other projects to which he was committed made him bow out early. Then I was fortunate in meeting Norman Benner of San Jose, an artist craftsman of the very first rank—imaginative, incredibly careful, sensitive and thoroughly devoted to the central idea. Though he was joyously willing, it still took us five years to complete the project. His work is simply impeccable.

I felt that I knew pretty much what was needed. The very first thing was to arrange for the best possible hand position, disregarding all pre-existing keys and levers, and to equalize the key travel and spring tensions. These two factors are critically important in rapid passages, when finger motions are at their best only if tensions and distances traveled are more equalized. Many keys are already good but others needed attention.

If you examine Figure 2 you will see how I feel the clarinet should be held (by me)! The angle of the clarinet to the mouth is critically influenced by the jaw configuration. The left hand works best when coming to the rings at about a 45° angle. I studied the motion of the left hand and its fingers, finger lengths and strengths, and arrived at a mechanism which allowed that hand to be in a natural position, so that when brought down to the clarinet the fingers had only to close toward the thumb, with no motion of the hand itself and no individual finger adaptation. This means that the left forefinger is poised *over* both the A and A♭ keys in a natural way; thus the passage $A^1/F\sharp^1$ or vice versa is a single one, the two *pads* affected coming down or up exactly as one, with no sliding of the forefinger.

Ex. 2

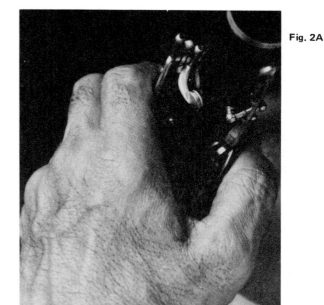

Fig. 2A

Fig. 2

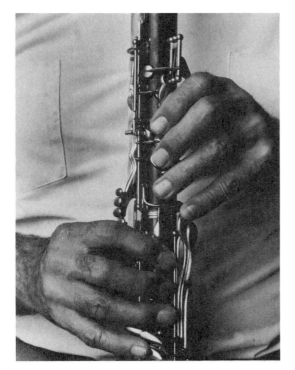

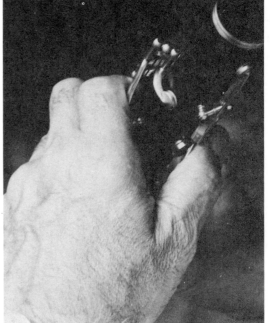

Fig. 2B

Adopting this position (Figures 2A & 2B) had the further advantage of placing the left little finger in the simplest position to manipulate the long E/F♯(B/C♯) levers (see Figure 2). Notice how very little thumb motion is necessary between Figures 2A & 2B.

To effect this I made an enlarged thumb plate beautifully contoured to the shape of the thumb. It is the most wonderfully solid feeling to close one's thumb on, because it furnishes a truly steady and substantial support for the whole hand, stabilizes the instrument and incidentally makes possible an F/G trill (Example 3) with the thumb rather than the usual

Ex. 3

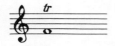

out-of-tune trill with the A♭ key. No change of fingering was involved beyond getting the 'feel' of the new platen. The thumb (and consequently the hand) is never forced into an unnatural position (see Figure 3).

The A and A♭ keys were re-designed (Figure 4) to give the same travel for each key, and to have the keys operate at the same angle as the finger approach. The A key's new fulcrum makes the key and finger operate from the same angle. Furthermore, increased space was needed between the A key and that for the A♭. In quick chromatic passages you will notice that many players tend to 'smudge' these two tones. The reason is that both are played with very nearly the same part of the forefinger. The separation has had another happy effect—it allows the A♭ lever to be further out from the clarinet, nearer to where the operational part of the forefinger really is (further down on the finger itself).

Fig. 3

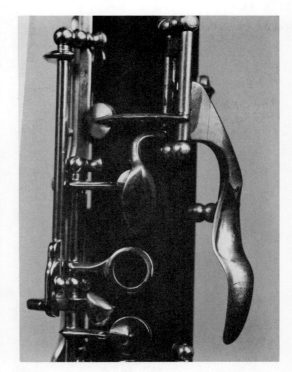

Fig. 4

The mechanism is arranged on a much simpler and more secure basis—a simple reversing action of the two rods (Figure 5). Once in adjustment it simply cannot get out, except by damage to the keys or pads. This is absolutely sure, and far better than the conventional levers which cross over each other at right angles. The flat spring on the A is eliminated. The 'throw' of the A key (and A♭ also) has been too little, and there has been cross friction at the junction of the key arms. The action on mine is beautifully light. Finally, by shaping the A♭ key functionally one can play a nicely in-tune $A♭^1/A^1$ trill by holding the A♭ with the 2nd joint of the 2nd L finger and trilling the A key with the L forefinger. However rapid the passage, the hand is not distorted in using these keys; the fingers are able to act from their proper fulcrum (base) (Figure 5).

We built a little extension on the 2nd L ring mechanism which can be operated together with the L 1st finger on the rare occasions when there is a tremolo

Ex. 4

trem.

or 12va

in a solo passage (Figures 1 & 4).

A little arm under the C/G♯ pad arm takes down the 2nd L ring. This makes a fine E♭ /B♭ on my clarinets with 1L, 3L, C♯ /G♯ key, plus the thumb. It does not change any existing tone or tuning on the clarinet (Figures 1 and 6).

I had always been unhappy (and who has not?) with the right hand trill keys (Figures 6 & 7).

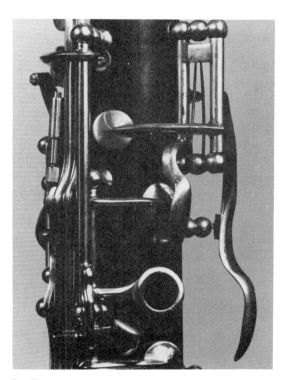

Fig. 5

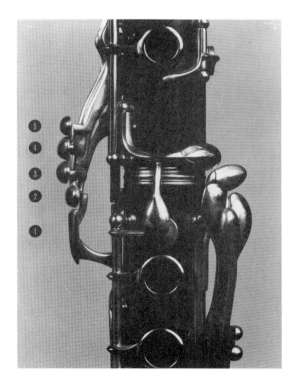

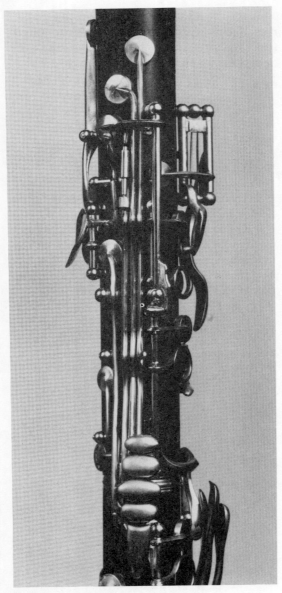

Fig. 7

Problem one: the tuning of the two top trill keys. Problem two: the positioning of the R E♭ /B♭ lever (much too low or cramped for most people). All was easily solved by a fresh approach, principally by drilling a new tone hole between the two top trill tone holes. This made necessary a total of five levers on that side, operated as follows: the E♭ /B♭ lever (#1)* as normal, except the spatula is much larger, more conveniently shaped and higher, right under the finger in the finger's normal position. Its outer post is higher to make the angle of the key conform to the direction of the hand approach. The adjoining F♯ /C♯ lever (#2) is more conveniently positioned in relation to the E♭/B♭ one (canted as the E♭/ B♭), and carries it down simultaneously. Lever #3 produces a superb B♭ when used in conjunction with the normal A key. On commercially available Mazzeo clarinets this B♭ is produced by pressing the A key plus R rings 1, 2 and 3 plus the R F/C key. Here lever #4 takes down lever #3 and together with the A key produces a beautifully in-tune throat tone B natural—first time in the history of the clarinet! It stops the wheel on my chromatic Strobotuner dead center. Lever #5 takes down levers #4 and #3, and together with the A key produces a beautifully in-tune C natural, the strobe again being stopped dead center. The advantage of these keys is enormous: for the first time it is possible to produce B natural and C natural with a chalumeau quality, and *absolutely* in tune. On the numerous occasions when one or two of these notes are required in a low register passage, the quality can be kept uniform by not involving the clarion register. The ease of manipulation in rapid passages is incredible, and even more important, the easy control of very soft passages involving these notes. These are now 'honest sounds, whether sustained or trilled, and all are perfectly in tune (see Example 5).

* These key numbers are those of Figure 6.

Ex. 5

Though the additional tone hole required adds to the total volume or capacity of the bore, I found that even with the most critical tuning, voicing, or speaking evaluations there was no discernible change in the instrument.

B♭¹ is normally fingered as on the conventional Mazzeo clarinet (see Chapter 21).

The L E♭/B♭key has been shortened, as has the R B /F♯ (Figure 1). The latter makes it more certain that the high D♯³/ E♭³ is not flattened by the 3rd R finger (especially of larger hands) slightly overlapping the adjoining tone holes on either sides. Additionally the action is cleaner, being closer to the fulcrum and requiring a shorter 'drop. This key is pressed with the tip of the 3rd finger RH. The shortening of the E♭/B♭ key leaves much more room for the third L finger, and allows an easy downward slide to produce E♭/C (B♭/G) legato—an advantageous fingering not often enough used. It too is played with the tip of the finger.

Ex. 6

My clarinets have articulated action for the E/F♯ (B/C♯). This is standard on the Mazzeo 21M model, and I would never be without it. I have known many players who have had it added to their plain Mazzeo or plain Boehm models (Figure 1).

I have included a L A♭/E♭lever. In one form or another, this lever (Figure 8) has been around for a long time on full

Boehms, Mazzeo 21 M's and Oehlers. The usual (and entirely valid) objection has been that the A♭/E♭arm between the low E/F♯ arms forces the F♯/C♯spatula too far out of position for the hand. The very clever Lennie Gullotta, a wonderful technician, solved this in a most ingenious way, designing a shape which can be applied to any plain or Mazzeo model Boehm— and very simply too. The arm for the A♭/ E♭ spatula lies *outside* that for the F♯/C♯, its tubing riding over one of the already existing post installations, with the spatula then extending over to its usual place.

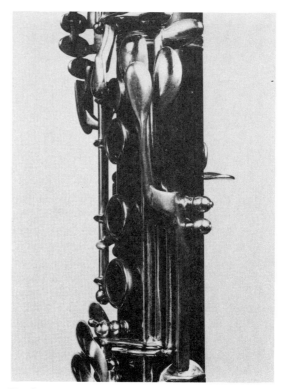

Fig. 8

In addition to its conventional usage as an alternate little finger operation, I find it immensely useful in passages involving high G³ and A³ in succession (see Example 7).

Ex. 7

Depending on the sequence of notes before and after, you can play G³ to A³ either

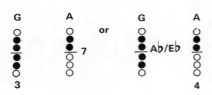

One thing which has always puzzled me: why most players persist in fingering G³ with this combination

and at the same time complain about the tuning of their high tones D³ to F♯³. The tones from C♯³ to F♯³ are nothing more than overblown E² to A² (using the 1st L tone hole as an effective register vent), and G³ to B♭³ being further overblown C♯³ to F³. Actual tuning of these tones varies widely with instruments, depending on the player, mouthpiece, barrel, etc. My point is simply that G³ with the 3rd L finger raised is too sharp. Because everyone tries to play in tune, the embouchure is relaxed when playing this tone with the 3rd finger in raised position. But this means that neighboring tones are also affected when they are played in conjunction with G³—I am speaking specifically of tones from D³ to F♯³, and these tones

generally cannot afford any flattening. Try this simple experiment:

Maintaining a constant embouchure, play a slow chromatic scale from C♯³ through G³ using the indicated fingering for G³.

You will find the G³ to be beautifully in tune if you have played with each tone at its best centered quality. Now while holding this fingering, making no embouchure or other change, simply raise the 3rd L finger. You will notice the G³ will become wildly sharp. It doesn't take much practice to get used to the correct fingering (3rd finger L down). For some players one problem may develop—a difficulty of making a legato at first from D³ or E³ to G³. An extremely simple solution (while getting used to this idea) is to make the legato to the G fingered as

for a split second, then *quickly* lowering the 3rd L finger. The finger change (when done properly) is inaudible, and you wind up with a beautiful slur plus a finely toned and tuned G³.

The register key (Figure 3) has been shaped in combination with the enlarged thumb spatula or platen, and its aperture adjusted (together with a smaller tone hole) to produce optimum overblown

12ths. This makes it much easier to play very delicate and soft entrances on any notes from

Ex. 8

especially A^2 to C^3, as well as better tuning the overblown 12ths of the clarion register. The covered thumb hole makes for a more resonant, better tuned $F\sharp^1$. I do not use the register hole for the throat B♭ (ever!), so the register vent can have one single, solitary and efficient function—its own. It no longer has to do double duty.

Finally—I do not have a particularly fast L little finger trill, so I added an extension to my C♯/G♯ key to make possible an easy trill C/C♯ ($G^2/G^2\sharp$ or E^3/F^3) with the R forefinger (Figure 6). A great comfort. This used to be on many clarinets in the early days of this century.

The net result is a clarinet which has not changed existing fingerings (except for my R trill keys) but has a most wonderful, more solid, almost sensuous feeling to the keys. I have been playing these clarinets for seven years, in some of the most demanding chamber music as well as solo pieces, and am delighted to report that there is nothing I wish to change. My London tailoring experience has paid off.

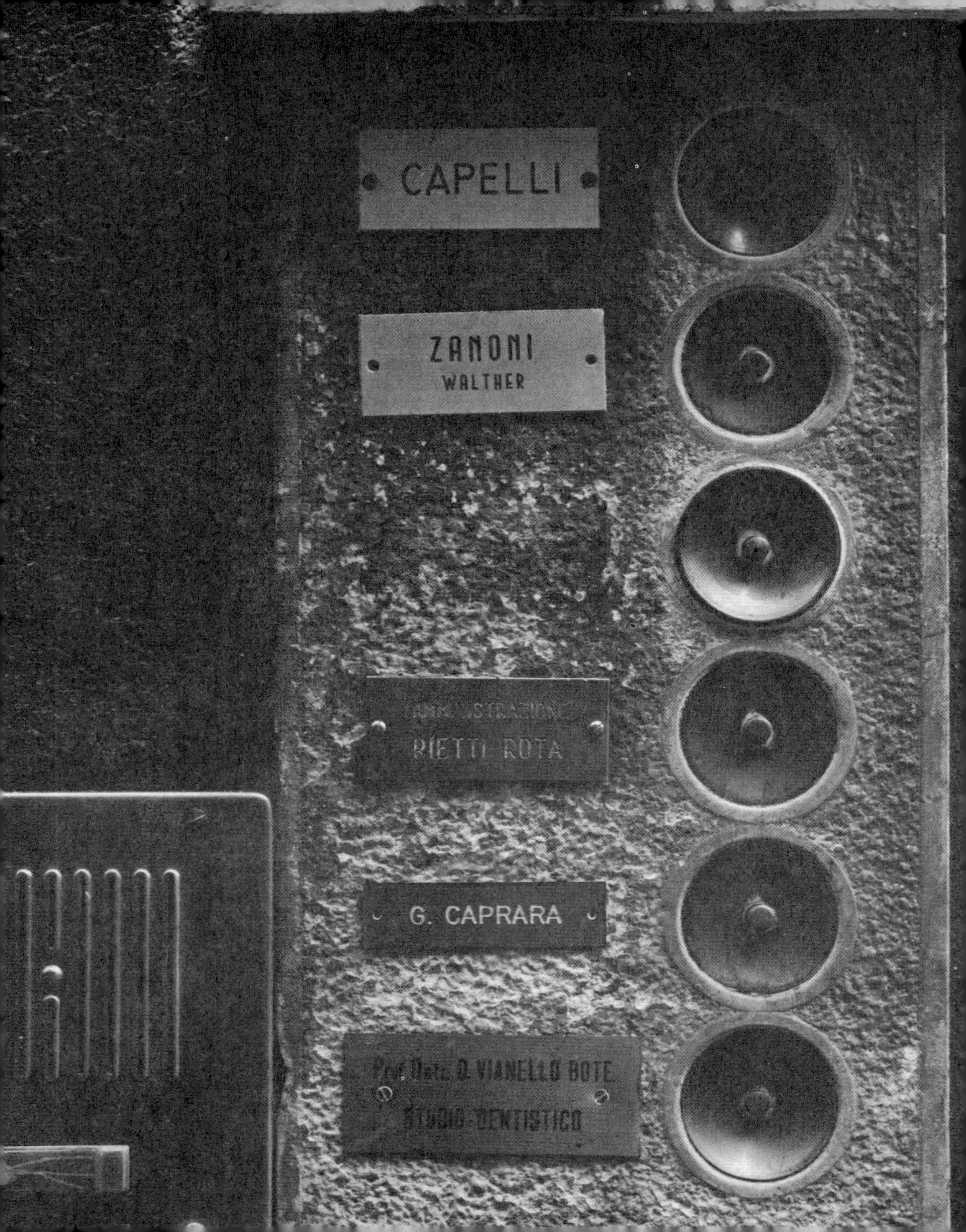
CAPELLI
ZANONI
WALTHER
RIETTI-ROTA
G. CAPRARA

PART VI
REFERENCE MATERIALS

Chapter 23:
WHAT TO PLAY & HOW TO SOUND

If you are of a Christian faith you will have a *Bible* in your house; if in a Judaic household, the *Talmud*; a Mohammedan, the *Koran*; a Mormon, *The Book of Morman*; a countryman, the *Sears Roebuck Catalogue*; and if one of today's younger generation, *The Whole Earth Catalogue*. But—if you are a woodwind player you must have the Himie Voxman/Lyle Merriman *Woodwind Ensemble Music Guide*. If additionally you can be identified as a clarinettist, you also must have Wayne Wilkins' *The Index of Clarinet Music*, and Richard Gilbert's *Discographies I and II*.

Strong words these. But in my extensive library of clarinet and general chamber music references these three works are my most used sources. For repertoire use, these three works practically supplant all the usual sources for such material (Altman, Rendall, Stubbins, Thurston, Cobbett, Kroll, Weston, Grove, et al). Progress is best nurtured by a thirst for knowledge, and if you have this thirst, and these reference texts, you will be best informed. As the U.S. Patent Office, the

electronic, and the sound people would say, they represent 'the state of the art.' Let me deal with each book separately.

The Voxman/Merriman work is a jewel. It is of such continual use to me that I have a copy on each floor of my house. After months of daily use I can only find one fault with it—the title. While it is, of course, of most interest to woodwind players, it is also true that it appears to be comprehensive even as to music coupling winds with strings and other instruments. So really it is a volume which might be better identified as 'Ensemble Music Guide (of particular interest to woodwind players).'

It is superbly organized, so one reaches across the desk for it without the sense of starting a long and possibly elusive search. It is a timesaver. While the approach to listing categories of instrumentation has been unique with each author of such works (and some are excellent) this is the first one I have ever seen the organization of which could easily be adopted as a universal one. The overall categories are '2 instruments', '3 instruments', etc., to '13 instruments,' then a section for 'choirs' followed by another for 'voice and instruments,' and concluding with a 'publisher's key.' Each of these categories is divided into logical groupings, and the easiest way to explain is to illustrate the division of one category, three instruments. In order these are: 3 flutes - 3 flutes, collections - 3 oboes - 3 clarinets - 3 clarinets, collections - 3 bassoons - 3 saxophones - 3 saxophones, collections - 3 woodwinds - 2 flutes, keyboard - 2 oboes, keyboard - 2 clarinets, keyboard - 2 bassoons, keyboard - 2 woodwinds, keyboard - 2 woodwinds, keyboard, collections - woodwind, brass (including horn) - woodwind, strings - woodwind, brass, strings - woodwind, brass, keyboard - woodwind, string, keyboard - 3 instruments (including harp) - 3 instruments (including guitar) - 3 instruments (including percussion) - 3 instruments (including recorder) - 3 instruments (including tape). The sequence couldn't be easier to understand. Each has its own page reference, so you can easily find exactly the section you wish.

I cannot conceive running a music store dealing in ensemble music without a counter-copy of this book. The chamber music (or ensemble) player doesn't exist who has not had the experience of going into a music store to order some more (or even less) esoteric item and been told that the dealer didn't know where to get it. When you find the piece you want, look for the publisher's name on the same line, then turn to the key to the publishers and you have the whole story.

Purists may decry the presence of some transcriptions, but chances are they overlook the facts that:

1. some of the transcriptions are superbly suited to the instruments;
2. the purists themselves were young once;
3. there is need for such transcriptions;
4. the one you don't like you do not have to buy.

One of the best tests for a book of this kind is to examine really carefully an area of particular interest to you. For me this was woodwind, strings and keyboard. Naturally the woodwind was a clarinet. Despite having practically every pertinent reference book right here in the house and (I thought) every piece for such combinations, I found several not known to me. On examination I learned that the publishers of these were somewhat off-beat (as some people would say, they were not in New York!), but the music was valuable.

Incidentally, do not be dissuaded by learning that a piece is out of print. My usual practice is to mail a postcard directly to the publisher. A few such cards can do the trick. Publishers are, after all, interested in selling their publications and they suffer from insufficient exposure to the field of instrumentalists, so the more they know of your personal wants the better their response. Dealers often try to turn you off on certain requests, generally because they do not know where to turn for the particular item. Give them the title, publisher's name and address—or better yet, urge them to get a copy of this book. You will be helping the cause of ensemble music, and yourself. The one problem which remains is that this book, like any similarly intended list, is out of date, even on publication. Hopefully the demand will be sufficient to warrant frequent updated versions. Indeed the next edition is already in progress.

Following a great human tradition, when something new is invented anywhere in the world, or some wonderful action is taken, it is inevitable that practically the same thing is happening elsewhere. So it is with the Voxman/Merriman opus. Almost in the same mail with it I received *The Index of Clarinet Music* by Wayne Wilkins (who also publishes indices for violin and flute). *The Index of Clarinet Music* follows the intention of its title, thus including methods, studies, solo pieces w/wo piano, a vast graduated array of groups of all kinds, and solos with orchestra, or band, as well as a short list of books. Though I personally find the organization of the Voxman/Merriman book more lucid and easy to work with, it is a fact that I could not do without the Wilkins work. It has one enormous advantage—an intention to issue yearly up-dating supplements. My subscription has already gone in for the next 5 years. To my knowledge this is the first time in my years of teaching that

I have ordered anything musical from Arkansas. I am going to keep my eye on that state from now on! Helpful to the clarinet fraternity is the separate listing of music for E♭, alto, bass and contrabass clarinets. My hat (beret) off to Mr. Wilkins. If you are a serious clarinet performer or teacher you cannot do without these Voxman/Merriman and Wilkins volumes. Needless to say, each has music not listed in the other, an inevitability, since sources will have differed. And now since you know where to find *what* to play let us turn our attention to *how* it should sound.

Past generations have had to be content with the examples set by the pupil's teacher, or the players in that particular area. No more. The sounds of all schools of clarinet playing are now at your feet. I guess I mean 'available to your ears'! *The Clarinetists' Discography* I and II lists an extraordinary array of clarinetists. Volume II is intended to be used with Volume I which was published some time ago. I find it absolutely fascinating to have the Messrs. (or should I say Ms?) Amadeo, Boskovsky, Brymer, Cahuzac, de Peyer, Deplus, Draper, Errante, Etlinger, Geuser, Hamelin, d'Hondt, Klocker, Kovacs, Lancelot, Langenus, Leister, Ludwig, Lurie, McCaw, McLane, Stalder, Thurston, Weber, Wlach and Wright playing for me only, in my own studio.

Here one must be cautious. It is easy enough to understand the absence of the great players whose careers antedated recording, but it is also easy to overlook the unevenness of the representation of the clarinet fraternity as a whole if we consider only the names in these discographies. The availability of tape recording, the availability of recording situations, the personal drive and organizational abilities of certain players do much to bring us some of our finest playing, as well as some not quite so distingushed. But we must

not overlook distinguished players without the drive for personal promotion, or solo performance, who sat quietly in their chairs, carried their responsibilities with great distinction, but never (or rarely) recorded their interpretations of solo or small ensemble works.

One such comes immediately to mind: Manuel Valerio, for many years the second clarinet of the Boston Symphony Orchestra and first clarinet of the Boston Pops Orchestra. He made some of the most beautiful tones I have ever heard from *any* clarinet, then or since. Try to find some of the Pops recordings made in the 30s, 40s, and throughout the 50s and you will see why I think so. There should have been a goodly number of recordings of Langenus, one of the most musical clarinettists ever, Dick Waller, principal of the Cincinnati Symphony, and certainly one of America's finest clarinettists, is unknown to most record enthusiasts. There are many others. I make note of these players, not for the professional (who already knows them) but for younger players, lest they believe that if a player is 'not in print' he is not to be considered among the great.

Richard Gilbert, the author of the discographies, and the moving force behind the Grenadilla Society (which is bringing us an abundance of previously unavailable treasures) has done a great job of organizing his material. The principal lists are arranged alphabetically by (1) composer, (2) player, (3) collections (by players), (4) reviews, (5) critiques, (6) Grenadilla Society publications, plus various appendices (deletions, record companies' addresses, publishers' lists, key, etc.). The discography has a strong personal stamp to it, and thus when one has become acquainted with the general attitude of Mr. Gilbert, the critiques become very interesting indeed. Personally I find the 'review' section of limited value. So many reviewers are presented alongside one another that their writing is meaningless unless one happens to be acquainted with the individual writer's abilities and bias. Anyhow I harbor a lifetime horror of most music critics. I would like to see them become (or better, replaced by) reporters, who would deal with the facts of a performance, and not parade their own musical knowledge or ignorance.

The great thing about the discographies is that you can now survey a broad spectrum of clarinet sound and style, thus avoiding one's own possible provincialism. You can hear the Mozart clarinet quintet performed by some 36 or more different clarinettists, all schools of playing being well represented.

Gilbert's publishers' list has addresses, and I strongly second his suggestion that you write in support of the re-issuing of out-of-print recordings. Clarinet players, and ensemble players generally, can become a very substantial lobby, and this seems to be the day of lobbies. We may even have an office in Washington some day! I will ever be in Gilbert's debt, and I wouldn't even try to get along without the discographies.

And all of this brings me to some thoughts about listening. There are many dimensions in listening, each with its own ramifications. Too often, I find people's opinions of playing qualities influenced by the choice of repertoire. This, of course, should have nothing to do with the judgment as to playing quality (except as to style). Sometimes I find the listener carried away by a *certain* quality—such as brilliance of performance. Now brilliance, digital virtuosity, rhythmic verve et al, are to be judged, and hopefully admired—but each for its own sake. Each is *not* an all-inclusive summation of a player. Worse still is being blinded by a player's reported reputation (good or bad) and hearing only what the reputation has told you.

I can readily recall that one of today's prominent players—a very fine musician, with not the most impeccable stylistic sense, a rather ordinary tone quality, wonderful rhythmic vitality—has turned in an absolutely brilliant performance of one of the most difficult major concerti. And I am interested to note the number of clarinettists who are lured by this one display of pyrotechnics into calling this player the 'greatest ever.'* And so in varying degrees do I hear judgments of other players.

Let us be more rational, more fair (to ourselves and to the judged performers). Be discriminating. Notice *what* it is that you do admire—and be aware of the other qualities less well put forth. It will make you all the more receptive and able to listen open-mindedly for a better presentation of those other qualities. Consider basic tone quality, tuning, phrasing interest, technical freedom (tonal and digital), rhythmic clarity and interest, stylistic honesty, ensemble aptitude—each as a separate thing as well as inter-related—and then I think you will agree that *no* clarinettist is really so good in all of these qualities as to blot out your awareness of excellence in these factors among others.

Tone quality is of many kinds, but I am continually dismayed by the number of players who developed their tone unthinkingly. Not only were they not seeking to follow in the clearly defined footsteps of one admired master, but they were not even pursuing their own muse. I believe those players who play with the most beautiful and interesting tones are the ones who approached tone production with a dream, or example, of what they sought. Their sounds did not just happen. That is why these discographies, intelligently used, can be of inestimable value to each one of us.

* Please do not write to ask his name!

Chapter 24:
MY USUAL TEACHING MATERIALS

I say 'usual' because they vary with each pupil. Though I taught a good many beginners in my earlier teaching most of my professional life has been spent teaching players of college, or conservatory, age or beyond—with only an occasional high school pupil. Therefore I do not feel qualified to write in any detail as to materials available for the earlier levels. But, since my text is mostly concerned with basics, it can be read and applied by pupils at any level. As to actual methods— I recently examined a couple which seem admirable: *Learn to Play the Clarinet!* by Frederick Jacobs and *Learn to Play the Clarinet* by William Eisenhauer and Charles F. Gouse. Despite the wonderful track record of the school band programs in the United States it is only relatively recently that I have seen increasing evidence of the wiser teachers recommending private instruction after the inspirational group indoctrination period. I have always been saddened to learn of the number of pupils who stopped playing upon graduation from high school, and I have felt that this was at least somewhat due to an insuffi-

cient study-closeness to their instruments. Only a continual scrutiny of all elements of a pupil's progress will make for the quality of playing which we most admire.

As to my own choices of material, let me say that I have no fixed order of study. It varies with each pupil. I try to prescribe what that moment in the study program most needs. Let me begin by listing methods, with perhaps a few words about certain ones.

1. Gay—Méthode Progressive e Complète
2. Klosé—Méthode Complète de la Clarinette
3. Langenus—Complete Method for the Boehm Clarinet (Vol. 2 and 3)

I use the Eugene Gay method as the backbone in the earlier period of working with a pupil. It is discussed at length in Chapter 17. Its particular virtues are the well-graded and diversified studies. I consider it the best graded of all methods. But, of course, along with it, and increasingly as the pupil progresses I add a good deal of supplementary material so that the pupil has a good diet of all the material needed to keep all aspects of control in focus. The Klosé 'Méthode' has many wonderful virtues. It includes some of the best-ever instructional writing for the clarinet. In its present form I find it less comprehensive than I like, and to this end I am embarked on a massive up-dating and enhancement of it. It is my hope to make it the backbone of a progressing clarinet instruction routine, and it will be published by the Alfred Publishing Co. Date of publication has not yet been announced because as yet I am not even sure of the date of completion. Volume 2 of the Langenus 'Method' is used in the early stages, but the Volume 3 material is quite valuable in latter stages, though the writing is rather closely related to clarinet 'possibilities' rather than to challenges.

Here it is well If I explain the collective way in which I use all teaching material. Upon examining Chapter 16 on scales you will see that some work is done with scales every week. This is one of the most important points of focus. Some time each week is spent with certain technical studies, with material related to phrasing, orchestral studies, etudes and solo pieces for clarinet alone, major clarinet and piano and chamber music works, as well as a generous sampling of 20th century material, and occasional special writing or research projects. From time to time I request the performance and recording of an etude or solo sonata as a whole. The pupil brings the recording to the lesson to be played, whereupon I ask him to make editorial comments as it progresses. It is so important to develop the habit of continual critical evaluation. Then I am able to comment not only on the performance itself, but on the pupil's expertise (or lack) in evaluation. They *must* become fine editors for, after all, you really play your clarinet with your ears!

The following is my 1978/79 list. Full titles are given in the bibliography. All of this may seem like an overwhelming number of items, but remember that as each patient is not expected to have administered *all* the medicines which a doctor prescribes, neither should a pupil be expected to work with this entire list.

Ferling—16 Etudes
Gabucci—60 Divertimenti
Gambaro—10, 12 and 21 Caprices
Gay—24 and 30 Etudes of Style
Gillet—Etudes re 'Technique supérieure'
    (see Chapter 16)
Hite—Melodic & Progressive Etudes
    (1st 2 volumes only)
Jeanjean—Progressive & Melodic Etudes
    (selected few from the 3 volumes),
    18 Etudes
Jettel—Modern Technique Studies
Klosé—20 Etudes after Kreutzer &
    Fiorillo, 30 Studies after Aumont
Kroepsch—416 Studies
Lancelot—15 Etudes
Lester—The Advancing Clarinetist
Manevich—10 Studies
Noferini—6 Serial Studies
Périer—Etudes: 20 of virtuosity, 22
    modern, 30 re style & interpretation,
    and 3 volumes of classic sonatas
Polatschek—12, and Advanced Etudes
Rose—26, 32 and 40 Etudes
Ruggiero—20 Divertimenti
Sarlitt—25 Etudes
Stevens—12 Melodic Studies
Uhl—48 Etudes

SCALE STUDIES

See Chapter 16.

GENERAL STUDIES

Balassa—Collection of Etudes
Bitsch—12 Studies in Rhythm
Blancou—40 Studies
Bozza—12 Etudes, 14 Studies of
    Mechanism
Dubois—12 Etudes
Ensor—Baroque Studies

ORCHESTRA STUDIES

By Bonade, Caillet, Drucker, Giamperi, Langenus, McGinnis, Temple-Savage—and also the orchestra parts for the principal works of Beethoven, Brahms, Strauss, various other standard composers, and especially, modern French composers.

SPECIAL STUDIES

Finger—Geer

Altissimo register—Drushler, Heim

Multiphonics—Bozza (Graphismes), Rehfeldt (New Directions). This last is
indispensible if you are interested in
the subject. They are, however, not
my dish of tea, yet it is impossible
not to be involved with them. I am
eagerly awaiting production of the
Marchi clarinet which overblows in
twelfths and seventeenths, thus making production of a range to G^4
(that's right, G^4!) easily possible.

Solfeggio oriented—Bordogni, Dufresne,
Starer.

SOLO MUSIC—(Clarinet alone)

I place a great deal of emphasis on these.
They are excellent in that they make it
necessary for the student to get the entire
feel of the form (architecture) of the
piece, make him wholly dependable as to
rhythmic determination, color, etc. There
is no one to hide behind or to lean on—
you either make a successful performance
or you do not. It is these which we most
often record, to have the recordings self-
analyzed. Though many are excellent for
concert performance others fall more
exactly into the category of etudes (as
opposed to exercises). Naturally my list
varies from year to year, more than with
other forms, and it is obviously strongly
representative of recent writings.

Antoniu—3 Likes. 1973
Arma—Petite Suite
Babin—Divertissement Aspenois
Bavicchi—Sonata #2
Ben-Haim—3 Songs w/o Words
Becucci—A pouffer de rire
Binet—Chanson de Louisette

Bornyi—1983 (with tuning bar)
Braun—3 Movements
Chagrin—Improvisation
Cheslock—Descant
Constant—For Clarinet
Dennisow—Sonata (1972)
Donizetti—Study
Dubois—Sonata Breve
Eitler—Ansias
Escher—Piece, Op. 84
Gelbrun—Partita
Heider—Inventio II
Hovhaness—Lament
Jacob—5 Pieces
Jenni—Musica Della Primavera
Jettel—5 Grotesken
Jolivet—Ascèses
Kardos—Solo Sonata
Karg-Elert—Sonata, Op. 110
Krenz—Musica
Kunc—Pastoral Fantasy
Kupferman—5 Singles
Kurtz—Fantasy
Laderman—Serenade
Laporte—Reflections
Levy—Soliloquy
Lourié—The Mime
Mather—Etude
Mayer—Raga Music
Milano—4 Arabesques
Mimaroglu—Monologue I
Moore—Ragtime & Variations on
Irish Themes
Osborne—Rhapsody
Perle—Sonata #2
Persichetti—Parable XIII
Pleskow—2 Bagatelles
Pousser—Madrigal I
Rosza—Sonatina, Op. 27
Rychlík—3 Szenen
Schneider—Partita
Simeonov—Poème
Stalvey—PLC Extract
Sternburg—12 Grotesken
Stravinsky—3 Pieces
Sydeman—Sonata

Taranu—Improvisation
Tisné—Envocation pour Ellora
Wellesz—Suite
Whittenberg—3 Pieces

CLARINET & PIANO
with orchestra (piano reduction), and CHAMBER MUSIC

Again my list varies from year to year, but always includes the staples of the clarinet repertoire (these are a must for all pupils): Beethoven, Berg, Brahms, Crusell, Debussy, Hindemith, Martinu, Milhaud, Mozart, Nielsen, Poulenc, Schumann, Spohr, Stravinsky, Wanhal and Weber. Note: the Mozart includes the violin and piano sonatas. The 1978/79 list also includes such composers as Arma, Bassett, Bezanson, Binet, Danzi, Donizetti, Eberl, Etler, Eybler, Finzi, Haik-Ventoura, Haubiel, Hovhaness, Jacob, Jolivet, Kauder, Krenek, Kupferman, Lees, Levy, Lutoslawski, Manevich, Mann, Molique, Moszumanska-Nazar, Nixon, Penderecki, Pokorny, Rameau, Archduke Rudolph and Starer.

BOOKS

Ammer—*Musician's Handbook of Foreign Terms*
Ferguson—*Keyboard Interpretation* (invaluable for study of ornaments in music)
Thurston—*Clarinet Technique*
Stein—*The Art of Clarinet Playing*
Voxman—*Woodwind Ensemble Music Guide*
___ *Woodwind Solo and Study Material Music Guide*
Hindemith—*Elementary Training for Musicians*

Levarie & Levy—*Tone: A Study in Musical Acoustics*
Benade—*Fundamentals of Musical Acoustics*
Rendall—*The Clarinet* (3rd revised edition by Philip Bate)
Kroll—*The Clarinet* (revised by Diethard Riehm)
Brymer—*Clarinet*
Weston—*Clarinet Virtuosi of the Past*
___ *More Clarinet Virtuosi of the Past*
Rehfeldt—*New Directions* (also listed under multiphonics)

Notice that this book list is not in alphabetical order, but is roughly the order I suggest for acquisition.

P.S. (Private: to teachers only)—One reason for the length of the music lists, and for the changes each year (which bring in some of the latest publications) is . . . "how many times do I have to hear one more etude by so-and-so" . . . and how many times have I heard this said by busy music teachers? That's what comes of the constant re-hearing of the old chestnuts. I like it better my way, then it is always fun and exciting.

PART VII
ACOUSTICS

Chapter 25:
A CLEAR VIEW OF SOUND

Enthusiasm now impells me to write about a book which I feel is undoubtedly the most valuable I have read in the past quarter century: *Fundamentals of Musical Acoustics* by Arthur H. Benade of Case Western Reserve University. The publisher is Oxford University Press.

The subject is usually forbidding, but my enthusiasm is aroused by Dr. Benade's wonderfully sensitive attention to musical values, and by his stunningly clear statement of just about everything acoustical which is important to music-making. The author's organization is such that if a graphic analogy of it could be made it would be judged an object of beauty. His style is lucid, personal, almost neighborly. However, this is not 'popularized' science, and reading the text takes great attention. Every phrase and formula has to be masticated (even Fletcherized!) for full savoring. But the rewards are so rich that no serious musician should be without this book.

A word of advice: you may feel, after careful reading of the introductory chapter, that you can skim into the area of your particular interest. I urge you not to do so. Carefully following Benade's development of information will give such a comprehensive view of the subject that you will then be better able to move into your own especial area. His grasp of every conceivable aspect of the subject is so complete and his presentation so lucid that, when coupled with his musical slant, the whole becomes extraordinarily alive. If you have even limited training in mathematics you will have no trouble in following his illustrations and equations; they are very ingenious. He reveals his sympathies when he says that "almost everything in this book has had the benefit of extensive *rehearsal* (italics mine) in both spoken and written form." Nice choice of words!

For me the most important aspect of the whole book is the matter of pitch identification and the perception of the various partials and their functions. Since this has such bearing on tone quality in performance, Benade's explanation is of prime importance to any musician. It is spelled out in exquisite form and is of almost unbelievable helpfulness in making music better. The interaction of all parts of a tone from its inception through promotion and reception becomes understandable and, even more important, useful to each of us. How wonderful to find together in one volume all that material which he identifies as 'Musical Acoustics: The Meeting Place of Music, Vibration Physics, Auditory Science, and Craftsmanship.' His very specific definition of 'sanitary' versus 'musical' sounds will be welcomed by musicians, since most have been frightened away from laboratory (sanitary) sounds. He writes in our language of musical sounds in practical use. His adjustment techniques, discussed in the brass and woodwind chapters, show a very practical musical turn of mind, and are eminently useful to a performer—and to a manufacturer.

The clarity of each section is considerably enhanced by a series of terse, numbered statements (each a summing up), 'Digressions' (which amplify interesting related points); illustrations; problems (which challenge the reader); and notes (which give reference sources—happily appearing at the end of sections to which they apply, instead of being lumped at the end of the book).

The major factor in making the material digestible and coherent is the 'route' he follows in his sequence of subject matter and discussion. He commences with impulsive sounds, the relation of sounds and motions, and the identification of the qualities in a sound and its decay. Then he continues through a full examination of struck and plucked instruments, room acoustics (including the listener's contributions and limitations), loudness, acoustical phenomena governing the musical relationships of pitch, successive tones (reverberations, melodic relationships and musical scales) to a discussion of all the instrument families. These are followed by a most helpful chapter on half-valved octaves, burrs, multiphonics and wolf tones. The current proliferation of experiments with multiple sounds from single instruments makes this chapter most timely.

The chapter on variations in perceived loudness is facinating and should be of great help to those players who measure loudness by their input rather than the outcome. There are many of these about! And by cultivating their ability to identify the harmonic components of their sounds they would learn not only to assess their own loudness, but to 'center' each tone for greater resonance and better timbre values. They would also improve the overall tuning of their instruments, not merely with embouchure or other body adjustments, but with adjustments of the instrument.

Benade's discussions of pitch 'wander-ings' or deviations from the confines of the tempered scale are perceptive and helpful. Especially so are his remarks about the individual decay rates of a tone's components and the effect of these on one's sense of pitch, which demonstrate that group playing has continual need of 'bending' to give the illusion of overall in-tuneness.

Naturally I read the chapters relating especially to the clarinet with particular interest (but only when I arrived at them in sequence!). Since everyone uses adjectives to describe tone color, I welcomed his correlating these subjective terms with objective values of cut-off frequencies. Equally welcome were his clear, unambiguous statements as to the effects of closed and open tone holes, as well as of tone hole shapes. Most of all I warmed to to his discussion of the problems which manufacturers and players have brought upon themselves in trying to produce fairly accurately tuned twelfths in the face of the use of only one register hole. Is not this the time to break loose and really do something about this? After all, present expertise has rid us of the problems of earlier days in producing trouble-free mechanisms for double register keys. As a matter of fact, with the Mazzeo models of clarinets the two register holes could be ideally placed acoustically, since neither of them is needed to produce the throat B♭. Two other especially noteworthy passages dealt with the effects of wall materials, and radiation of sounds from woodwinds (of especial interest in making recordings).

For most of my life I have been a fairly regular observer of birds and hence a fairly regular user of telescopes. Early on I learned that while looking with one eye it was best to keep the other open. Coincidentally, I also found out in the early years of my musical life that I could shut out the sounds of one instrument when two were playing together, or indeed hear only one instrument out of a mass. And it was not necessary for either to be an oboe or trumpet; it could even be a flute. During my symphonic years, when my mind was allowed untold hours of 'travel time to far places' during extended rests in the music, I could actually not hear the music around me. The only problem was to develop a time sense which would bring me back to the scene a couple of measures before I was to play my part. Maybe my ears were receiving signals, but I was oblivious to them. Also I find no problem with shutting out tape hiss when listening to a badly engineered magnetic tape. Thus you will understand my especial interest in Benade's discussion of focussing attention on a particular source of sound, and the efficacy of a single ear. Notice yourself how, in a welter of conversations, you can editorially extract and hear only the one you wish.

Thorough as Benade's book is, it raises or leaves unsolved some musical mysteries: in my youth I sometimes practiced for hours in complete darkness (I mean *complete*) and I recall feeling that my hearing was more acute while doing this. Benade analyzes the problems and frustrations of listening through earphones. The isolation would seem to be somewhat analogous in these two situations, but the results are evidently quite different. Any clues?

I have known a few occasions in my life when two solo instruments (a flute and oboe, for instance) playing in unison were incredibly well in tune. The tones were so fused that one could not distinguish either the flute or oboe sonorities. It is what Toscanini described as a 'floboe.' What happened acoustically? If there is an answer in this volume I have missed it.

A continual mystery to me is the tuning and resonance changes which are possibly effected within an instrument when it is used for a period by another player. I have heard many performers say that they hesitated or refused the loan of a particular instrument to a poor student, or even to a capable colleague, because after its return the instrument would not 'play' as well in tune or tone as before. I have had this impression in my own experience. Putting aside all questions of mechanical adjustments, etc., is there any basis in fact for this?

One more fascinating question arises from Benade's statement on the tolerance of tuning errors in a group of strings, by a kind of neutralization, resulting from the spread in the tuning of their partials (about 20 cents). I have noticed a somewhat similar effect when listening to a very large group of clarinets, which do not have the same error margin. Yet the overall tuning seemed tolerable indeed. Was this an illusion? Or was I merely being charitable to my clarinet colleagues?

Benade the scientist-musician has written a book that deserves to be the cornerstone of a fine musician's library. It not only answers many questions, but stimulates questions. This stimulus is wonderful, and I am grateful. Knowing this book I now cannot imagine being without it.

PART VIII
"SONGS MY MOTHER TAUGHT ME"

Chapter 26:
DUTCH UNCLE LECTURE
by *Oom* Rosario Mazzeo*

Some years ago, when I was teaching at Tanglewood in the Boston Symphony's Berkshire Music Center, I gave a talk which I called my "Dutch Uncle Lecture," or *Songs My Mother Taught Me*. It touched on many things concerning the business of music which everyone knew, thought he knew, or anyhow should have known. My background, both as a personnel manager and clarinettist, made me feel naturally avuncular on this subject. It proved so popular that I have been asked many times to put it into print.

My concern is with instrumentalists, whether as orchestra players, chamber music performers, or soloists. It is amazing how many opportunities for engagements, promotions, etc., are lost because of lack of adherence to the decorum expected of an artist. Any one detail may not seem *that* important generally, but in particular circumstances each may loom large indeed, perhaps not in your mind— but very likely in the minds of those with whom you are involved. Anyhow—why go to the trouble of learning to play well

(and it is considerable trouble!) and then throw your chances away by something which may be interpreted as a boorish action?

The over-riding word in your vocabulary as an instrumentalist should be 'service.' Service to your instrument. Service to your composer. Service to your colleagues. Service to your audience. And service to music! All of these things go into the makeup of a professional musician. The Italian language has a fine distinction in their two words *musicista* and *musicante*. The first means an artist, the second a street musician of scanty training. Each may have his own dignity, but the demands on the former are considerably more.

In this day and age, with the multiplicity of opportunities open to an instrumentalist, each must be prepared to use his talents in a number of ways. Teaching is in the forefront of these. It is the one thing that most instrumentalists like to do in addition to their playing. Towards this end be sure to have as fine an academic background as possible. Move towards every degree you can acquire. At least a B.A., if possible an M.A., and hopefully a Ph.D. should be your goals. Many opportunities in our best schools and universities are available only to those possessed of proper training. Sometimes the same position will be available to a person having any one of these three degrees—*but* the salary will be markedly higher if you have one of the advanced degrees.

In my own personal acquaintance and work with a great many of today's (and yesterday's) conductors, I have never known one who gave a hoot whether the player he was auditioning had a perfor-

---

* 'Uncle' in the Netherlands.

mance degree or not. The playing itself, when properly displayed, gave all the necessary evidence of the fullness of musical training. Therefore I have always recommended that my pupils get academic degrees rather than performance degrees, these being so much more valuable in obtaining a teaching position.

We read with fascination of some not-so-admired doings of fellows like Mozart, Beethoven and Wagner. This is small excuse for imitating their weaker moments or allowing our reputations to be sullied by credit, or moral misbehavior, excessive drinking, lack of punctuality or any characteristic which is not generally admired. Let us keep in mind that we are not Mozarts and Wagners. At the moment when a conductor or manager has a decision to make concerning you, any lapse may turn him in favor of someone else. This may sound prissy, but I assure you I have seen hundreds of opportunities (including some great ones) lost because of some such shortcoming.

Always see that your instrument is in proper playing order. Excuses are sometimes interesting, occasionally amusing, but—never acceptable. It doesn't take much effort always to carry a music stand, always to have a sturdy case that keeps your music flat. This last, in an orchestral situation, together with a firm resolve *never* to mark parts with a pen, to make only such marks as can be erased (after all, the next fellow may prefer another fingering!), to keep your folder in order, to see that all music is accounted for, all go to making the librarian your friend. Librarians' offices are often near those of conductors—and somehow when a librarian has a beef about a player, he seems to like to do it when the conductor is within hearing, knowing that he will have from the conductor a certain sympathy about the care of parts.

Professional musicians today are members of the American Federation of Musicians, and are active members of one or more locals. Rules for the well-being of your local should be strictly observed, because like traffic violations, your lapses will somehow follow you everywhere you go. Someone, somewhere will remember something about you at a moment when you fondly wish that this someone didn't exist. Today, more and more locals are allowing the auditioning of players from other locals when vacancies are announced in an orchestra. This is wonderfully healthy to our musical life, since it makes for better quality orchestras. However do not feel you can ride roughshod over a local member in the town where you are being heard. The rule always stands that, everything else being equal, the local player gets the job. You will find partisanship now and then. People *are* people, and partisanship is one human quality.

When you are seeking employment subscribe to certain standard habits:

1. Always typewrite your application and all correspondence relating thereto.
2. Have available a well drawn up *curriculum vitae* and *keep it up to date,* since the last items usually have the most meaning. In today's world of duplicating machines this is a very easy matter.
3. If there is any remote chance of traveling abroad, be sure to have a passport. After all there is no use of having a tux if you can't travel!
4. Passport photographs need not be poor ones. The self-made ones in the dime store machines don't make you look your most intelligent. Most portrait photographers have special (and surprisingly low) rates for which they

will make excellent ones.

5. Be sure to have an address on your letterhead. Envelopes are often thrown away upon opening.

Auditions, though usually difficult to live through, are a necessary evil. No one has yet come up with a better (and workable) way to judge a player. When you present yourself for a hearing, keep in mind that the entire committee as well as the conductor are gathering impressions. You may open your instrument case in their presence. Is it a sloppy jumble of this, that and the other thing—including some folded music? Have some standard repertoire ready to play. Most conductors prefer a slow movement of either Bach or Mozart and a fast one. They expect you to know the most standard works in the repertoire, but not necessarily the wild piece they included in their last program. There used to be a great emphasis on sight-reading, but fortunately this is becoming a thing of the past. The interest will be in how you structured the music, not in whether you missed a G♯ somewhere along the line. Your instant observation of clefs, key signatures, time signatures, tempo indications, etc., will have far more meaning than mere note accuracy, though they do like the right notes.

Progressive and intelligently run auditions are conducted in somewhat like the following manner. You will be asked to play a piece of your choice—perhaps with slow and fast movements. Do not choose some esoteric wonder which the committee doesn't know. They will begin by judging the piece and not you! Besides, they will have sent you a list sometime prior to the session of the things from the orchestral literature which they want to hear, and perhaps a concerto of their choice. As for sight reading—they will give you something which you cannot

possibly have known, then ask you to spend fifteen or twenty minutes preparing it (while the next applicant is playing his prescribed repertoire), after which they expect you to play it well. After all, they are interested in how you are going to play at concerts *after* having rehearsed. The better audition sessions (preliminaries at least) are held behind screens.

Women should be sure not to wear high heels. All the prejudices against women in orchestras have not yet been forgotten, even though it is generally agreed that women make better troupers.

Don't expect to play a sonata at an audition. They want to hear you, not the pianist. Incidentally your solo piece should be one that their pianist can read easily. Generally speaking it is not a good idea to bring your own pianist unless he is a very good one. Keep in mind that theirs will (or should) be a good one, and if yours is less so some of the impression he makes will rub off on you.

Be sure that your instrument is tuned well. If you find that you are not in tune—stop. They would rather wait while you tune, than to have to listen to you play out of tune.

You have been engaged! Now what?

Let me take up the subject of contracts, starting with one you may have. You have learned about an opening in an orchestra a step or two or three above the one you are in. You believe that you are good enough to win the post. You prepare diligently. You travel hundreds (perhaps thousands) of miles to the place of audition. You play well. You are offered the post.

At this point, just as all that you wished for is about to come true, you have a real quandary—you did not really expect to win, and therefore had not dealt with your *present* contract.

My feeling, after many years of facing

this problem with players, is that you should make a clean, simple statement to those offering you a new contract. After all, if you are good enough for them to have selected you, they undoubtedly expect you to hold a current contract. So do not be evasive. It will make them lose faith in you, and will to some extent govern their future actions with you. Ask for time to request a release (being sure, of course, that you have a firm offer in hand). Unless the auditions are too close to the coming season, the chances are good that your request will be granted. If your orchestra hasn't enough time to replace you, then it would have been better for you to not have played the audition at all.

Read your new contract. It will probably concern itself only with length of season, weekly or annual wage, and formula for renewal or non-renewal. Since most of the conditions regarding hours, services, etc., undoubtedly tie in with the local union contract, be sure to read the agreement with the union too. I have seen a good deal of bitterness develop because a player felt that the management was imposing special conditions on him, when these had actually been agreed upon by the player's fellow musicians and union officers.

The written word is a fine starting point. At the risk of sounding a little pollyanish let me say that a truly successful engagement is one which you approach with the same attitude I recommended for playing in tune with a colleague—be sure to contribute at least 101 percent of the effort! The more you contribute to making the orchestra better, the greater your ultimate reward.

Managers have a hard row to hoe. Don't plague yours about problems he can't solve. His job is to get the show on the road, keep it there, and bring it home safely. Only to an extent can he control conditions at halls, especially in tour situations. Keep in mind that sloppy managers simply don't last; they are eroded away by the continual grinding of musicians. If your manager has been around for a good while, the chances are that he knows what it is all about and will respect you all the more if you take your place alongside him as a real trouper. All money and other contractual dealings should be with him. Do not go over the head of the manager and make a request of the trustees or conductor unless you do it with the full knowledge of the manager—otherwise you stand the risk of losing his support. If you have a really good case, it may be easier for him as well as more effective for you if you go to his superiors *with his blessing*.

Conductors. Ah yes! Conductors. They are paid to please the audience. They had better please the trustees. They ought to please the composer. They want to please themselves. They try to please the ladies' committee. Above all they have to please you. Otherwise they do not get results. No one can see through a conductor sooner than the players of his own orchestra. Any shoddiness of character, slackness of endeavor, lack of truly critical and self-effacing attitude, and other deficiencies are obvious to those ladies and gentlemen who face his baton every day.

Don't create unnecessary problems for him. The conductor may be a personal friend of yours, but keep this friendship away from the orchestra; otherwise you will build up resentment among your colleagues.

If there is some ambiguity, or an error, in your part—and you know or suspect the correct answer, do not try to demonstrate your carefulness and devotion to righteousness by publicly asking him for the answer. You are only holding up the rehearsal and making him impatient, because if he knows you to be a good and careful player he will also know that the answer is readily available to you without bothering him. Your action is only a form of 'Look Ma, watch me.'

Since conductors do not know *all* the answers, by all means avoid asking yours any questions if you suspect he does *not* know the answers. A great conductor will say "I don't know"—the lesser type (but still possibly very successful) can only glare—and remind themselves to put a mark on your score card. Your aspiration ought to be anticipation of the conductor's any requests, never to have him call on you for something you did do and should not have, or did not do and should have. Try to restrict his attention to you only for such occasions as wanting more or less of what you are otherwise doing well. Best of all, of course, is to have him only smile happily at you! If he accuses you of making a mistake (and you did not) don't take the trouble of telling who *really* did it. Remember that old one about 'honor among thieves.' Let the other fellow confess his own mistakes—he will remain longer as your friend.

Life has many mysteries which remain unsolved. For me, there is one which adds up to thousands of hours of lost rehearsal time—and with rehearsal time costing as much as it does, I wonder why conductors persist in counting measures laboriously and aloud, somewhere to somewhere—no one else knows where. Then, when he has finished counting, he announces *first* the number of measures (at which point you can do nothing), and *then* the letter or rehearsal reference number. How much better if he had said "Before letter—" and then proceeded to count aloud. The moment he finished counting the orchestra would be instantly ready to start, since it would have fol-

lowed the whole process. Ah me!

Speaking of keeping the librarian's friendship, never take your music home to study it without telling him. Think of the poor fellow, checking all the music folders just before the concert, finding a part missing—meanwhile you are in your car driving to the concert (therefore unreachable). He cannot know for sure if you took it or not. Remember him also in those desperate moments when you are at rehearsal, and so preoccupied that you reach into your pocket and find only the inevitable ball point pen. Don't! Desist—or you will lose his friendship. Keep in mind also that corrections should be made clear enough to be understood by a substitute—or by your successor. Phrasing marks should be lightly made, because it seems that each conductor wants it 'the other way.'

When you are starting a new reed, check it with some tuning device. It's so easy to stay with a reed which sounds well, and perhaps plays easily, but which you should discard because it tunes your instrument differently. How many oboe players have I seen who forced the orchestra up or down (and tempers *up*) only because their reeds sounded well to them—though not at normal pitch.

Get to a rehearsal or concert sufficiently early to adjust your chair and general position comfortably, to see and play easily. You will lose the affection of the colleague sitting behind you if you do this five seconds before the rehearsal starts. Along with this is the matter of weaving or posturing. Some players feel that they do not achieve their fullest expression unless their bodies sway—then their souls really speak. If you have to do that ask the conductor to give you a seat behind the orchestra, preferably backstage.

Good concert decorum indicates that

you should behave with dignity on the stage before, during and after a performance. Only a general sense of disorder can result from your yelling at a colleague sitting at some distance to arrange a ride after rehearsal, or to give him your opinion of the latest Dodgers game. It is not necessary to come on the stage long before the appointed time (indeed many European orchestras have the players file on together just before the performance, come to their seats, sound their tuning notes, and then sit quietly until the conductor comes on, almost immediately). And don't practice all the solos and difficult passages loudly. Don't give the show away; you are not doing previews.

Your dress should be whatever is prescribed—and this seldom includes ankle socks. If you are sitting on a raised stage the result will be a great sight of hairy legs. Ladies, if you are wearing short skirts (mini skirts are singularly unadapted to appearances on stage with an orchestra) please leave your sexy stockings at home, wear something unobtrusive. Though black and white are usually prescribed as the colors to wear there is no reason why styling should be too restricted, but it should not be flamboyant.

Horn players especially please note: it is necessary to drain your instruments. It does not help appreciation of the music, or your playing, to make the audience aware of this. I knew one horn player who persisted in raising his horn above his head and then slowly rotating the instrument to gradually drain it. He wasn't a very good horn player and this may have been his only moment of glory before the audience!

Taxes. Yes, taxes. The music profession, by reason of its generally itinerant nature is somewhat suspect among tax authorities. Keep a full diary and accounts—especially if you are doing 'general busi-ness.' The International Musician each year publishes excellent tax hints. Make it your business to read them. Credit cards are very helpful in accounting for your traveling expenses.

Inevitably—after years of playing in an orchestra, when you have reached the umpty-umpth performance of Brahms' Fourth Symphony—you will find some boredom creeping in. If you don't do something about it you will wind up hating music. You would be surprised at how many of the older symphony players dislike playing. And even if they don't dislike it they find that their playing loses spark, and becomes merely routine. Chamber music and solo playing helps. The best players among the thousands I have known are those who indulged in a good deal of performing outside the orchestra.

Teaching is also a good antidote, besides being a source of extra, always necessary, income. It has the virtue of keeping you in touch with the younger generation, and forces the continual analysis of technical problems—a help even to *your* playing.

I make a great plea for hobbies unrelated to music. The time and generally introspective attitude necessary to develop a fine music career need balance away from music. Again, speaking from a lifetime of experience, I would say that the *un*happiest musicians I have known were those whose interests centered solely towards playing their instruments.

Never lose sight of the fact that playing abilities decline earlier than the usual retirement ages, especially for winds. Indeed, the New York Philharmonic Orchestra's pension system used to be based on the idea that wind players would retire five years earlier than strings. Be conscious of your pension equities, so that you, and not the management, make the decision as to when you should retire. The ego which develops through a lifetime of performance doesn't take enforced retirement easily.

Lastly remember that you are a member of your community, and as such you should interest yourself in some civic activities. Somehow musicians seem to feel that they, as a class, are exempt from such responsibilities, and usually involve themselves less than the average non-music-career person.

I always admired an illustrious colleague who said that the ideal way to a happy, full and long orchestral life was to be blissfully impersonal in the orchestra during all work sessions, to carry more than your share of the musical load, to make sure that the manager truly recognizes your merits when it is contract renewal time, and to forget the orchestra when you step across the threshold of your own home.

Now you are entitled to say 'BUT I KNEW ALL THAT.'

Chapter 27:
EXTRA-CURRICULAR MUSICIANS
A Personal View

Every time I have heard a school band or orchestra, I could not help wondering what the future held for these dedicated instrumentalists. In my many years as Personnel Manager of the Boston Symphony Orchestra, with my close involvement with the Berkshire Center at Tanglewood, and as a personnel adviser to various conductors and orchestras throughout the country, I learned where some of the most talented eventually went. Some occupied posts in symphony orchestras, many were teachers in schools ranging from elementary through our largest universities, and some pursued solo careers of one kind or another.

But I also wondered what happened to those who were not so dedicated to their instruments as to pursue them single-mindedly. Did they just stop playing once their in-school instruction had ceased? Or did they go on to study privately so as to be able to make music recreationally? In what other ways had their music education affected their lives? Also I was interested in those who had lessons through-

out their student years but had not been able to pursue professional careers. These questions needed answers.

Music, as exemplified by school band and orchestra programs, attracts a wonderful aggregation which for a few years lives together making music, then gradually separates into categories or subdivisions of people who:

1. find music the choice for their life's work.
2. find music a necessity, but do not want to make playing an instrument their life's focus.
3. have a stronger interest in a non-music career, but maintain a tie with music, perhaps as hobbyists, often making significant musical contributions.
4. choose other directions, only to find later in life that music is after all the love to which they want to return.

My life, ranging over many aspects of music (I dare say more than most performers), has brought me into contact with an extraordinary array of musical people, and without hesitation I can say that some of the most interesting were in categories 2, 3 and 4. I think of them as heroes of music—ironically unsung. Most of them undoubtedly prefer it that way, but all would happily acknowledge the importance of music and music education in their lives. It is to these that I now address myself.

A good many years ago I returned from a concert tour to find a volume on my desk. The title, absolutely fascinating to me, was *Clarinet Music From 1700 to 1870* by L. Revea and George S.F. Orsten. The authors were unknown to me. The book was a gold mine of information assembled in a very scholarly way. Naturally I wrote a very grateful thank-you letter, and this commenced a fairly regular correspondence with the authors, then living in Colorado. Every letter from them brought helpful information. By chance, a couple of years later, I was going out to Colorado for some concerts and discovered that I had a three- or four-hour wait in Denver between planes. I wrote to the Orstens, inquiring if by any chance they might happen to be in Denver at that time, and would they care to visit with me at the airport. Arrangements concluded, we met at the appointed time, they with armloads of early editions of music from our period of mutual interest.

After the interval of so many years I still have a vivid recollection of our wonderfully stimulating talk, during which I learned a great deal. The book has gone through several editions but is presently out of print. Never a week goes by that I do not consult my copy profitably. What is of particular interest is that though Revea is a performing musician (clarinet and basset horn) George is fundamentally a physicist whose work has taken him all over America. Presently he is teaching at Amherst College and though involved in a number of other projects, he continues his inspiring interest in musicology.

Speaking of scientists makes me think of my ebullient friend and an IBM computer wizard, Daniel Leeson. Dan's work is wide ranging, taking him to all corners of the globe—but withal he has found time to indulge his enthusiasm for the basset horn. Some of the most hilarious letters I have ever read have been his reports of evenings in the New York area when he assembled groups of professional musicians to play early wind music. Though this included such gems as the Mozart *Serenade* for thirteen instruments, it also included some non-gems by non-Mozarts. If ever you have heard some of these eighteenth and early nineteenth century pieces, you will understand Dan's

report that "the more we played, the more we got to laughing, until finally the hilarity reached uncontrollable proportions—and we had to stop playing." Nonetheless his constant searching for and study of early music has made him an authority on clarinet and basset horn music of that period. Witness his excellent articles in the *Instrumentalist*. He now lives in the Stanford area in California, and I keep hearing reports of his continued explorations into his favorite repertoire. He too is an unsung hero.

Most of us do not take time to realize the amount of effort needed behind the scenes to make our musical organizations tick. A glance backwards makes me recall Winnie Davis Crane, a friend of my Tanglewood days. Winnie Davis, a stunning woman, is an amateur pianist married to Bruce Crane of the Crane Paper Company. The most notable of her many accomplishments was founding and guiding the Pittsfield Community Music School. Over these many years she has hovered discreetly in the background, always seeing that everything was organized as it should be, and that the proper forces were brought to bear. Sufficient money was raised so that music education of real quality could be available on a year-round basis in a community somewhat removed from big cities. This was long before the proliferation of community music schools. She was a real pioneer.

In contrast, the most flamboyant music patron I know of, was Mrs. Jack Gardner of Boston. I cannot quite say that we were next door neighbors because there was one building between us. This one building was the Boston Museum of Fine Arts, therefore the distance to her house ('palace') was about a quarter of a mile. I could have shortened this slightly by cutting across the grass, or I could even have canoed across, there being a stream running through the Fens.

This would have been an appropriately romantic way to approach her 'palace,' certainly one of the most unusual buildings anywhere. Alas, I never knew her personally, since she was a generation ahead of mine, but I went there so often that I felt I did. Even though she was not alive one could feel her presence everywhere—in the general ambience, the paintings, the gardens, the furnishings, the building, the extraordinary flower garden in the inner court—a particular delight in the spring—and then, music.

She was a great patroness, and in her day probably single-handedly sponsored more music than any other individual in the Boston area. Even long before she built the 'palace' she gave sumptuous "music parties" at which she entertained all the artistic greats of the day. She was an early and vigorous champion of the then new Boston Symphony Orchestra and was without doubt the most enthusiastic sponsor for the earliest Boston Pops Concerts. If only she could have lived to see them flower under Arthur Fiedler she would have been swept off her feet!

Her enthusiasm knew no bounds, whether professional or amateur musicians were involved. She often engaged groups of New England Conservatory students to play for her guests, or else had the Kneisel Quartet, or Charles Martin Loeffler (a prominent violist-composer of the day, alas not sufficently played now). The opening concert at the inauguration of her 'palace' was performed by a large group from the Boston Symphony under Gericke. She even had Paderewski give a private concert for her alone. Nellie Melba sang for her, and the painter John Singer Sargent, whose 'El Jaleo' is so dramatically shown there, used to play the piano informally for her and her guests. Her sponsorship and support projects were a significant part of the music scene for a generation. That is what loving music can accomplish.

In Stratham, New Hampshire there lives a remarkable woman and dear friend, Cecilia Saltonstall. Married to a busy surgeon, Dr. Henry Saltonstall, Cecilia, in the midst of bringing up four children and maintaining a busy household, has found (or made) the time to indulge her love for chamber music, in which she plays the viola, violin, flute and recorder, and to organize all kinds of educational opportunities in music for young and old alike. She is the 'Mrs. Music' of the Exeter area.

As if this were not enough she assembled and published a vast catalog of music for small orchestras. This comprehensive reference is of inestimable value to all small groups. She has now completed an up-dated version.

Her literary and musical heritage was a rich one. An aunt, Catherine Drinker Bowen, an enthusiastic violinist, is known to all of us as a great biographer of historical personages. Her father, Henry S. Drinker, a lawyer and music scholar, founded the 'Accademia dei dilettanti' in Philadelphia, a group of several hundred amateur singers and players who met regularly to study the cantatas and oratorios of Bach, and works by Mozart, Beethoven, Brahms and others. In order to cope with the lack of good English translations, he undertook the massive job of making suitable English texts himself. These are all available to any choral group by applying to the H.S. Drinker Library at the Westminster Choir School at Princeton, New Jersey.

Right here in Carmel we have another dear friend, David Hagemeyer, who exemplifies all that is ideal in non-professional music-making. A surveyor by profession and a violist by passion, he will play chamber music at any hour of any day at the drop of a hat (western, eastern, or beret). I think it is the bee which can smell others at incredible distances, and it must be some such faculty which Dave has. If anyone comes anywhere near Monterey with an instrument, David's sensors tell him at once.

For many years there has been a great Christmas Season Chamber Music 'Bash' in Carmel. Dave and his friends (the principal one Mel Jacobsen, an eye specialist) rent a big house in Carmel for the holiday season. Each of the fifteen to twenty-five who come, brings an instrument, plenty of rosin, music, and a sleeping bag. For two weeks the house knows no silence— day or night. Come the first of the year they happily return to their various corners of California to await the next season.

And speaking of chamber music . . . many years ago at Tanglewood, when I was in charge of making chamber music assignments for some one hundred fifty to two hundred players a week, there came to my desk a charming woman who wanted to play the violin, who did not want to play in the orchestra, who wanted to play only chamber music, who wanted to have a double assignment each week, and who particularly wanted to play with persons not orchestra-oriented. She had a busy summer with us. I like to think it was there that the seedling which later came to life as the 'Amateur Chamber Music Players, Inc.' sprouted.

As many of you know, Helen Rice has for many years published a catalog of instrumentalists who wish to play chamber music. Each is listed with address, telephone number, instrument, and a self-evaluation as to playing ability and interests. The idea is simply that no matter where you are there is a chance you can find someone to play with. I have heard many reports of players in America, Europe, and Asia, who on arriving in a far city phoned a local listed player with the net result being a happy evening of chamber music playing with congenial colleagues, and often life-long friendships. Maybe this is the time for you chamber music buffs to become members. Write the Amateur Chamber Music Players, Inc., P.O. Box 547, Vienna, Virginia 22180. Bravo to Helen, whose project thrives.

I recall many happy occasions of music-making by and with another close friend of ours, Dr. Peter Strykers. Peter, born and educated first in Holland, studied piano with great fervor. Music was reduced to second place as he went on to become an eminent doctor in Berkeley, where he has lived for many years. But he is passionately devoted to his beautiful two-manual Hubbard and Dowd harpsichord, and upon it he performs with great taste. His music-making is so intensive that a great deal of the spirit rubs off on anyone anywhere near him.

Another to whom music mattered much was Jacob Kaplan, a Justice of the Massachusetts Supreme Court. He claimed that it was only his music that kept him happily on balance. He studied the clarinet with me for a good many years, insisting that 'it cleared his mind' by compelling him to concentrate so.

Since so much of my life was spent in and around Symphony Hall in Boston it is inevitable that I have heard many tidbits of its past history. One of the more fascinating was about Debussy's *Saxophone Rhapsody*. Mrs. Richard J. Hall, a Boston Brahmin, learned to play the saxophone and performed whenever possible— including an appearance at the *Societé Nationale* in Paris. She had commissioned Debussy to write a piece for her, and though he had already spent the money, he just could not face the idea of writing it. He thought it ridiculous when he had seen her in a pink frock playing such an 'ungainly' instrument, and he did not want to have a work of his contribute to a similar spectacle. That he did finally complete a sketch of the work, and that it has come into the repertoire, is due only to the persistence of Mrs. Hall. I used to think of her as I sat on the stage looking over the audience of Boston *grandes dames*, and wonder how many of them were cooking up musical projects. Or playing the saxophone.

The most meaningful interrelationship I have known between music and another profession has been the career of Ansel Adams. We have known each other since 1951 and have visited often in Boston and now in Carmel, where we both have come to live by the sea as neighbors. Ansel, who is undoubtedly the best-known photographer anywhere, is at the peak of a career so distinguished it seems to overshadow his great interest in music and the depth of his musical sensibility. It only seems so; his skill as a pianist was so great that he had to face a career decision and for various reasons turned to photography. Over the years he has played the piano only occasionally, but always with deeply earnest intent, and with outstanding ability. He has an absolutely uncanny sense of tone quality, and a sense of phrasing which can only be described as great. I have made occasional home tape recordings of his playing and their quality was such that when I played these tapes for such astute listeners as Pierre Monteux and Charles Munch they speculated aloud on the known masters who they thought it might be. Rubinstein? Gieseking? Serkin? The same sense of form, of tone color, and of the poetry of pre-visualization which made possible his wonderful photographic masterpieces was continually evident in his playing. Or should I say it the other way around? Look at how his photographs sing!

I submit that great contributions to music are not restricted to practicing musicians. Even among one man's friends are many who earn their bread elsewhere but perform the non-musical wonders offstage which make the musical wonders onstage possible, or who undertake the multitudinous allied functions which advance the cause of music. For them there is no monetary reward, 'only' a lifetime of deep personal satisfaction.

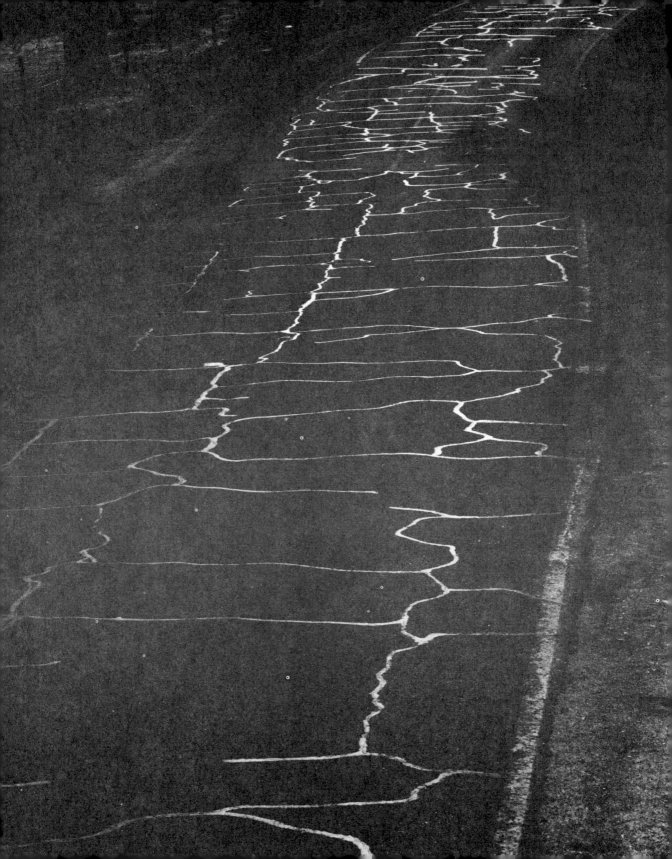

Appendix — 1

THE CLARINET MASTER CLASS

The Clarinet Master Class articles appeared in the *Bandwagon,* a publication of The Selmer Company, beginning with Volume 15, # 3 issued in October 1967. *The Bandwagon* is issued at irregular intervals throughout the year. There have been two methods of identifying issues, the first by volume, number and date, and latterly by number only.

Class Number	Class Title	*Bandwagon* Number
1	Untitled	Vol. 15 #3 - Oct. 1967
2	Fibrecane Joins the Boston Symphony	Vol. 15 #4 - Nov. 1967
3	The Arts of Tonguing	Vol. 15 #5 - Dec. 1967
4	Some Notes on Auxiliary Keys	Vol. 16 #1 - Feb. 1968
5	Untitled	Vol. 16 #2 - May 1968
6	A Guide to Scale Studies (cont'd.)	Vol. 16 #3 - Sept. 1968
7	A Guide to Scale Studies (cont'd.)	Vol. 16 #4 - Dec. 1968
8	Untitled	#55
9	A Library for Clarinettists	#56
10	Untitled	#57
11	Untitled	#58
12	Tuning — some rules and iron clad maybes	#59
13	Untitled	#60
14	Untitled	#61
15	Untitled	#62
16	Untitled	#63
17	The Real Basis of Staccato	#65
18	Forward with the Boehm Clarinet	#66
19	Non-existent	
20	Thinking Will Make It So	#68
21	Protecting the Inner Lip	#70
22	Tonguing (The Subject Which Never Ends) Included Rule of the Tongue: Tips for Slips of the Trade by *Deborah Abbott*	#71
23	A Reference Library for Clarinettists	#72
24	E$\flat$ ^{1}/B$\flat$ ^{2}	#73
25	Minute — But Not Minutiae	#74
26	Eugene Gay's Clarinet Method— The Most Efficient Tool of All–Part I	#75
27	Eugene Gay's Clarinet Method–Part II	#76
28	What to Play & How to Sound	#77
29	The California Custom Clarinet	#78

Note: The Clarinet Master Classes # 5, 6, 7 and 8 were also issued in a one volume booklet form by The Selmer Company in 1969.

Appendix — 2

A FEW BOOKS CONCERNING REED MAKING

Bonade, Daniel. *The Clarinetist's Compendium.* Kenosha, Wisconsin: Leblanc Publications, Inc. (1962): Ch. 4.

Jaffrey, K.S. *Reed Mastery.* Jaffrey, 78 Liverpool Street, Summer Hill, N.S.W., Australia, 1956. 50 pp.

Opperman, Kalman. *Handbook for Making and Adjusting Single Reeds.* New York: Chappell & Co., 1956. 40 pp.

Rendall, F. Geoffrey. *The Clarinet.* 3rd rev. eds. by Philip Bate. London: Ernest Benn Ltd. (1971): Ch. 6.

Spratt, Jack. *How to Make Your Own Clarinet Reeds.* Stamford, Conn.: Jack Spratt Woodwind Shop, 1956. 24 pp.

Stubbins, William H. *The Art of Clarinetistry.* Rev. ed. Ann Arbor, Michigan: Ann Arbor Publishers, Ch. VI.

Willaman, Robert. *The Clarinet and Clarinet Playing.* Salt Point, New York: Willaman (1949): Ch. III.

Bibliography

MUSIC
(Of particular interest to clarinettists)

Antoniou, A. *3 Likes. 1973.* Bärenreiter & Neuwerk, Heinrich-Schütz-Allee, 35 Kassel, Wilhelm-shöhe, Germany.

Arma, Paul. *Petite Suite.* Henry Lemoine & Cie., 17 Rue Pigalle, Paris 9e, France, 1967.

Babin, Victor. *Divertissement Aspenois.* Augener, London, 1952, (hereafter referred to as Augener).

Balassa, G. *Collection of Etudes.* Editio Musica Budapest, PF.322, Budapest 5, Hungary.

Bavicchi, John. *Sonata No. 2.* Oxford University Press, Inc., 200 Madison Avenue, New York 10022, (hereafter referred to as Oxford).

Becucci, ?. *A pouffer de rire.* Editions Durand & Cie, 4 Place de la Madeleine, 4 Paris 8e, France, 1973, (hereafter referred to as Durand).

Beer, Joseph. *Quintet for Clarinet, horn, and 3 viole-d'amour.* Breitkopf & Härtel, Leipzig, (hereafter referred to as Br. & H).

Beethoven, Ludwig van. *Septet, Opus 20.*

——. *Symphony No. 3 in E♭ major.* (Eroica).

Ben-Haim, P. *Three Songs Without Words.* Alexander Broude, Inc., 225 West 57th Street, New York 10019.

Berlioz, Hector. *Symphonie Fantastique.*

Binet, F. *Chanson de Louisette.* Durand.

Bitsch, Marcel. *Douze Etudes de Rythme.* Alphonse Leduc, 175 Rue Saint-Honoré, Paris, France, 1957, (hereafter referred to as Leduc).

Blancou, V. *40 Studies.* Leduc.

Bonade, Daniel. *Bonade Orchestral Studies.* Leblanc Publications, Inc., 7019 30th Avenue, Kenosha, Wisconsin 53141, (hereafter referred to as Leblanc).

Bordogni, Marco. *20 Solo Studies for Clarinet.* Southern Music Co., 1100 Broadway, Box 329, San Antonio, Texas 78292, 1969, (hereafter referred to as Southern).

Bornyi, Lajos. *1983* (with tuning bar). Waterloo Music Co., Ltd., 3 Regina Street N., Waterloo, Ontario, Canada, 1973, (hereafter referred to as Waterloo).

Bozza, Eugène. *12 Etudes.* Leduc.

——. *14 Studies of Mechanism.* Leduc, 1948.

——. *Graphismes.* Leduc, 1975.

Brahms, Johannes. *Quintet in B minor, Opus 115.* Simrock Edition.

——. *Sonata in F minor, Opus 120 # 1.* Wiener Urtext Edition, Musikverlag Ges. m.b.h. & Co. K.G., Wien. (hereafter referred to as Wiener).

——. *Sonata in E♭ major, Opus 120 # 2.* Wiener.

——. *Symphony No. 2 in D major.*

——. *Variations on a Theme of Haydn.*

Braun, Yehezkiel. *3 Movements.* Israel Music Institute, P.O. Box 11253, Tel-Aviv, Israel, 1973, (hereafter referred to as Israel Music).

Caillet, Lucien. *Orchestral Passages from Modern French Repertoire.* Durand.

Campagnoli, Bartolomeo. *Duet* (transcription).

Chagrin, Francis. *Improvisation.* Augener, 1955.

Cheslock, Louis. *Descant.* Oxford, 1971.

Constant, Marius. *For Clarinet.* Salabert, Paris, 1975.

Dennisow, E. *Sonata (1972).* Hans Gerig Musikverlag, Drususgasse 7-11, D-5 Cologne, Germany.

Donizetti, Domenico Gaetano Maria. *Study.* Henry Litolff Verlag (Peters), 1821.

Drucker, Stanley. *Orchestra Excerpts.* Vol. V-VIII. International Music Co., 511 Fifth Ave., New York 10017, (hereafter referred to as International).

Drushler, Paul. *The Altissimo: A Partial Approach.* Shall-u-mo Publications, P.O. Box 2824, Rochester, New York 14626, 1978.

Dubois, Pierre Max. *12 Etudes.* Leduc.

____. *Sonata Breve.* Leduc, 1965.

Dufresne, Gaston. *Develop Sight Reading for Radio, T.V., Symphony.* Edited by Roger Louis Voisin. Charles Colin, 111 West 48th St., New York, 1954.

Dvorak, Antonin. *Concerto for 'Cello and Orchestra.*

Eisenhauer, William and **Gouse, Charles F.** *Learn to Play the Clarinet.* Alfred Publishing Co., Inc., 15335 Morrison St., Sherman Oaks, CA 91403, 1971, (hereafter referred to as Alfred).

Eitler, Esteban. *Ansias.* Mercury Music Co., New York, 1951.

Ensor, C. *Clarinet Studies from the Baroque Period.* Spratt Music Publishers, 17 W. 60th St., New York 10023.

Escher, P. *Pièce pour clarinette seule, Opus 84.* Edition Kneusslin, Amselstrasse 43, Basel 24, Switzerland.

Ferling, W. *16 Etudes.* Leduc.

Gabucci, A. *60 Divertimenti.* G. Ricordi & Co., Via Salomone 77, Rome, Italy, 1957, (hereafter referred to as Ricordi).

Gambaro, Giovanni Battista. *10 Caprices, Opus 9.* Ludwig Doblinger Verlag, Dorotheergasse 10, Wien, Austria.

____. *12 Caprices.* Ricordi, 1971.

Gambaro, Vicenzo. *21 Caprices.* Ricordi, 1971.

Gay, Eugene. *Méthode progressive et complete.* (2 vol.). Gerard Billaudot Editions Musicales, 14, Rue di l'Echiquier, Paris 10e, France, 1932, (hereafter referred to as Billaudot).

____. *24 Etudes de Style.* Billaudot, 1971.

____. *30 Etudes de Style.* Billaudot, 1971.

Geer, Gloria. *The Clarinet Handbook.* Gloria Geer, Box 8, 2008 Jackson St., Hollywood, Fla. 33020, 1975.

Gelbrun, A. *Partita for clarinet, 1969.* Israel Music.

Giamperi, A. *Orchestral Studies.* Ricordi, 1960.

Gillet, Fernand. *Exercices sur les Gammes, les Intervalles et le Staccato.* (3 vol.). Leduc, 1968.

____. *Exercices pour la Technique Superieure de la Clarinette.* Leduc, 1964.

Hamelin, Gaston. *Gammes et Exercices.* Leduc, 1930.

Heider, Werner. *Inventio II.* Ahn & Simrock, Mommsenstrasse 71, 1000 Berlin 12, Germany.

Heim, Norman. *The Development of the Altissimo Register for Clarinet.* Swift-Dorr Publications, 17 Suncrest Terrace, Oneonta, New York 13820.

Hibbard, William. *Bass Trombone, Bass Clarinet, and Harp.* E.C. Schirmer Music Co., 112 South St., Boston, Mass. 02111.

Hindemith, Paul. *Sonata for clarinet and piano.* Edition Schott, 48 Great Malborough St., London W.I., England, 1940, (hereafter referred to as Edition Schott).

Hite, David. *Melodic & Progressive Etudes.* (Vol. I & II). Southern.

Hovhaness, Alan. *Lament.* C.F. Peters Corp., 373 Park Ave. South, New York 10016, 1967.

Jacob, Gordon. *5 Pieces.* Oxford, 1973.

Jacobs, Frederick. *Learn to Play the Clarinet.* Alfred, 1969.

Jeanjean, Paul. *18 Etudes.* Alfred.

——. *Etudes progressives et melodiques.* (3 vol.). Leduc.

——. *Vade-mecum du clarinettiste.* Leduc, 1927.

Jenni, ?. *Musica della Primavera.* Associated Music Publishers, 866 Third Ave., New York 10022, 1974, (hereafter referred to as Associated).

Jettel, Rudolf. *5 Grotesken für Solo Klarinette.* Eulenburg, m.b.h., Grütrasse 28, 8134 Adliswil, Zürich, Switzerland, 1971.

——. *Special Studies for Attainment of Modern Technique.* Ibid.

Jolivet, André. *Ascèses.* Billaudot, 1968.

Kardos, István. *Solo Sonata for clarinet.* General Publishing Co., P.O. Box 267, Hastings-on-Hudson, New York 10706, 1970.

Karg-Elert, Sigfrid. *Sonate, Opus 110.* Wilhelm Zimmermann Musikverlag, Zeppelinallee 21, 6000 Frankfurt, Germany, 1925.

Kauder, Hugo. *Sonata No. 2.* Southern, 1974.

Klosé, Hyacinthe Eléanor. *Méthode Complète de la Clarinette.* Leduc, 1942.

——. *30 Studies after Aumont.* Leduc.

Krenz, J. *Musica.* Polskie Wydawnictwo Muzyczne, Krakowśkie, Przedmieście 7, 00-068 Warszawa, Poland, 1959.

Kroepsch, F. *416 Progressive Daily Studies.* Carl Fischer, Inc., 62 Cooper Sq., New York 10003, (hereafter referred to as Fischer).

Kunc, Bozidar. *Pastoral Fantasy, Op. 59.* Rongwen Music Inc., 56 West 45th St., New York 10036, 1959, (hereafter referred to as Rongwen).

Kupferman, N. *5 Singles.* General Music.

Kurtz, S. James. *Fantasy.* Sam Fox Music Sales Corp., 62 Cooper Sq., New York 10003, 1966.

Laderman, Ezra. *Serenade.* Rongwen, 1958.

Lancelot, Jacques. *15 Etudes.* Editions Musicales Transatlantiques, 14 Ave. Hoche, Paris 8e, France.

Langenus, Gustave. *Complete Method for the Boehm Clarinet.* (Vol. 2 & 3), Fischer.

——. *Clarinet Cadenzas.* Fischer.

Laporte, André. *Reflections.* J.W. Chester Ltd., Eagle Court, London EC I, England, 1971, (hereafter referred to as Chester).

Lester, L. *Advancing Clarinetist.* Fischer, 1969.

Levy, Ernst. *Soliloquy.* 1971 mss.; copies may be obtained from the composer at Chemin de Joulen, 1110 Morges, Switzerland.

Lourie, A. *The Mime.* Rongwen, 1958.

Manevich, A. *10 Studies.* International.

Mather, Bruce. *Etude.* Canadian Music Centre, 1962.

Mayer, John. *Raga Music.* Alfred Lengnick & Co., Purley Oaks Studios, 421a Brighton Rd., South Croydon, Surrey, England, 1958.

Mazzeo, Rosario. *Mazzeo Clarinet Manual.* (See book bibliography).

___. *A Guide to Scale Studies.* (See book bibliography).

McGinnis, R. ed. *Orchestral Excerpts.* (4 vol.). International.

Milano, R. *4 Arabesques.* Theodore Presser, Bryn Mawr, Pennsylvania 19010, (hereafter referred to as Presser).

Mimaroglu, I. *Monologue I, 1958.* Seesaw Music Corp., 177 East 87th St., New York 10028.

Moore, M. *Ragtime and Variations on an Irish Theme.* Western International Music, Inc., 2859 Holt Ave., Los Angeles, CA 90034.

Mozart, Wolfgang Amadeus. *Rondo No. 4* (K. Anh. 229 c. 1783).

___. *Quintet in A major, KV 581.* Johann André, Offenbach-an-Main.

___. *Trio in Eb major.* (Kegelstatt) K. 498. Br. & H.

Noferini, Giordano. *6 Studi di tecnica seriale.* Ricordi, 1970.

Offenbach, Jacques. *Overture to Orpheus in the Underworld.*

Osborne, Willson. *Rhapsody.* Peters, 1958.

Périer, A. *Recueil de Sonates.* (3 vol.). Leduc, 1931.

___. *22 Etudes Modernes.* Leduc, 1930.

___. *20 Etudes de virtuosité.* Leduc, 1935.

___. *30 Etudes.* Leduc, 1930.

Perle, G. *Sonate No. 2.* Presser, 1967.

Persichetti, Vincent. *Parable XIII, Opus 126.* Elkan-Vogel Co., Inc., c/o Presser, 1974.

Pleskow, ?. *2 Bagatelles.* American Composers Alliance, New York.

Polatschek, Victor. *Advanced Studies for the Clarinet.* G. Schirmer, Inc., 866 Third Ave., New York 10022, 1947, (hereafter referred to as G. Schirmer).

Pousseur, H. *Madrigal I.* Universal Editions, Karlplatz 6, Wien 1, Austria, 1963.

Rose, Cyrille. *26 Etudes.* Billaudot.

___. *32 Etudes.* Fischer, 1913.

___. *40 Etudes.* Costallat, Paris.

Rosza, M. *Sonatina, Opus 27.* Rongwen, 1958.

Ruggiero, G. *20 Divertimenti.* G. Zanibon, Piazza Dei Zignori 24/26 35100 Padova, Italy.

Rychlík, J. *3 Szenen.* Hans Sikorski Musikverlag, Johnsalle 23, 2 Hamburg 13, Germany.

Ravel. *Bolero.*

Rimsky-Korsakov. *Scheherezade.*

Sarlitt, H. *25 Etudes de Virtuosité.* Leduc, 1932.

Schneider, W. *Partita.* Moseler Verlag, 3340 Wolfenbuttel, Germany.

Schubert, Franz. Ballet Music from *Rosamunde.*

___. *Symphony No. 8 in B minor.* (Unfinished).

Sibelius, Jan. *Symphony No. 1.*

Simeonov, Blago. *Poème.* Waterloo, 1974.

Slonimsky, Nicolas. *Thesaurus of Scales and Melodic Patterns.* Coleman-Ross Co., Inc., New York, 1947.

Spohr, Louis. *Concerto No. 1 in C minor.* 1808. Peters

Stalvey, Dorrance. *Plc Extract.* Salabert, Paris, 1975.

Starer, Robert. *Rhythmic Training.* M.C.A. Music, 445 Park Ave., New York 10022, 1969.

Sternburg, Friwi. *12 Grotesken.* V E B Fr. Hofmeister, Leipzig.

Stevens, Halsey. *Twelve Melodic Studies.* Peer International Corp., 1740 Broadway, New York 10019, 1971.

Stiévenard, Emile. *Practical Study of the Scales.* G. Schirmer, 1909.

Strauss, Richard. *Till Eulenspiegel's Merry Pranks.*

Stravinsky, Igor. *l'Histoire du Soldat.* Chester, 1920.

Sydeman, W. *Sonata.* C.F. Peters, 373 Park Ave., So., New York 10016, 1967.

Taranu, Cornel. *Improvisation.* Leduc, 1977.

Tausch, Franz. *Concerto in E♭ major.* c. 1844.

Temple-Savage, R. *Difficult Passages.* Boosey & Hawkes, P.O. Box 130, Oceanside, New York 11572.

Tisné, A. *Invocation pour Ellora.* Billaudot, 1972.

Tchaikovsky, Peter Ilyich. *Symphony #4.*

Uhl, Alfred. *48 Etuden fur Klarinette.* Edition Schott, 1940.

Verdi, Giuseppe, *Aida.*

Voisin, Roger Louis. (See Dufresne).

Wellesz, Egon. *Suite, Opus 74.* Rongwen, 1958.

Whittenberg, C. *3 Pieces, Opus 29.* McGinnis & Marx, 201 West 86th St., New York 10024, 1970.

BOOKS

Abbott, Deborah. *Rule of the Tongue: Tips for Slips of the Trade.* Bandwagon # 71. (See Appendix 1).

Altmann, Prof. Dr. Wilh. *Kammemusik-Katalog,* 6th ed. Verlag von Friedrich Hofmeister. Leipzig, 1945.

Ammer, Christine. *Musician's Handbook of Foreign Terms.* New York: G. Schirmer, 1971. 71 pp.

Benade, Arthur H. *Fundamentals of Musical Acoustics.* New York: Oxford University Press, 1976. 596 pp.

Bonade, Daniel. *The Clarinetist's Compendium.* Kenosha, Wis.: Leblanc Publications, Inc., 1962. 17 pp.

Boretz, Benjamin and **Cone, Edward T.** *Perspectives on Notation and Performance.* New York: W.W. Norton & Company, Inc., 1976. 212 pp.

Brymer, Jack. *Clarinet.* (Menuhin Music Guides). London: MacDonald & Jane's, 1976. 259 pp.

Cobbett, Walter Willson. *Cobbett's Cyclopedic Survey of Chamber Music.* London: Oxford University Press, 1963. 3 vols.

Cone, Edward T. (See Boretz, Benjamin T.).

Cooper, Grosvenor and **Meyer, Leonard B.** *The Rhythmic Structure of Music.* Chicago: The University of Chicago Press, 1960. 212 pp.

Copland, Aaron. *What to Listen for in Music.* Rev. ed. New York: Mentor Books, 1957. 192 pp.

Ferguson, Howard. *Keyboard Interpretation.* New York: Oxford University Press, 1975. 211 pp.

Gilbert, Richard. *The Clarinetists' Solo Repertoire.* New York: The Grenadilla Society, 1972. 100 pp.

____. *Clarinetists' Discography II.* New York: The Grenadilla Society, 1975. 150 pp.

Gillespie, James E., Jr. *Solos for Unaccompanied Clarinet. An Annotated Bibliography of Published Works.* Detroit: Information Coordinators, Inc., 1973. 78 pp.

Giokas, Dennis G. "Mozart's Trio, K. 498." *The Clarinet.* Vol. 5 # 2. International Clarinet Society, James Schoepflin, Department of Music, Washington State University, Pullman, Washington 99164. Pp. 12-13.

Grove, Sir George. *Dictionary of Music and Musicians.* 5th ed. London: MacMillan & Co., Ltd., 1954.

Hindemith, Paul. *Elementary Training for Musicians.* Rev. ed. New York: Associated Music Publishers, 1949. 237 pp.

Jaffrey, J. S. (See Appendix 2).

Kroll, Oskar. *The Clarinet.* Rev. by Diethard Riehm. New York: Taplinger Publishing Company, 1968. 183 pp.

Langwill, Lyndesay G. *An Index of Musical Wind Instrument Makers.* 5th ed. Lindsay & Co. Ltd. 17 Blackfriars Street, Edinburgh. (1977) 308 pp.

Levarie, Sigmund and **Levy, Ernst.** *Tone: A Study in Musical Acoustics.* The Kent State University Press, 1968. 248 pp.

Levy, Ernst. (See Levarie).

Machlis, Joseph. *The Enjoyment of Music.* 4th ed. New York: W.W. Norton, 1977. 702 pp.

Matthay, Tobias. *Musical Interpretation.* New and enlarged ed. Boston: The Boston Music Company, 1913. 168 pp.

Mazzeo, Rosario. *Musings from Mazzeo.* Published intermittantly and without date from

1962 into the 1970s. Elkhart, Ind.: The Selmer Company.

——. *The Clarinet Master Class.* (See Appendix 1).

——. *A Guide to Scale Studies.* (See Appendix 1).

——. *Mazzeo Clarinet Manual.* Philadelphia: Henri Elkan, 1959. 37 pp.

Merriman, Lyle. (See Voxman, Himie).

Opperman, Kalman. (See Appendix 2).

Orsten, George S.F. and **Revea, L.** *Clarinet Music from 1700 to 1870.* Published privately, 1965. 110 pp.

Rehfeldt, Phillip. *New Directions.* Berkeley, Ca.: The University of California Press, 1978. 144 pp. plus 1 LP recording.

Rendall, F. Geoffrey. *The Clarinet.* New ed., rev. by Philip Bate. London: Ernest Benn Ltd., 1971. 206 pp.

Revea, L. and **Orsten, George S.F.** *Clarinet Music from 1700 to 1870.* Published privately,

Spratt, Jack. (See Appendix 2).

Stein, Keith. *The Art of Clarinet Playing.* Evanston, Ill.: Summy-Burchard, 1958. 80 pp.

Stubbins, William H. *The Art of Clarinetistry.* Ann Arbor, Mich.: Ann Arbor Publishers, 1965. 329 pp.

Thurston, Frederick. *Clarinet Technique.* 3rd ed. New York: Oxford University Press, 1977. 94 pp.

Voxman, Himie and **Merriman, Lyle.** *Woodwind Ensemble Music Guide.* Evanston, Ill.: The Instrumentalist, 1973. 280 pp.

——. *Woodwind Solo and Study Material Music Guide.* Evanston, Ill.: The Instrumentalist, 1975. 395 pp.

Weston, Pamela. *Clarinet Virtuosi of the Past.* London: Robert Hale, 1971. 292 pp.

——. *More Clarinet Virtuosi of the Past.* Pamela Weston, 1 Rockland Road, London SW15 2LN, England. (1977) 393 pp.

Wilkins, Wayne. *The Index of Clarinet Music.* Music Register, P.O. Box 94, Magnolia, Arkansas 71753. (1975) 143 pp. plus 1976/77 and 1977/78 Supplements.

Willaman, Robert. *The Clarinet and Clarinet Playing.* Robert Willaman, Salt Point, New York. (1941) 241 pp.

Wolff, Konrad. *The Teaching of Artur Schnabel.* (A Guide). London: Faber & Faber, 1972. 189 pp.

ACKNOWLEDGMENTS

The author and publisher express their thanks and appreciation to those who have allowed permission for the use of quotations and musical examples used in this book.

Alphonse Ledue & Co. for the quotations of the Hamelin's *Gammes et Exercises* and Gillet's *Exercises sur les Gammes, la Intervalles et le Staccato*

Gerard Billaudot editor and Eugene Gay for all examples of the *Method* by Eugene Gay

MCA Music for Robert Starer's *Rhythmic Training*

B. Schott Sohne for Hindemith's *Sonata for Clarinet and Piano*

Alfred Publishing Co., Inc. for Jeanjean's *'Vade-Mecum de Clarinettiste'*

Coleman-Ross Company, Inc. for Nicolas Slonimsky's *Thesaurus of Scales and Melodic Patterns*

E. C. Schirmer Co. for Stiévenard's *Practical Study of the Scales*

Also Deborah Abbott, George and Revea Orsten, Daniel Leeson, Winnie Davis Crane, Cecilia Saltonstall, David Hagemeyer, Helen Rice, Dr. Peter Strykers, and Ansel Adams

All photos by Rosario Mazzeo

INDEX